Understanding Global Crises

Understanding Global Crises

An Emerging Paradigm

Assaf Razin

The MIT Press
Cambridge, Massachusetts
London, England

MIT Press books may be purchased at special quantity discounts for business or sales promotional use. For information, please email special_sales@mitpress.mit.edu.

This book was set in Palatino LT Std by Toppan Best-set Premedia Limited, Hong Kong.

Printed and bound in the United States of America.

Library of Congress Cataloging-in-Publication Data

Razin, Assaf.
Understanding global crises : an emerging paradigm / Assaf Razin.
    p. cm
Includes bibliographical references and index.
ISBN 978-0-262-02859-2 (hardcover : alk. paper)
1. Financial crises. 2. Investments, Foreign. I. Title.
HB3722.R39 2014
338.5′42—dc23
2014016733

10 9 8 7 6 5 4 3 2 1

To my grandchildren Iddo and Neeve, with a cautious measure of optimism, and love

Contents

Preface

Remember Lev Tolstoy's famous passage from *Anna Karenina*: "Happy families are all alike. But, every unhappy family is unhappy in its own way." Tolstoy's allegory has been used before to describe fittingly key features that separates one financial crisis from another. However, financial crises also have some common story lines: banking crises, credit frictions, market freezes, asset-price booms and busts, and currency crises. A challenge to any new research is the integration of disparate threads into a coherent analytical whole. Indeed, the recent research into financial crises has pursued an attempt to integrate major crisis elements, to take account of the connections among different elements of a crisis, and to understand the impact a multiple-origin financial crisis exerts on economic activity.

The purpose of this book is to account for crises in recent history; to identify the main streams of microeconomic and macroeconomic theory that can explain the emergence and resolutions of crises; and to describe key policy insights that crises generate. The book surveys models that integrate financial frictions into macroeconomics and monetary economics. Along the way, the book provides many pertinent references from the literature. These references may be used to deepen the reader's understanding of complex analytical issues and the interactions among various driving forces that lie behind global financial crises.

Back in the early 1990s, I started exploring balance of payment crises among countries with high external imbalances. I embarked then on a project with Gian-Maria Milesi-Ferretti (1997, 2000) concerning current-account sustainability issues, which are based on precautionary lending, collateral, and willingness to repay external debt, in addition to intertemporal solvency considerations. In the two-thousand-year-old *Mishnah*, Rabbi Akiva used to say: "everything is given on collateral, and a net is spread over all the living. The store is open, the Storekeeper extends credit, the ledger is open, the hand writes, and whoever wants to borrow may come borrow."

I was increasingly interested in learning more about the various channels and forces that lie behind global financial and economic crises.

This book is the outcome of that learning process.

I have naturally included these features in my lectures to both graduate and advanced undergraduate students. The lectures on which this book is based may help interested economists understand the nature and the key elements of global financial crises. To prepare for this intellectual journey, I start by detailing recent histories of crises. Then, I present basic analytical elements of the theories of financial and currency crises. Ultimately, I describe the way these elements fit together in macroeconomic analysis of global crises, based on recent progress in developing New Keynesian macroeconomic analysis.

Overview

Financial crises, triggered by bursting asset bubbles and marked by bank failures, sharp tightening of credit and downfall of international trade, international capital flow reversals, collapsing exchange rate regimes, and the crumbling of the monetary economy into a liquidity trap, all generate extreme disruptions of the normal functions of financial and monetary systems. As a consequence, crises also upset the normal functioning of the real economy: they depress output and curtail employment. The combination of a deep recession and failing financial institutions creates acute difficulties for monetary and fiscal macroeconomic management.

Financial institutions and financial markets are crucial for the workings of the modern economy. They enable efficient transmission of resources from savings to productive investment opportunities, and they provide risk-sharing possibilities so that investors can take risk in order to innovate and accumulate capital, thereby advancing growth and prosperity. In a subtle way, financial institutions and financial markets also enable the aggregation of useful information, which can guide decisions concerning investment and consumption on a more rational basis. Likewise, federal monetary arrangements, such as the U.S. single-currency area and others in the past, are created to facilitate trade and financial transactions among countries, thereby improving business efficiency. Financial and currency crises mark severe disruptions of the normal functioning of the real economy and may lead to long periods of depressed economic activity. Monetary arrangements that are based on a faulty political, institutional, and economic architecture, such as the European Monetary Union, put their member states into a "monetary cage," akin to the gold standard, and could cause member-state economies to underperform gravely relative to the "uncaged" potential.

Contents

This book aims at parsing and explaining some key forces that feature in every one of the global and regional financial crises and monetary crises that erupted in the world economy over the past decades. The text presents historical accounts of the recent major financial crises and then proceeds to present and explain the main streams of theories on the financial crises that featured in these historical episodes: banking crises and panics; credit frictions and market freezes; currency regime crises, births and bursts of asset bubbles, and conflicting forces behind the volatility of international capital flows.[1]

The book also deals with the emergence of a new paradigm: the development of the late twentieth- and early twenty-first-century macroeconomic analytical framework from the pre-2008 paradigm of modern macroeconomic thinking that served as the workhorse of policy making. The old model had been used to provide the theoretical underpinning for monetary and fiscal policy making in the period known as the Great Moderation. But, as part of the intellectual awakening after the 2008 global crisis, there is a surge of remodeling efforts aimed at the development of an analytical framework that can underpin monetary and fiscal policy making in the era of the Great Recession.

While the surveys presented in this book are extensive, they should not be viewed as a comprehensive review of research on financial crises. The literature on financial crises is simply too large for such a comprehensive review.

Acknowledgments

During the past few years, I have used earlier drafts of this book in graduate and advanced undergraduate courses at Cornell University, Tel Aviv University, Georgia's International School of Economics at Tbilisi (ISET), the University of Munich, Croatia Central Bank, Serbia National Bank, Moscow's New Economic School, Georgetown University, Shanghai University of Finance and Economics, Xiamen University, and Warwick University. Chapters of the book were also presented at seminars and conferences: the Federal Reserve Bank of San Francisco, the European Economic Association Congress, and the 2012 annual meeting of the Society for Economic Dynamics.

Chapters of this book draw heavily on previous works. Chapters 2 and 3 are based on Razin and Rosefielde (2011, 2012), and chapter 9 draws on Binyamini and Razin (2008). I thank Steve Rosefielde and Alon Binyamini for allowing me to include these pieces in the book. Key parts of chapters 5, 6, and 7 draw heavily on the review of theories of financial crises in Goldstein and Razin (2013a, 2013b). I asked Itay Goldstein to be a coauthor of this book but, rather modestly, he declined the offer.

I gratefully acknowledge useful comments on earlier drafts of the book by Eswar Prasad, Elhanan Helpman, and three anonymous reviewers and competent research assistance by Ori Katz, Tianli Zhao, and Andrey Prelin.

1 Introduction

1.1 Two Camps

The recent global financial crisis, which began with the subprime mortgage crisis and exploded on September 15, 2008, with the collapse of the Lehman Brothers bank, took much of the economic profession by surprise. The panic after the abrupt closure of Lehman Brothers triggered a deep depression that took place around the globe. Although there were ample early-warning signs as well as sound microtheories about financial fragility, no coherent macroeconomic theory existed. Economists failed to consider adequately and to put into a coherent analytical framework the destabilizing cumulative effects of financial deregulation, hedge funds, electronic trading, financial entrepreneurship, moral hazard, regulatory laxness, regulatory hazard (such as "mark to market"), Phillips curve–justified persistent monetary ease, subprime mortgages, derivatives and mortgage-backed securities, one-way-street speculation leading to risk-shifting incentives, "too-big-to-fail" financial intermediaries, hard asset bubbles (real estate, commodities, energy), structural deficits with fiscal hidden liabilities, special interest transfers, global imbalances—all these because economists had come to believe that policy makers had learned how to tame the financial beast decades after the Great Depression. With the advantage of hindsight, more than half a decade after the global crisis, both the strengths and weaknesses of the economic consensus that existed before the 2008 crisis can now be discerned and appraised, with an eye toward parsing the future directions of research.

The global financial crisis that erupted in the United States instantaneously swept across Europe. Like the United States, the European Monetary Union (EMU) was ripe for a crash. It had its own real estate bubble (specifically in Ireland and Spain), had indulged in excessive deficit spending, was financially deregulated, and had rapidly expanded credit (partly through derivatives). A critical piece of the financial crisis and its perplexing aftermath is global imbalances, often called the global savings glut. This means that some nations (e.g., China) underconsume and overexport, while other nations such as the United States overconsume and overimport, devaluing the latter's currency and pressuring its Federal Reserve to keep interest rates too high for the purpose of stimulating recovery (Bernanke 2005).[1] The global imbalance view was valid as far as it went but failed to account for the related phenomena of asset inflation and bank failures in debt-ridden nations. Asia's liquidity glut flooded into the wide-open, lightly regulated American shadow banking system (including mortgage institutions) and inundated many smaller countries such as Iceland, Ireland, and Estonia sparking speculation and asset bubbles that soon burst with dramatic adverse effects on risk perceptions in the world's short-term interbank loanable funds market. Burst asset price bubbles reduced the worldwide lending ability of banks, a problem compounded by tightened loan requirements limiting the access of banks to emergency credit infusions. The international dimension coupling the East and West beyond the obvious trade linkages wasn't only important for its restrictive impact on monetary policy; it was also a key element in the larger global financial crisis (Minsky 1982; Tobin and Golub 1998). Macroeconomic policy management moreover was therefore further complicated by external shocks and the complexities of international policy coordination.

Figure 1.1, pioneered by Eichengreen and O'Rourke (2009), demonstrates a startling point. The first year of the 2008–2009 slump in industrial production (and indeed also in trade in other charts, not shown, that the authors produced) was fully comparable to the first year of the great global slump from 1929 to 1933. It appears on reflection that the recent financial panic, and the Great Recession that followed, stunned the macroeconomic profession because a consensus had emerged that the modern state regulatory mechanisms (including automatic fiscal stabilizers) had reduced the business cycle oscillations in output and employment to a degree where fine tuning could be achieved merely by controlling short-term (and, derivatively, through arbitrage, also long-term) interest rates through a consistent monetary rule, without fiscal policy assistance or fortified financial regulation. The recent crisis has some similarities with the Great Depression. It appears that in both cases, the trigger is a credit crunch following a sudden burst of

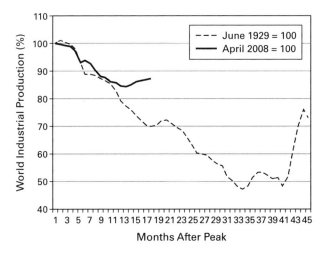

Figure 1.1
World Industrial Production. *Source*: FRED; originated in the work of Eichengreen and O'Rourke (2009).

asset-price and credit bubbles. Figure 1.1, which tracks the behavior of world industrial production during the Great Recession, indeed shows a common pathway in the initial phases of the two crises. However, differences in financial institutions and policy reactions may explain the divergence of tracks after the initial stages.[2] Recovery of world industrial production starts much earlier in the Great Recession than in the Great Depression. Periods of depressed output are significantly shorter in the former than the latter, thanks to different policy reactions and improved financial and budget institutions. This does not amount to a claim that economists understand how to use fiscal policy and supplementary monetary instruments to recover optimally or prevent future reoccurrences, given the often destabilizing expectations of the private sector due to conflicting incentives, finance fragility, and politically gridlocked governments. Rather, it means that complacency based on incomplete knowledge of how the system works is no longer tenable, and reassessment of past output, employment, and finance stabilizing measures is in order.

Pre-crisis conventional wisdom held that business cycle oscillations were primarily caused by productivity shocks that lasted until price- and wage-setters disentangled real from nominal effects (Lucas 1975, 2000, 2003), or monetary shocks, in view of staggered wage and price adjustments. These real and monetary shocks sometimes generated inflation or deflation, which it was believed was best addressed with monetary policy. Accordingly, central bankers were tasked with the mission of maintaining slow and stable inflation. Zero inflation and deflation were shunned because they purportedly were incompatible with full capacity and full employment (Phillips 1958; Phelps 1967; Friedman 1968) and well-managed monetary policy. Although central bankers were supposed to be less concerned with real economic activity, many came to believe that full employment and 2 percent inflation could be sustained indefinitely by *divine coincidence*.[3] This coincidence was said to be made all the better by the analytical discovery that real economic performance could be regulated, in theory, with a single monetary instrument, the short-term interest rate. Evidently, arbitrage across time meant that central banks could control economy-wide temporal interest rates, short and long, and arbitrage across asset classes implied that the Federal Reserve ("the Fed") could similarly influence risk-adjusted rates for a diverse set of securities. Fiscal policy, which had ruled the roost under the influence of crude Keynesianism from 1950 to 1980, in this way was relegated to a subsidiary role of macroeconomic stabilization. This view was aided by macroeconomic theorists' beliefs in the empirical validity of friction-free Ricardian-equivalence arguments and skepticism about lags and political grid-locks, which makes discretionary fiscal policy as a stabilization tool practically irrelevant.

It is also true that the financial sector likewise was given short shrift in macroeconomic theory, because financial sector prudential policy was perceived as regulatory only, affecting structural performance but not business cycle performance, rather than as an aggregate demand management issue. The consensus view held that automatic stabilizers such as unemployment insurance should be retained in order to share privately uninsurable risks. Federal deposit insurance was preserved to deter bank runs, and commercial banks' credit and investments continued to be regulated to prevent moral hazard under the federal deposit insurance, but otherwise finance was lightly supervised, especially "shadow banks," hedge funds, mortgages, and derivatives.

The pre-crisis temporary convergence of views among macroeconomists was based on the post–World War II experience, with relatively nonsubstantial business cycles. But the Great Recession, which followed the financial crisis, was significantly different than other recent recessions (figure 1.2).

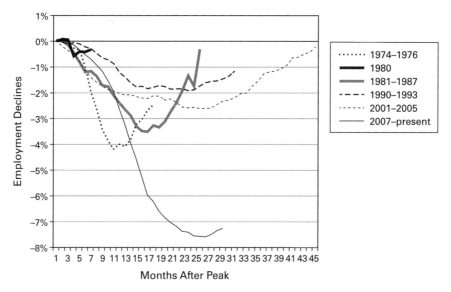

Figure 1.2
Employment Declines in Various U.S. Crises

Needless to say, most of the theorists now concede that the pre-crisis monetarist consensus was mistaken. Both recognize that with the Fed funds rate near the zero lower bound, the burden for stimulating recovery and short-term growth falls to nonconventional monetary policies, such as quantitative and credit easing. But the agreement stops here. From this point on, the profession has split into two contending camps.

The "Ricardian faction" contends that further overbudget spending with deficit to GDP ratios in many large nations such as the United States will drive up interest rates, crowd out private investment, and have negative stimulatory impact. This could easily generate recession (depression) coupled with a bout of high inflation (deflation), due to excessive commercial bank liquidity. This is reminiscent of Friedrich Hayek warning that a surge of excessive liquidity can misdirect investments leading to a boom followed by a bust.

However, members of the other camp, concerned about the non-Ricardian conditions, such as credit frictions, market freezes, liquidity traps, and deflation, see matters vice versa. They insist that austerity policies and deflation are the danger under depressed markets (which via the Bernanke doctrine implies a Great Depression with rising real wages and excess savings; see Bernanke 1983). They deduce that avoidance of disaster hinges on temporarily raising public spending to fill in the gap of shrinking private spending, continued central bank credit easing, and quantitative easing. They are aware that this could have inflationary ramifications, which is helpful to lower the real interest rate, but brush the soon-to-arrive inflation peril aside by claiming that speculators will absorb most of the idle cash balances governments are prepared to print, because with zero interest rate, money and bonds are perfect substitutes. At the same time, inflationary expectations are to be replaced by deflationary expectations. Moreover, they contend that excess base money can be drained from the system, whenever banks decide to resume lending, but not fully, during a long period of de-leveraging by households and firms. And, as icing on the cake, they proclaim that large multiplier effects during depression-like situations will not only raise employment but also provide the wherewithal to repay the government debt. They also emphasize the longer-term implications of deep unemployment that create a segment of the labor force that may become unemployable.

Notwithstanding these disagreements, the bottom line, therefore, is that the pre-2008-crisis faith in just one monetary lever, ensuring stability and growth, happened to be wishful thinking. The dynamics of macroaggregates depends on heterogeneous expectations, information, and contractual and credit frictions of erstwhile utility seekers under incomplete information, in morally hazardous and incomplete financial markets, subject to sundry shocks. Policy management is correspondingly complex, particularly in the presence of de-leveraging and liquidity trap conditions; and still more challenging in imperfect regulatory regimes where low inflation is targeted to ensure full employment and rapid economic growth, susceptible to moral hazard, adverse selection, coordination failures—the unavoidable characteristics of any financial intermediation. That is, we should not lose sight of the financial sector as a central pillar of the macroeconomic model. Fiscal policy also needs serious rethinking. The politically congenial notion that all deficit spending including tax rebates is equally efficacious and necessarily crowds out private sector spending is not valid, in view of the various frictions including politico-economic-based frictions, and a consensus needs to be forged on how governments attempting to resolve various conflicting economic and political interests can be disciplined to discharge their obligations responsibly, without squandering the benefits of deficit spending on special interests and rent seekers.

1.2 The Road Map

Part I of this book presents a recent history of global and regional financial crises in the past three decades. It surveys major financial crises that took place in the 1990s, the 2000s, and the 2010s: (a) the credit implosion leading to a severe banking crisis in Japan; (b) the meltdown of foreign reserves triggered by foreign hot-money flight from the frothy economies of developing Asian nations with fixed exchange rate regimes; (c) the global financial crisis; and (d) the euro-zone crisis.

Japan was slashed by a speculative tornado in 1986–1991. It was localized, brief, and devastating, with allegedly paralytic consequences often described as the "lost decades" (1986–2013). The phenomenon was a selective price bubble, disconnected from low and decelerating GDP inflation all the way to deflation, as well as more vigorous but diminishing rates of aggregate economic growth converging asymptotically toward zero, or worse.

The Asian financial crisis that erupted in 1997 was triggered by a foreign capital flight, which induced liquidity and credit implosion. It began as a run on Asian banks by foreign short-term depositors and expanded into an assault on government foreign currency reserves, sending shock waves as far as the shores of Russia and of Argentina.

The global financial crisis triggered the deepest and longest recession since the Great Depression of the 1930s. The defining event of the 2008 global financial crisis was a "hemorrhagic stroke": a paralytic implosion of the loanable funds markets. The post–September 2008 emergency was caused by the terrifying realization that major financial institutions, especially those connected with hedge funds, could not cover their current obligations either with asset sales or short-term bank credit because confidence in the value of their assets had been lost, and short-term lending suddenly ceased. People everywhere were panicked at the prospect of cascading financial bankruptcies, where the securities of failed companies contaminated the value of other assets, triggering margin calls, shuttered credit access, lost savings, bank runs, stock market crashes, liquidity crises, universal insolvency, economic collapse, and global ruination.

The global financial crisis, which erupted in the United States, instantaneously swept across Europe and triggered the euro-zone crisis. Like the United States, the European Monetary Union was ripe for a crash. As mentioned earlier, the EMU had its own real estate bubble (specifically in Ireland and Spain), had indulged in excessive deficit spending, was financially deregulated, and had rapidly expanded credit (partly through derivatives). Policy responses and recovery patterns for key European Union members such as Germany, France (within the euro zone), and the United Kingdom (outside the euro zone) were similar. However, after the bubble burst and the crisis began unfolding, it became clear that the euro-zone plight differed from America's in one fundamental respect. There was no exact counterpart of euro-zone GIIPS (Greece, Ireland, Italy, Portugal, and Spain) in the United States. Some American states had overborrowed, but the sovereign debt crisis didn't place individual states at deflationary risk or threaten the viability of the federal union. Not so for some members within the euro zone.

Part II of this book reviews the analytics of financial fragilities, which underlie banking crises, and credit frictions, which underlie debt crises. These fragilities and frictions are rooted in coordination failures, incentive problems, asymmetric information, risk-shifting behavior, and excessive optimism among participants in collateralized debt markets. Each and every one of these forces is present in global financial problems that occurred over the past decades.

Banks are known to finance long-term assets with short-term deposits. The advantage of this arrangement is that it enables banks to provide risk sharing to investors who might face early liquidity needs. However, this also exposes the bank to the risk of a bank run, whereby many creditors decide to withdraw their money early. The key problem is that of a coordination failure, which stands at the root of the fragility of banking systems: When more depositors withdraw their money from a bank, the bank is more likely to fail, and so other depositors have a stronger incentive to withdraw.

A key policy question is how to avoid the damages from coordination failures and runs in the financial system. While insurance has been effective, its implications for moral hazard have to be considered carefully, and so there is room for more research on the optimal deposit insurance policy. Using recent developments in economic theory, global-games models enable analysis of the benefit of insurance in mitigating runs against the cost in generating moral hazard, leading to characterization of optimal insurance policy. In the above models of financial institution failures, the focus was on the behavior of depositors or creditors of the banks. However, problems in the financial sector often arise from the other side of the balance sheet. The quality of loans provided by the banks is determined in equilibrium, and frictions exist that make banks cut on lending to protect themselves from bad outcomes.

While basic economic theory suggests that in equilibrium, prices adjust so that supply equals demand and no rationing arises, it shows that this will not occur in the credit market because of the endogeneity of the quality of the loan. There are two key frictions that stand behind rationing: moral hazard and adverse selection. A large recent literature studies the implications of such frictions for lending, especially the implications of moral hazard. If a borrower has the ability to divert resources at the expense of the creditor, then creditors will be reluctant to lend to borrowers. Hence, for credit to flow efficiently from the creditor to the borrower, it is crucial that the borrower maintains "skin in the game"; that is, that he has enough at stake in the success of the project, and so does not have a strong incentive to divert resources. This creates a limit on credit, and it can be amplified when economic conditions worsen, leading to a crisis.

Part III of this book reviews the analytics of currency crises and balance of payments crises. Currency crises occur when the country is trying to maintain a fixed exchange rate regime with capital mobility but faces conflicting policy needs such as fiscal imbalances or a fragile financial sector that need to be resolved by independent monetary policy. An important aspect of financial crises is the involvement of the government and the potential collapse of arrangements it creates, such as an exchange rate regime. Many currency crises (e.g., the early 1970s breakdown of the Bretton Woods global system) originate from the desire of governments to maintain a fixed exchange rate regime that is inconsistent with other policy goals. This might lead to the sudden collapse of the regime. The literature on currency crises begins with the first-generation and second-generation models.

Such models are highly relevant to the current situation in the European Monetary Union. In the basis of the theory of currency crises is the famous international finance tri-lemma, according to which a country can choose only two of three policy goals: free international capital flows, monetary autonomy, and the stability of the exchange rate. Countries in the euro zone now realize that in their attempt to achieve the first and third goals, they have given up on the second goal, and so have limited ability to absorb the shocks in economic activity and maintain their national debts, triggered by the global financial crisis. Coordination problems among investors and currency speculators aggravate this situation and may have an important effect on whether individual countries in Europe are forced to default and/or leave the monetary union.

The third-generation models of currency crises connect models of banking crises and credit frictions with traditional models of currency crises. Such models were motivated by the East Asian crises of the late 1990s, where financial institutions and exchange rate regimes collapsed together, demonstrating the linkages between governments and financial institutions that can expose the system to further fragility.

Part III also addresses international capital flows with information frictions that are prone to the so-called sudden-stop phenomenon, whereby capital inflows unexpectedly dry up. Economists tend to favor capital mobility across national borders as it allows capital to seek the highest rate of return, adjusted for risk. Unrestricted capital flows further offer several advantages. First, international flows reduce risk through diversification of lending and investment. Second, global integration of financial markets can contribute to the spread of best practices in corporate governance, accounting standards, and legal practices. Third, global mobility of capital limits the ability of governments to pursue bad policies. In an integrated world capital market, with perfect information, all forms of capital flows are indistinguishable. Information frictions are important elements needed in order to differentiate between equity tradable debt and loan flows, as well as between various types of equity flows. Foreign direct investment (FDI) has proved to be resilient during financial crises. For instance, in East Asian countries, such investment was remarkably stable during the global financial crises of 1997–1998. In sharp contrast, other forms of private capital flows—portfolio equity and debt flows, and particularly short-term flows—were subject to large reversals during the same period. If domestic and foreign investors differ in their information sets regarding future stock market returns, there exists an efficiency-based pecking order of capital flows among debt foreign investment, portfolio foreign investment, and direct foreign investment.

Part IV of this book deals with key developments of the emerging macroeconomic paradigm: from an analytical framework that features full capital-market arbitrage, smooth credit, Ricardian-equivalence properties, representative agents, and efficient monetary management, to the framework with multiple agents, which incorporates debt frictions, liquidity traps, and relatively ineffective monetary management and provides a role for fiscal policy in aggregate demand management. The analytical framework based on the frictionless paradigm captures well the role of globalization forces and the reduction in inflation in the 1990s Great Moderation era. The multiple-agent, market-friction revised analytical framework captures some key features of the Great Recession that occurred in the aftermath of the 2008 global financial crisis. It gives insight about the macroeconomic effects of debt over-hang on economic activity and inflation, when the monetary policy rate reaches its lower bound.

Finally, this book concludes with an epilogue that presents some ideas for further research.

I   Recent Financial Crises

Carmen Reinhart and Kenneth Rogoff (2009), surveying centuries-old crises, have discovered startling qualitative and quantitative parallels across a number of standard financial crisis indicators in 18 postwar banking crises (see also Chancellor 2000). They found that banking crises were protracted (output declining on average for 2 years): asset prices fell steeply, with housing plunging 35 percent on average and equity prices declining by 55 percent over 3.5 years; unemployment rose by 7 percentage points over 4 years, and output fell by 9 percent. Two important common denominators were reduced consumption caused by diminished wealth effects and impaired balance sheets resistant to monetary expansion when interest is at its lower bound (liquidity trap).

2 The 1990s and Early 2000s

This chapter surveys major financial crises that took place in the 1990s and early 2000s: (a) the credit implosion leading to a severe banking crisis in Japan; (b) the meltdown of foreign reserves triggered by foreign hot-money flight from the frothy economies of developing Asian nations with fixed exchange rate regimes economies.[1]

Financial institutions, banks, and shadow banks (financial institutions providing credit through the derivative trade) are typically arbitrageurs. They borrow short at low rates, lending money long for higher returns. Many also offer a wide range of fee-generating services, including packaging and distributing derivatives.[2] Like any other business, their fortunes are affected by fluctuations in aggregate demand and supply—flourishing in good times, and floundering in bad. Their health in this way partly depends on the prosperity of others, but the relationship is asymmetric because financial institutions together with monetary authorities determine the aggregate supply of money and credit. Financial institutions are special. They are strategically positioned to lever directly and indirectly more than most other businesses, to expand the aggregate money and credit supplies, to create debt, and to affect speculatively stock, commodity, and real estate prices. Self-discipline and competent regulation are essential but are too often compromised by the lure of easy profits and a regulatory desire to foster financial innovation. Financial crises contract aggregate money and credit, diminish the income velocity of money, and jeopardize the profitability, solvency, and survivability of firms throughout the economy. In the most dire cases, they can wreck national economic systems (*systemic risk*).

Financial crises vary in frequency and intensity. There were three major crisis events during the past 20 years: the Japanese "zombie bank" debacle, the 1997 Asian financial crisis (broadened to include

Russia in the period 1998–1999 and Argentina in the period 2001–2002), and the global financial crisis of 2008. The first two were respectively local and mostly regional, but the third was worldwide. Two were exacerbated by Keynesian liquidity traps and debased sovereign debt (as tax revenues dropped and bailout money surged), and all were severe, but none approached the 1929 Great Depression's ferocity. They provide interesting clues about how a black swan catastrophe (Taleb 2010) might have unfolded, but are more useful for learning how to deter and mitigate future financial crises and recessions (depressions) in perpetually changing technological, regulatory, developmental, transitional, and psychological environments.

This broad perspective is essential because although historical patterns are instructive, they cannot be relied on entirely either to identify causes accurately or to predict future events. Things never are completely the same (continuity), as human societies change, learn, adapt, and evolve. On one hand, recent crises have much in common with the Great Depression. All followed asset bubbles. They started in the financial sector and gradually spread to the real sector. During these crises, many financial institutions either defaulted or had to be bailed out. The Japanese and 2008 global crises appear to have begun with burst bubbles that dried up credit and drove short-term interest rates toward zero. On the other hand, the crises of the 1990s and 2000s displayed even more differences judged from the Great Depression benchmark. Institutions, policies, financial innovation, globalization (versus autarky), regulation, deregulation, floating exchange rates, and reduced financial transparency have profoundly altered the potentials, conditions, dynamics, and rules of the game. Domestically, nations have established and expanded an alphabet soup of oversight and regulatory agencies including the 1933 Glass-Steagall Act (repealed in 1999), the 1933 Federal Deposit Insurance Corporation (FDIC), and the 1934 Securities and Exchange Commission (SEC).

Internationally, the world today is still being swept by a wave of globalization, characterized by rapidly growing foreign trade, capital movements, technology transfer, direct foreign investment, outsourcing of product and parts, information flows, improved transport, and even increased labor mobility. This contrasts sharply with a post–World War I universe in retreat from the prewar globalization wave that began in the 1870s, and the protectionist, beggar-thy-neighbor, isolationist, and autarkic tendencies of the 1930s. The pre–Great Depression international exchange and settlements mechanism underpinning the old regime has vanished. The gold standard and the 1944 Bretton Woods system (which established the International Monetary Fund [IMF] and World Bank Group) fixed and adjustable peg exchange rate mechanisms are no long with us, replaced since the early 1970s by flexible exchange rates exhibiting a distinctive pattern of core-periphery relations that some describe as Bretton Woods II.[3] Free-trade globalization has been evangelically promoted by the 1947 General Agreement on Trade and Tariffs (GATT), its 1995 World Trade Organization (WTO) successor, and diverse regional customs unions, while the IMF provided currency and crisis support, and the World Bank provided development assistance. Many claim that as a consequence of these institutional advances, emerging nations including China and India have not only been able to catch up rapidly with the West, but in the process accelerated global economic growth above the long-run historical norm, buttressing prosperity and dampening business cycle oscillations.

Scholarly and governmental attitudes toward managing financial crises and their consequences likewise bear little resemblance to those prevailing after World War I and through the early years of the Great Depression. Back then, Say's law and government neutrality were gospel. What goes up must and should come down. If financial and related speculative activities raised prices and wages excessively, it was believed that the government should let those responsible reap what they sowed by allowing prices and wages freely to adjust downward and firms to go belly up. There was some, but very little, room for stimulatory monetary and fiscal policy. The Keynesian revolution as it has gradually unfolded and evolved radically altered priorities and attitudes toward macrocausality and appropriate intervention. Its seminal diagnostic contribution lay in showing the decisive roles of price rigidities and credit crises in causing and protracting depressions. Sometimes, depressions began when real wages were too high, inducing output and credit to fall. On other occasions, depressions were engendered by financial crises (sharp contractions in loanable funds [credit], and consequent liquidity crises), and then inured by "sticky wages and prices." Regardless of the sequencing, Keynes claimed that two gaps—the first a supply shock, the second impairments of the Walrasian automatic wage and price adjustment mechanism (invisible hand)—created double grounds for fiscal intervention. Policy makers accordingly made the restoration of full employment and economic recovery their priorities, dethroning neutrality in favor of activist fiscal and supportive monetary intervention. Where once it was resolutely believed that eradicating anticompetitive practices and empowering the market were the best strategies for coping with financial crises and their aftermaths, Keynesians, neo-Keynesians, and post-Keynesians all now believe that fighting deflation and stimulating aggregate effective demand are the highest goods, even if this means rescuing those who cause crises in the first place and tolerating other inefficiencies. These attitudes are epitomized by Ben Bernanke's unflagging commitment to bail out any institution that poses a "systemic threat" and to print as much money as it takes (quantitative easing [QE]) (Bernanke 2012), while governments around the world push deficit spending to new heights (sometimes passively due to unexpected slow economic and tax revenue growth), tempered only by looming sovereign debt crises. These attitudes also are evident in growth accelerating excess demand strategies and prosperity promoting international trade expansion initiatives.

This characterization of novel aspects of the post–Great Depression order would have been complete two decades ago but is no longer because it conceals a penchant among policy makers to square the circle. Governments today are intent on restoring aspects of pre–Great Depression laissez-faire, including financial sector liberalization and decontrol, at the same time as they press disciplined, globally coordinated monetary and fiscal intervention. One can imagine an optimal regime where regulatory, simulative, and laissez-faire imperatives are perfectly harmonized, but not the reality. Consequently, the most novel aspect of the 1990s and 2000s may well be the emergence of a global economic management regime built on contradictory principles that can be likened to stepping full throttle on the accelerator while intermittently and often simultaneously slamming on the regulatory brakes.

Which subsets of these factors, including the null subset, appear to best explain the Japanese, Asian, and 2008 world financial crises and their aftermaths? Let us consider each event separately and then try to discern larger, emerging patterns.

2.1   Japan's Financial Crisis: The Lost 1990s and Beyond

Japan was slashed by a speculative tornado in the period 1986–1991, commonly called the *baburukeiki* ("bubble economy"). It was localized, brief, and devastating, with allegedly paralytic consequences often described as *ushiwanaretajunen* ("two lost decades"). It started a long period of stagnation (figure 2.1). The phenomenon was a selective price

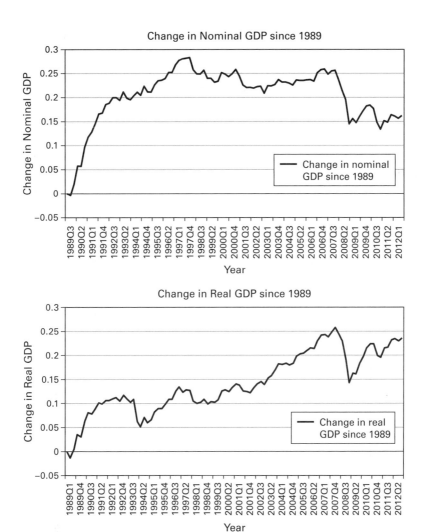

Figure 2.1
Japan's Stagnation

bubble, disconnected from low and decelerating GDP inflation, as well as more vigorous but diminishing rates of aggregate economic growth converging asymptotically toward zero, or worse (after the bubble burst, 1992–2010). The bubble was most conspicuously manifested in rabid land- and stock-price speculation, but also affected Japanese antiques and collectibles (like high-quality native ceramics and lacquerware). The Nikkei 225 (Neikei Heikin Kabuka) stock market index rose from below 7,000 in the early 1980s to 38,916 on December 29, 1989, plummeted to 30,000 seven months later, and continued to fall with fits and starts thereafter before reaching a 27-year low of 7,055 on March 10, 2009. In January 2011 it hovered around 10,000. At its height, Japan's stock market capitalization accounted for 60 percent of the planetary total, but by 2011 the worth of Japan's market capitalization was a pale shadow of its former glory. The real estate story was similar. Condo prices increased 140 percent between 1987 and 1991, on top of already globally sky-high values, then plummeted 40 percent by 1994.[4] At the bubble's apex, the value of a parcel of land near the emperor's imperial palace in Tokyo equaled that of the state of California. By 2004, prime "A" property in Tokyo's financial district had slumped to less than 1 percent of its peak, with the total destruction of paper wealth mounting into the tens of trillions of dollars. The speculative frenzy predictably ended badly but also displayed uniquely Japanese characteristics.

Thanks to deflation and low rear output growth, in nominal terms Japan's GDP in 2013 is no higher than it was in 1991.

The immediate cause of the crisis was financial; an institutional willingness to accommodate domestic hard asset speculation in lieu of low, zero, and even negative returns on business investment and consumer savings accounts. Corporations and households, having piled up immense idle cash balances during the miraculous "Golden Sixties" and subsequent prosperity through 1985, and encouraged to believe that the best was yet to come despite diminishing returns to industrial investment, seized on stock and real estate speculation as the next great investment frontier. They succumbed to what savvy Wall Street calls a "bigger pig" mentality, persuading themselves that fortunes were at their fingertips because whatever price little pigs paid today for stocks, real estate, and collectibles, there always would be bigger pigs tomorrow willing to pay more. Banks capitulating to the frenzy began binge lending, rationalizing that clients always would be able to repay interest and principal from their capital gains, until one fine day they ruefully discovered that there were no bigger pigs at the end of the rainbow. This epiphany, coupled with a panic-driven free fall in asset values and capitalization, left bankers in both a predicament and a quandary.

The predicament was that by regulatory rule, slashed asset values required bankers to contract loan activity and force borrowers to meet their interest and principal repayment obligations even if this meant driving clients into bankruptcy. The quandary was that Japanese cultural ethics strongly proscribe maximizing bank profits at borrowers' expense. Through thick and thin, Japanese are trained from birth to support each other communally, subordinating personal utility and profit seeking to the group's well-being. Watching out first for number one is never the right thing to do, as it is in competitive, individualistic societies. Tough love is not an option; burden sharing is the only viable course,[5] which in this instance meant refusing to "mark capitalizations to market," seeking government assistance, and stalling for time hoping that with patience, clients' financial health eventually would be restored. This judgment was not wrong. Japanese corporations operating under the same cultural obligation immediately began earmarking revenues from current operations for debt reduction at the expense of new capital formation and refrained from new borrowing to cover the gap. Banks for their part not only maintained the fiction that outstanding loans were secure, but also provided cash for current corporate operations and consumer loans at virtually no cost above the bare minimum for bank survival. Moreover, they kept their lending concentrated at home, instead of seeking higher returns abroad.

These actions averted the broader calamities that typically accompany financial crises. Japan did not swoon into hyperdepression (GDP never fell, growing 1.7 percent per annum in the period 1990–1993),[6] or experience mass involuntary unemployment. The country was not swept by a wave of bankruptcies. There was no capital flight, sustained yen depreciation, deterioration in consumer welfare, or civil disorder. However, Japan's economy deteriorated fast into a liquidity-trap equilibrium, where fiscal policy becomes more potent whereas conventional monetary policy is not. There was need for temporary government deficit spending, quantitative easing, comprehensive financial regulatory reforms, and high-profile criminal prosecutions. Interest rates already were low, and although the government did pursue deficit spending, arguably it did matter less than in a strictly Keynesian universe because Japanese industrial workers in large companies were employed for life (*shushinkoyo*). For pedestrians on *hondori* ("main street") who blinked, it seemed as if nothing had happened at all beyond a moment of speculative insanity.

However, matters looked very different to Western macrotheorists and Japanese policy makers, particularly those who erroneously believed that deficits and loose monetary policy are the wellsprings of sustainable rapid aggregate economic growth (as distinct from recovery). But, their prescription for Japan's "toxic asset" problem was to bite the bullet, endure the pain, and move on swiftly to robust, ever expanding prosperity. Given ideal assumptions, biting the bullet is best because it doesn't sacrifice the greater good of maximizing long-term social welfare for the lesser benefits of short-term social protection. Advocates contend that the Japanese government fundamentally erred in condoning bank solicitude for the plight of endangered borrowers and in abetting banks with external assistance because these actions transformed otherwise healthy institutions into "zombie banks" (the living dead),[7] unable to play their crucial role in bankrolling investment, technology development, and fast-track economic growth.

Their claim has some disputed merit (Miyajima and Yafeh 2007),[8] but also is seriously incomplete. It is true that Japanese growth has been impeded by zombie banks, deflation, the liquidity trap conjectured by Paul Krugman early in the 1990s,[9] faulty banking policy, and the aftermath of stock and real estate market speculation, but it should have done much better because its competitiveness has substantially improved. Stock market and real estate values denominated in yen are where they were three decades ago, while prices elsewhere across the globe have soared. Japan is more competitive now on inflation and exchange rates bases against much of the world than it was in 1990. Moreover, the government has tenaciously pursued a zero interest, loose money policy, in tandem with high deficit spending that has raised the national debt to 150 percent of GDP. If Japan's growth retardation was in fact primarily due to insufficient zombie bank business credit, government stimulus should have mitigated much of the problem.

There is an explanation for Japan's almost three lost decades that has little to do with two concurrent and isolated speculative incidents, one in the stock market, the other in real estate, with scant sustained effects on production and employment. The advantages of Japan's postwar recovery and modernizing catch-up diminished steadily in the 1980s and were fully depleted by 1990, when its per capita GDP hit 81 percent of the American level. Thereafter, Japan's culturally imposed, anticompetitive restrictions on its domestic economic activities became increasingly pronounced, causing its living standard to diminish to 73 percent of America's norm. Japan at the end of the 1980s was poised to fall back, with or without a financial crisis, and it is in this sense that the almost three lost decades are being erroneously blamed on the bubble and its zombie banking aftermath.[10] Yes, there were eye-popping speculative stock market and real estate price busts, but they weren't the national economic debacles they are usually painted to be, either in the short or intermediate term.

This interpretation raises a larger issue that cannot yet be resolved, but nonetheless is worth broaching. Does Japan's fate presage China's future? When the advantages of catch-up are depleted, when China's population grays, as Japan's has begun to,[11] and when the delusion of permanent miraculous growth subsides, will the end of days be punctuated with a colossal speculative bust, followed by uncountable lost decades? Perhaps not, but still it is easy to see how history may repeat itself.

2.2   The 1997 Asian Financial Crisis and Out-of-Region Spillovers

The Asian financial crisis that erupted in 1997 was a money and credit implosion induced by foreign capital flight (see Stiglitz 1996; Fratzscher 1998; Radelet and Sachs 1998; Rajan and Zingales 1998a).[12] It began as a run on Asian banks by foreign short-term depositors and expanded into an assault on government foreign currency reserves, sending shock waves as far as the shores of Russia and of Argentina.[13] Banks were decimated by acute insolvency. They did not have the cash on hand to cover mass withdrawals of short-term deposits because these funds had been lent long, sparking asset fire sales, slashed capitalizations, and credit and money contractions, which in turn triggered widespread business failures, depressions, and mass unemployment. In 1997–1998, Thailand's GDP plummeted 8 percent, Indonesia's 14 percent, and South Korea's 6 percent (Maddison 2003a). Foreign capital flight (repatriation of short-term deposits), compounded by insufficient government foreign currency reserves, soon compelled steep devaluations that increased import costs, reduced *command national income* (domestic purchasing power including "command" over foreign imports), disordered balance sheets, and otherwise diminished real national consumption.

These events, unlike Japan's financial crisis 7 years earlier, were triggered by foreign capital flight rather than domestic stock and real estate meltdowns and were not quarantined. The crisis started in Thailand and spread rapidly to Indonesia, South Korea, Hong Kong,[14] Malaysia, and the Philippines, with smaller reverberations in India, Taiwan, Singapore, and Brunei. Fledgling market communist regimes in China, Vietnam, Laos, and Cambodia were spared runs on their banks and foreign currency reserves by stringent state banking and foreign exchange controls: They experienced secondary shocks from diminished regional economic activity, but otherwise escaped unscathed.

The root cause of the runs on Asia's banks and foreign reserves was the foreign-financed Asian economic development and East–West interest rate differentials. After World War II, Asia became a magnet for both foreign direct and portfolio investment, driving foreign debt-to-GDP ratios above 100 percent in the four large ASEAN economies (Thailand, Malaysia, Indonesia, and the Philippines) in the period 1993–1996, and causing local asset market prices to soar (real estate and stocks). Rapid, near-double-digit GDP growth contributed to the asset boom, inspiring confidence that investments were safe because Asia's miracles were expected to continue for the foreseeable future. The GDP growth rates of Thailand, South Korea, and Indonesia during the decade preceding the Asian financial crisis were 9.6, 8.2, and 7.2 percent per annum, respectively (Maddison 2003b). At the same time, Asia's high interest rates attracted the *carry trade*: short-term borrowing of low-yielding currencies such as the Japanese yen and their subsequent short-term investment in high-yielding foreign bank deposits and similar liquid debt instruments. Short-term "hot" money (including large sums from Japanese financial institutions searching for positive returns on near-money instruments well after Japan's financial crisis ended) poured into the region, creating what increasingly came to be perceived as a pan-Asian bubble economy, exacerbated by *crony capitalism*,[15] severe political corruption, and instability (especially in Thailand, Malaysia, and Indonesia).

Foreign investors steeled by their faith in Asian miracles at first were not perturbed by the frothiness of the Orient's markets, but the swelling bubble, compounded by surging current account trade deficits, undermined their confidence. Speculators, hot-money carry traders, and other investors gradually grasped that the high returns they were reaping could be wiped out by catastrophic devaluations and began planning for the worst, realizing that those who fled early would

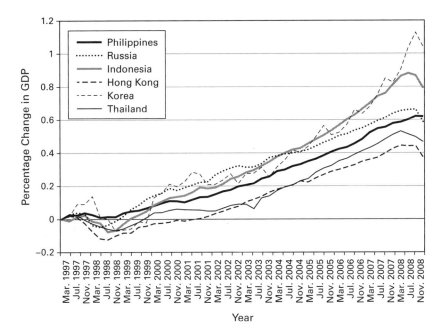

Figure 2.2
Gross Domestic Product and the 1997 Crisis: East Asian Countries and Russia

preserve their wealth, and those who dallied would be left holding an empty bag. The incentive to flee was increased further by developments outside the region. America's Federal Reserve chairman, Alan Greenspan, began nudging U.S. interest rates higher to deter inflation, creating an attractive safe haven for hot-money hedging, made more appealing by the prospect of an appreciating dollar. The effect of the 1997 regional crisis on East Asia and Russia is plotted in figure 2.2.

The precise combination of factors that ignited full-throttle capital flight is open to dispute. Southeast Asian export growth dramatically slowed in spring 1996, aggravating current account deficits. China started to out-compete its regional rivals for foreign, directly invested loanable funds. The domestic asset bubble began to pop with stock and land prices in retreat, forcing large numbers of firms to default on their debts. No doubt for these and many other reasons including asymmetric information (Mishkin 1999), opacity, corrupt corporate governance, and crony capitalism, foreign investors rushed for the exits in early 1997, symbolically culminating in the Thai government's decision on July 2, 1997, to abandon its fixed exchange rate, allowing the value of its baht to freely float. Over the course of the next year, the baht's value fell 40 percent. The Indonesian, Philippine, Malaysian, and South Korean currencies swiftly followed suit, declining 83, 37, 39, and 34 percent, respectively.

Devaluation, stock and real estate market crashes, bankruptcies, mass unemployment, wilted interest rates, and heightened risk aversion dissolved the fundamental disequilibria that had beset the region before the fall, only to be immediately replaced by urgent new priorities. Downward spirals had to be arrested, economies stabilized, and steps taken not only to achieve rapid recovery, but also to foster structural changes supporting long-term modernization and growth. Thai economic planners and their counterparts elsewhere in the region had a coherent overview of what needed to be done (mundane partisan squabbles aside) but, unlike the Japanese 7 years earlier, sought external foreign assistance from the International Monetary Fund, the World Bank, the Asian Development Bank, and individual nations including China to finance balance of payments deficits and facilitate structural adjustment. Japan did not run a current account deficit during its crisis, did not need foreign exchange rate support or structural adjustment assistance funding, and so relied entirely on its own resources, whereas the dependency of non-communist developing Asia on the developed West was placed in stark relief. The region of course could have gone it alone; however, its aspirations for fast-track convergence and countercrisis stimulus were clearly tied to its integration into the global financial system, and perhaps acceptance of some bad IMF conditionality as the price for the good.

There has been an extensive discussion over whether Washington Consensus–style monetary and fiscal stringency combined with mandated economy-opening structural reforms imposed by the International Monetary Fund helped or harmed Asia.[16] This issue is important, but only so for current purposes insofar as structural reforms increased or diminished the likelihood of future crises. The evidence to date on balance, despite strong claims to the contrary, favors the regional decision to follow the IMF's tough love advice. Asia accepted fiscal austerity and monetary restraint. It liberalized, amassed large foreign currency reserves, maintained floating exchange rates, and prospered. After enduring a protracted and perhaps excessively painful period of adjustment, Asia not only resumed rapid growth within the IMF's framework but also, when push came to shove in 2008, weathered the global financial shock wave better than most. It appears that although global financial liberalization does pose clear and present speculative dangers as IMF critics contend, the risks can be managed with prudence and discipline.[17]

Some have suggested that Russia provides a cogent counter–Washington Consensus example because having liberalized after its own financial crisis in 1997 and recovered, its economy was crushed by the 2008 financial crisis. The claim however is misleading on a variety of grounds. There simply is too much dissimilarity for the Russian case to be persuasive. Unlike Asia, Russia was mired in hyperdepression when it defaulted on its sovereign euro-denominated debt in 1997. It never received significant sums of direct and/or hot-money inflows into the private sector during the Yeltsin years, had a floating peg exchange rate, and received no IMF support after the ruble collapsed. Consequently, it is fatuous to lump Russia into the same basket with Asia (Shleifer and Treisman 2005; Rosefielde 2005; Vavilov 2010).[18] The systems and contexts of Asia and Russia are too disparate for them to be pooled. The same argument for different reasons applies to Argentina in the period 1999–2001. The crises in Russia and Argentina were both linked to sovereign debt issues, but their problematic pasts and roles within the global economic and financial system place them in separate categories.

Clarity in this regard is essential for gauging the historical significance of the Asian financial crisis. Some like Niall Ferguson contend that Asia's financial crisis was the first tremor of the second globalization age that emerged after the Bretton Woods international monetary and financial order collapsed in the late 1970s to early 1980s, weakly implying that future crises will mimic Asia's experience (Ferguson 2008, 2010). This is implausible. Asia's crisis provides an object lesson on the broad danger posed to a wide variety of economies in various stages of economic development by overly exuberant international financial liberalization, but does not offer a blueprint about how things must unfold.

3 The 2008 Global Crisis

The origins of the 2008 financial crisis can be traced to various milestones in the construction of the post–World War II American economy.[1] During the 1950s, Keynesianism became orthodox at the same time momentum built to rescind sundry New Deal and wartime restrictions on free enterprise including wage-price controls and fair-trade retail pricing (Miller-Tydings Act of 1937; McGuire Act of 1952; both rescinded in 1975 by the Consumer Goods Price Act). Deregulation in rail, truck, and air transportation during the 1970s, ocean transport in the 1980s, the natural gas and petroleum sectors in the period 1970–2000, and telecommunications in the 1990s created opportunities for asset value speculation, soon facilitated by complementary deregulation initiatives in the financial sector. The Depository Institutions Deregulation and Monetary Control Act (DIDMCA) of 1980 and the Garn–St. Germain Depository Institutions Act of 1982 both increased the scope of permissible bank services, fostered mergers, facilitated collusive pricing, and relaxed accounting rules (Moody's, for example, is permitted to accept fees from insurers it rates). Beginning in the early 1990s, banks shifted from the direct loan business to packaging and marketing novel debt instruments such as mortgage-backed securities (ultimately including subprime loans) to other financial institutions, and shortly thereafter President William Jefferson Clinton approved the Gramm-Leach-Bliley Act of 1999, enhancing business flexibility. The Glass-Steagall Act of 1933 (Banking Act of 1933) had compartmentalized banks, prohibiting those engaged in stable businesses like mortgages and consumer loans from participating in riskier stock brokerage, insurance, commercial, and industrial activities, the intention being to build a firewall against speculative contagion. The repeal of provisions banning holding companies from owning other financial companies ushered in an era of financial merger mania across old divisional lines, allowing companies like Citicorp and Travelers Group to unite.

These developments, replicated across much of the globe, were all positive from the standpoint of neoclassical microeconomic theory because they enhanced competitive efficiency, with the proviso that moral hazards and speculative abuses were optimally contained by residual regulations (liberalization). However, if residual laissez-faire (do whatever you want) regulations were inadequate, then ensuing financial crisis costs could easily outweigh deregulatory efficiency gains.

Clearly, there are legitimate grounds for conjecturing deregulatory involvement in the 2008 global financial crisis, but deregulation isn't the only suspect. The financial environment also was placed in jeopardy by revisionist Keynesianism. John Maynard Keynes was an apostate monetarist who devised and spread the notion of counter-depressionary fiscal deficit in his book *General Theory of Employment, Interest and Money* (Keynes 1936).

Keynes contended that the Great Depression had been caused by deficient aggregate effective demand brought about by negative income effects, prolonged by a liquidity trap, and he claimed that full employment could be easily restored by offsetting private hoarding (speculative idle cash balances) with government expenditure programs (deficit-financed state procurements and programs). Other things equal, Keynes insisted competitive markets could and would achieve perpetual full employment, if it were not for income (multiplier) effects, and this destabilizing force could be overcome without inflation through countercyclical government deficit spending and countervailing surpluses. There was no place in Keynes' universe for continually mounting "structural deficits," sovereign debt, and/or "managed" inflation that could feed speculation and cause financial crises.

Nonetheless, immediately after World War II, the U.S. government passed the Employment Act of 1946 prioritizing the attainment and maintenance of full employment (further codified and expanded in the Humphrey-Hawkins Full Employment Act of 1978). The law did not fix quantitative targets, but marked the Truman administration's expansion of federal powers to include macroeconomic administration, management, and regulation, without explicit constitutional sanction, and established the Council of Economic Advisors to aid presidential policy making, as well as the Joint Economic Committee of Congressmen and Senators to review executive policies.

These actions enabled Washington to go beyond the perimeters of Keynesian orthodoxy whenever full employment could not be sustained with transcyclically balanced federal budgets. The exclusion remained moot throughout much of the 1950s until William Phillips discovered (Phillips 1958), and Paul Samuelson popularized, the notion that full employment could only be maintained with "excess" monetary and/or fiscal stimulation accompanied by inflationary side-effects (Phillip's curve). Keynes, many concluded, was almost right. Deficit spending was essential, but it also should be applied no matter how much inflation it generates to secure the higher goal of full employment. Full-employment advocates insist that governments are "morally" obliged to deficit spend forever, a position still widely maintained despite demonstrations by Milton Friedman and Edmund Phelps that Phillips was wrong in the medium and long runs by omitting inflationary expectations, which drive wage adjustments to compensate for expected inflation.

The orthodox Keynesian straitjacket was loosened further by Walter Heller, chairman (1961–1964) of President John F. Kennedy's Council of Economic Advisors, who introduced across-the-board tax cuts as a counter-recessionary stimulus, even though this meant creating credit not just for investment, but for consumption as well. "Keynes' employment and income multiplier theory required stimulating investment as the only legitimate method for combating deficient aggregate effective demand" (the Works Projects Administration [1932] providing 8 million jobs, and later investment tax credits).

Heller argued that new investment creates new jobs, wages, and derivatively increases consumption, whereas deficit consumption spending via diminished marginal propensities to consume merely transfers purchasing power from one recipient to another, without increasing employment. Heller's revisionism brushed Keynes' concerns aside, making it possible for politicians to claim that any deficit spending that benefited them and their constituents would stimulate aggregate economic activity and employment, including intertemporal income transfers from one consumer's pocket tomorrow to the next today.

This logic was extended by falsely contending that deficit spending and expansionary monetary policy accelerate long-term economic growth. Although there are no grounds for claiming that structural deficits and lax monetary policy accelerate scientific and technological progress (the ultimate source of sustainable economic growth), policy makers could not resist the temptation to assert that deficit spending and inflation are indispensable for maximizing current and future prosperity. The ploy has been successful as a political tactic, making not only deficits and inflation seem more palatable, but also widening the door to compounding past abuses by upping the ante whenever the economy sours. The reflex of policy makers is not to retrench, but to do more of what caused problems in the first place.

Academic macroeconomists likewise succumbed to wishful thinking, brushing aside the speculative momentum embedded in postwar institutional liberalization and fiscal indiscipline. Influenced by Lucas (1975, 2000, 2003) and Kydland and Prescott (1982), the conventional wisdom of 2000–2008 came to hold that business cycle oscillations were primarily caused by productivity shocks that lasted until price- and wage-setters disentangled real from nominal effects. These shocks sometimes generated inflation, which it was believed was best addressed with monetary policy. Accordingly, central bankers were tasked with the mission of maintaining slow and stable, Phillips curve–compatible inflation. Although, central bankers were supposed to be less concerned with real economic activity, many came to believe that full employment and 2 percent inflation could be sustained indefinitely by *divine coincidence*.[2] This miracle was said to be made all the better by the discovery that real economic performance could be regulated with a single monetary instrument, the short-term interest rate. Happily, arbitrage across time meant that central bankers could control all temporal interest rates, and arbitrage across asset classes implied that the Federal Reserve could similarly influence risk-adjusted rates for diverse securities. Fiscal policy, which had ruled the roost in this way under the influence of orthodox Keynesianism from 1950 to 1980, was relegated to a subsidiary role aided by theorists' beliefs in the empirical validity of Ricardian-equivalence arguments and skepticism about lags and political priorities (De Grauwe 2010). The financial sector likewise was given short shrift, but this still left room for other kinds of nonmonetary intervention. The consensus view held that automatic stabilizers such as unemployment insurance should be retained to share risks in case there were any unpredictable shocks. Commercial bank credit similarly continued to be regulated, and federal deposit insurance preserved to deter bank runs, but otherwise finance was lightly supervised, especially "shadow banks," hedge funds, and derivatives.

A similar myopia blinded many to the destabilizing potential of Chinese state-controlled foreign trading. As postwar free trade gained momentum, liberalizers grew increasingly confident not only that competitive commerce was globally beneficial, but also that trade expansion of any kind increased planetary welfare. Consequently, few were perturbed after China's admission to the World Trade Organization (WTO) in 2001 either by the conspicuous undervaluation of the renminbi (RMB) fixed to support export-led development or by Beijing's ever-mounting dollar reserves. It was assumed that even if China overexported (at the expense of foreign importable jobs), this would be offset by employment gains in the exportable sector as China increased its import purchases. *Overtrading* as theory teaches is suboptimal, but not seriously harmful to aggregate employment and has the compensatory virtue of expanding international commerce.

However, a fly spoiled the ointment. The Chinese (and some others like Brazil) chose to hold low-return dollar reserve balances (hoarding), instead of importing as much as they exported, compounding a "saving glut" caused by a broad preference for relatively safe American financial assets.[3]

Beijing's dollar reserves grew from $250 billion in 2001 to $2.6 trillion in 2010. In a perfectly competitive universe, this would not matter because others would borrow these unused funds, but not so in a Keynesian world where rigidities of diverse sorts transform idle cash balances into deficient aggregate effective demand and simultaneously serve as a vehicle for financial hard asset speculation. For reasons that probably involve the Chinese Communist Party's desire to protect privileged producers in both its domestic importable and exportable sectors (implicit, stealth "beggar-thy-neighbor" tactics), Beijing became an immense source of global real and financial sector disequilibrium, contributing both to the 2008 financial crisis and its aftermath. Chinese leaders in its state-controlled foreign trade system had and still have the power to reset the renminbi exchange rate and increase import purchases, but they chose and are still choosing to do neither.

Factors that either triggered the 2008 financial crisis or that reinforced its severity could be listed as follows: (1) an evolving deregulatory consensus, especially concerning financial institutions; (2) a penchant for imposing political mandates on the private sector, such as subprime mortgages, student loan lending, and excess automobile industry health benefits, which drove GM and Chrysler into

bankruptcy in 2009; (3) the notion that government insurance guarantees, off-budget unfunded obligations such as social security, and mandated preferences to savings and loan banks were innocuous, despite
the $160 billion savings and loan debacle of the late 1980–1990s; (4)
deregulatory myopia and activist social policy, including the encour-
agement of subprime loans, adjustable rate mortgages (ARMs), and
tolerance of finance-based credit expansion, which flooded the globe
with credit[4]; (5) lax regulation of post–Bretton Woods international
capital flows (early 1970); (6) the "shareholder primacy" movement of
the 1980s that partnered Wall Street with CEOs to increase management's ability to enrich itself at shareholder expense, widening the gap
between ownership and control first brought to light by Adolf Berle
and Gardner Means in 1932; (7) an indulgent attitude toward destructive financial innovation apparent in the 1987 "program trading" and
2000–2002 "dot-com bubble" stock market crashes,[5] as well as the 1998
Long-Term Capital Management hedge fund collapse[6]; (8) a permissive
approach to financial auditing,[7] including mark to face valuation for
illiquid securities; (9) the creation of a one-way-street, too-big-to-fail
mentality that transformed prudent business activity into a venal speculative game on Wall Street, main street, and in Washington; (10) the
2001 Wall Street stock crash, which shifted speculative exuberance from
stocks to hard assets (commodities, land, natural resources, precious
metals, art, antiques, jewelry) and paved the way for the subordination
of individual stock market investment to institutional speculation[8]; (11)
credit easing in the wake of the dot-com bust, orchestrated by the
Federal Reserve, which started a consumer credit binge, reflected in
high consumption and low savings rates, adding fuel to the inflationary fires; (12) the events of September 11, 2001, the war in Iraq, and
massive tax cuts, which swelled America's federal budget deficit and
triggered a petro bubble (and broad-based commodity inflation); (13)
an epochal surge in global economic growth led by Brazil, Russia,
India, and China (BRIC) wrought by technology transfer, outsourcing,
and foreign direct investment, which induced a wave of speculative
euphoria; (14) Chinese stealth beggar-thy-neighbor renminbi undervaluation and dollar reserve hoarding, reflected in Chinese underimporting, a burgeoning American current account deficit, and an overseas
savings glut, which exacerbated inflationary pressures, raised prices
for American treasuries, and lowered interest rates (widely mischarac-
terized as "financing imports"); (15) the 2006 American housing bust,
which toxified mortgage and derivative financial instruments[9]; (16) the

emergence of "institutional" bank runs, where financial and nonfinancial companies flee repurchase (repo) agreements; (17) rapidly mounting sovereign debt in Iceland, several European Union states,[10] as well as similarly onerous debt obligations in California and Illinois; (18) a naive faith in *divine coincidence*; (19) a colossal regulatory blunder in imposing "mark to market" valuation (Fair Accounting Standard [FAS] 157) of illiquid assets increased separation of ownership from corporate control enabling top executives to compensate themselves excessively, including golden parachute perks. CEOs were institutionally encouraged to gamble with shareholders' money at negligible personal risk.

The 2008 global financial crisis thus was not just a garden-variety, white swan, business cycle event. It was a long time coming, and prospects for a repetition depend on whether underlying structural disequilibria, including political indiscipline, are redressed.[11]

3.1   The 2008 Shock Wave

The defining event of the 2008 global financial crisis was a "hemorrhagic stroke": a paralytic implosion of the loanable funds market that seemingly brought the global monetary and credit system to the brink of Armageddon. The September 2008 emergency was caused by the terrifying realization that major financial institutions, especially those connected with hedge funds, could not cover their current obligations either with asset sales or short-term bank credit because confidence had been lost in the value of their assets, and short-term lending suddenly ceased. People everywhere were panicked at the prospect of cascading financial bankruptcies, where the securities of failed companies contaminated the value of other assets, triggering margin calls, shuttered credit access, lost savings, bank runs, stock market crashes, liquidity crises, universal insolvency, economic collapse, and global ruination. All crises are ominous, but this one seemed as if it just might degenerate into a black swan debacle, equal to or greater than the Great Depression of 1929. After all, the U.S. Treasury and Federal Reserve had reassured the public that the forced sale of the "risk management" investment banking firm Bear Stearns to J.P. Morgan Chase on March 24, 2008, for 5.8 percent of its prior high value had fully solved the subprime loan, mortgage, and derivative securitization threat, but subsequent events revealed that Bear Stearns was just the tip of a potentially *Titanic*-sinking iceberg, with American and European banking losses in the period 2007–2010 estimated by the International Monetary

Fund to reach $1 trillion and $1.6 trillion, respectively.[12] An additional $4 trillion to $5 trillion was expected to be lost through 2011, and although the Dow Jones Industrial Average fully recovered from the September 2008 highs by December 2010, 42 percent of its value was wiped out at the stock market crash's trough.[13]

The other shoe began dropping on September 7, 2008, when the Federal National Mortgage Association (Fannie Mae) and the Federal Home Loan Mortgage Corporation (Freddie Mac)—specializing in creating a secondary mortgage market—were placed into conservatorship by the Federal Housing Financing Agency after new mark to market accounting regulations (FAS 157) created havoc in the mortgage industry.[14] At the time, Fannie Mae and Freddie Mac held $12 trillion worth of mortgages.[15] Three days later on September 10, 2008, the "risk management" investment bank Lehman Brothers declared bankruptcy after having failed to find a buyer or acquire a federal bailout to cover a $4 billion loss. Merrill Lynch, finding itself in similar dire straits, was sold to the Bank of America on the same day. Six days later, the Federal Reserve announced an $85 billion rescue loan to the insurance giant American International Group (AIG), also heavily involved in "risk management" securitization activities. The news ignited a wave of Wall Street short selling, prompting the SEC to suspend short selling immediately thereafter. Then on September 20 and 21, secretary of the Treasury Henry Paulson and Federal Reserve chairman Ben Bernanke appealed directly to Congress for an endorsement of their $700 billion emergency loan package designed to purchase massive amounts of sour mortgages from distressed institutions. Forty-eight hours later, Warren Buffett bought 9 percent of Goldman Sachs, another "risk management" investment bank, for $5 billion to prop the company up. On September 24, Washington Mutual became America's largest bank failure ever and was acquired by J.P. Morgan Chase for $1.9 billion.

These cumulating disasters, exacerbated by parallel developments in Europe and many other parts of the globe addicted to structural deficits, Phillips curve–justified inflation, financial deregulation, asset-backed mortgages, derivatives, electronic trading, and hard asset speculation, sent shock waves through the global financial system, including the withdrawal of hundreds of billions of dollars from money market mutual funds (an aspect of the shadow banking system), depriving corporations of an important source of short-term borrowing. The London Interbank Offered Rate (LIBOR; the reference interest rate at which banks borrow unsecured funds from other banks in the London wholesale money market) soared, as did TED spreads (U.S. Treasury bills versus Eurodollar future contracts), spiking to 4.65 percent on October 10, 2008, both indicating that liquidity was being rapidly withdrawn from the world financial system. In what seemed like the blink of an eye, the global financial crisis not only triggered a wave of worldwide bankruptcies, plunging production, curtailed international trade, and mass unemployment, but also morphed into a sovereign debt crisis. Countries such as Iceland, Ireland, Greece, Portugal, Italy, and Spain found themselves mired in domestic and foreign debt that dampened aggregate effective demand, spawned double-digit unemployment, and even raised the specter of European Union dissolution (Dallago and Guglielmetti 2011).

These awesome events, together with collapsing global equity, bond, and commodity markets, unleashed a frenzy of advice and emergency policy intervention aimed at stemming the hemorrhaging, bolstering aggregate effective demand, and repairing regulatory lapses to restore business confidence. FAS 157-d (suspension of mark to mark financial asset pricing) broke the free fall of illiquid, mortgage-backed asset valuations, offering some eventual support in resale markets. The Emergency Stabilization Relief Act bailed out system-threatening bankruptcy candidates through emergency loans and toxic asset purchases. FDIC savings deposits insurance was increased from $100,000 to $250,000 per account to forestall bank runs. The SEC temporarily suspended short selling on Wall Street. The government pressured banks to postpone foreclosures invoking a voluntary foreclosure moratorium enacted in July 2008. The Federal Reserve and U.S. Treasury resorted to quantitative easing (essentially printing money) to bolster liquidity and drive short-term government interest rates toward zero, effectively subsidizing financial institutions at depositors' expense. The federal government quadrupled its budgetary deficit in accordance with Heller's neo-Keynesian aggregate demand management tactic, concentrating on unemployment and other social transfers, instead of the direct investment stimulation advocated by Keynes.[16] Committees were formed to devise bank capital "stress tests," coordinate global banking reform (Levinson 2010), improve auditing and oversight, prosecute criminal wrongdoing including Ponzi schemes (e.g., Bernard Madoff),[17] and investigate regulatory reform of derivatives and electronic trading (Dodd-Frank Wall Street Reform and Consumer Protection Act of 2010).[18] In Europe, many imperiled banks were temporarily nationalized, and a series of intra–European Union austerity and rescue programs was launched. In the larger global arena, the International Monetary Fund, World Bank, and others provided emergency assistance, and the deep problem of Chinese state-controlled trading was puckishly broached.

With the advantage of hindsight, it is evident the American government's Troubled Asset Relief Program (TARP), including the "cash for clunkers" program, other deficit spending and quantitative easing, passive acceptance of Chinese underimporting (dollar reserve hoarding), continued indulgence of destructive speculative practices (program trading, hedge funds, and derivatives), together with regulatory reforms and confidence-building initiatives did not cause a black swan meltdown and the subsequent hyperdepression many justifiably feared.[19] Some of these same policies may deserve credit for fostering a recovery, tepid as it is, but also can be blamed for persistent, near double-digit unemployment, a resurgence of commodity, stock, and foreign currency speculation, and the creation of conditions for a sovereign debt crisis of biblical proportions in the years ahead when the globe is eventually confronted with tens of trillions of dollars of unfunded and un-repayable obligations.[20]

At the end of the day, it should not be surprising that the institutionalized excess demand disequilibrium of the American and European macroeconomic management systems would produce some relief, even though their policies were inefficient and unjust. Financial stability is being gradually restored, and output is increasing, but the adjustment burden has been borne disproportionately by the unemployed, would-be job entrants, small businesses, savers, pensioners, and a myriad of random victims, while malefactors including politicians and policy makers were bailed out.[21] Moreover, the mentality and institutions that created the crisis in the first place remain firmly in command. Incredibly, the Obama administration under cover of the Dodd-Frank Act already has begun mandating a massive expansion of the very same subprime loans largely responsible for the 2006 housing crisis and the 2008 financial debacle that swiftly ensued (Wallison and Pinto 2010).[22] This action and others like it will continue putting the global economy squarely at black swan risk until academics and policy makers prioritize financial stability over parochial, partisan, ideological, and venal advantage (Wedel 2009).

The Great Recession's low GDP growth in the United States, which followed the 2008 financial crisis, is shown in figure 3.1. The post–asset bubble recession in Japan, which followed the 1991 financial crisis, is

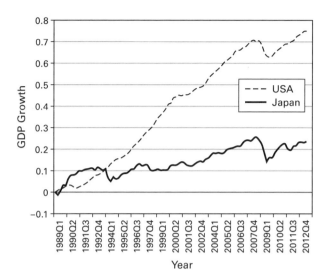

Figure 3.1
Two Great Recessions

also shown in figure 3.1 for comparison. In both cases, the interest rate reached its lower bound and government debt went sharply up. It appears, however, that the difference in the two recessions has to do not only with cyclical behavior but also with the relative decline in Japan's long-term growth trend.

3.2   Concluding Remarks

The *divine coincidence* is now seen for the pipe dream that it was, but there is no new consensus to replace it other than the pious hope that structural deficits, loose monetary policy, and better financial regulation (aggregate demand management) will foster prosperity, no matter how much gridlock exists among politicians and conflicts of interest among policy makers and special interests (White 2010). There seems to be little prospect that a constructive consensus soon will emerge capable of disciplining contemporary societies for the greater good by promoting efficiency, growth, and economic stability. The global economy is flying blind, propelled by panic and a herd mentality that spells troubles ahead.

4   The Crisis in the Euro Zone

The global financial crisis that erupted in the United States instantaneously swept across Europe.[1] Like the United States, the European Monetary Union (EMU) was ripe for a crash. It had its own real estate bubble (specifically in Ireland and Spain), had indulged in excessive deficit spending, had become financially deregulated, and had rapidly expanded credit (partly through derivatives).[2] Policy responses and recovery patterns for key European Union (EU) members such as Germany, France (within the euro zone), and the United Kingdom (outside the euro zone) were similar. However, after the bubble burst and the crisis began unfolding, it became clear that the euro-zone plight differed from America's in one fundamental respect: There was no exact counterpart of the euro-zone GIIPS (Greece, Ireland, Italy, Portugal, and Spain) in the United States.[3] Some American states had overborrowed, but the sovereign debt crisis didn't place individual states at deflationary risk or threaten the viability of the federal union. Not so for some members within the euro zone. During the U.S. savings and loan crisis in the 1980s, the southwestern American states received a transfer from the rest of the U.S. states equal to almost 20 percent of the southwestern states' gross domestic products. But, such a transfer has not been politically feasible among members of the EMU. The American experience therefore demonstrates that Europe's problem is not purely an economically failing single-currency area; the failure is political in an institutional sense. Politicians on both sides of the Atlantic can be uncooperative, but interstate disputes are more easily finessed under the American federal system than under the euro zone's weakly politically integrated system.

The global financial crisis involving the euro-zone periphery is mainly a balance of payments crisis, of the type akin to "sudden stop" in capital inflows (see Calvo 1998). Krugman (2014) observes that the cumulative current account deficits in the wake of the crisis are large for the euro-zone countries that plunged into the crisis. The crisis from sudden stop of capital inflows triggered, in turn, the sovereign debt crisis. The key mechanism behind the panic-based sovereign debt crisis was the belief among investors that the European Central Bank (ECB) would not behave as a lender of last resort. The belief was indeed confirmed in the initial phase of the crisis. In 2013, the ECB adopted the "whatever it takes" policy of (limited) sovereign bonds purchase. Recall that sovereign debt, for a member of the euro zone, is in effect denominated in "foreign currency"; that is, a national central bank cannot independently bail out the governments through purchasing their debt by printing its own currency—a point made forcefully by De Grauwe and Ji (2012). In contrast to the strong correlation between external deficits and crises in the euro zone, there is weak correlation between sovereign debt to output ratio and crises. Sovereign debt to GDP ratio in the wake of the crisis was not larger on average for the GIIPS countries (except Greece) than for other euro-zone countries (such as Belgium).

The disparity is easily traced to the EU and euro zone's special form of governance called *supranationality* (a partially sovereign transnational organization), which has largely been ignored in economic treatises about the costs and benefits of customs unions, economic communities, and monetary unions.[4] Until now, it has tacitly been assumed that supranational governance was as good or better than national economic mechanisms—that any policy regime accessible to nation-states could be replicated without dysfunction by supranational communities.

4.1   The History of European Integration

Nation-states before World War II never voluntarily surrendered their control over fiscal and monetary policy as part of a package to achieve political goals, even though they participated in international institutions like the League of Nations. The horrors of World War II, combined with cold war politics and the welfare state tide, however, propelled Europe along a novel supranational trajectory with some unintended consequences. On September 19, 1946, Winston Churchill gave a speech in Zurich advocating not only Franco-German rapprochement, but also a kind of United States of Europe, called a European "Third Way." He also advocated a "Council of Europe." It formed thereafter with the assistance of French foreign minister Robert Schuman. It mandated creation of supranational communities on the path to a fully democratic, integrated union.[5] The Schuman Declaration of May 9, 1950, reaffirmed the concept in conjunction with the formation of the European Coal and Steel Community (ECSC). It proclaimed the European Community as the world's first supranational institution, marking the "birth of modern Europe," and initiating an epoch where intra-European wars were impossible. The Soviet bloc formed a rival economic community, the Council for Mutual Economic Cooperation (CMEA), in 1949, but Comecon, as it is sometimes called, was more a body for policy exchange, like the Organization for Economic Cooperation and Development (OECD), rather than a supranational economic governance mechanism superior to national authorities.[6]

Schuman's utopian vision, which can be traced back to France's first socialist, Claude Henri de Rouvroy, the comte de Saint-Simon (1760–1825; see his 1814 treatise "On the Reorganization of European Society"), was the prelude to a succession of developments culminating in today's European Union: these included the European Economic Community (EEC), known as the Common Market (1958), the European Community (1967; together with the European Commission and the European Council of Ministers), the European Council (1974), the European Monetary System (1979), the European Parliament (1979), the Schengen Agreement (1985), the Single Market Act (1986), the Maastricht Treaty (1993) founding the European Union, and the European Monetary Union (2002), which inaugurated the euro.

Europeans are broadly pleased with European integration. There has been no intramember war, a common European identity has emerged, members are democratic and socially progressive, there is free travel, labor, and capital mobility within the EU space, the economy has been liberalized, and living standards have risen. However, EU economic performance has hardly matched Schuman's idealist claims for supranational communitarianism. Growth has been anemic, unemployment high, and moral hazard problems severe. Supranational governors have found it easier to agree on broad principles than to implement them and exercise fiscal discipline. Schuman felt sure that communitarians would be considerate, fair, self-restrained, and altruistic or could be tutored to act responsibly, but this proved to be the triumph of hope over experience. On one hand, the supranational deck was stacked in favor of overborrowing by the GIIPS countries and east Europeans. On the other hand, the GIIPS countries were misled into prematurely surrendering control over their monetary and exchange rate policy without receiving fiscal quid pro quos. As a consequence, the EU finds itself in an idealistically incorrect position, where the gap between rich and poor members is widening at a time when supranational institutional arrangements are forcing the GIIPS countries to extricate themselves from their predicament with painful and problematic deflationary tactics necessary to regain their competitive strength: the so-called internal devaluation.

The contradictory social democratic mandate to bring ever more relatively poor countries into the fold, boosting their creditworthiness with implicit guarantees, pressuring them to adopt the euro, and straitjacketing their fiscal options, while undermining fiscal discipline with sympathetic approval of entitlements and leveling, has solutions within a nation-state framework (a true United States of Europe) that could be simulated by a supranational organization. However, this is extraordinarily difficult to accomplish because Schuman's communitarian optimism was misplaced. The EU has yet to find a supranational architecture that reconciles his idealism with workable macroeconomic regulation.[7] It is in this sense that the aftermath of the 2008 financial crisis is more a culturally conditioned supranational institutional dilemma than a relatively simple matter of conventional international macroeconomic policy, and as such an overlooked element in the half-century-long debate on optimal economic and monetary unions and communities. If the EMU does eventually go the way of the CMEA, it won't be because economists failed to grasp the theory of unions and communities, but rather mainly because they didn't endogenize EMU supranational theory in institutional practice.

The power of this reconceptualization is best appreciated by contrasting received wisdom on optimal currency union theory as it pertains to the EMU with the behavior implied by Schuman's supranational utopian vision.

4.2   Experience Under the Monetary Union

The road to European monetary unification, the centerpiece of a full European Economic Community and Union, passed through the European Monetary System (EMS; 1979–1998) period, where eight member countries tried to dampen fluctuations in their foreign exchange rate parities.[8] They effectively pegged their currencies to the deutschemark in an effort to curb inflation and advance toward European monetary integration. The experiment failed. In 1992, important members of the EMS chose exit paths. Nonetheless, 11 members of the European Union upped the ante by choosing a solution that required more rather than less cooperation. On January 1, 1999, they created a common currency area (European Monetary Union; EMU) that effectively imposed a fixed exchange rate among all member countries. Participants surrendered their authority over national monetary policy and vested it in the supranational hands of the European Central Bank (ECB), forcing members to rely exclusively on fiscal and regulatory policy to manage macroeconomic disequilibria. The decision was an act of blind faith because many members failed to honor their Maastricht pledges to contain inflation and deficit spending prior to monetary union. Aspirants seeking EMU accession were supposed to hold inflation to no more than 1.5 percent per annum; to maintain a stable exchange rate with the Exchange Rate Mechanism (ERM) without devaluation; and to run public sector deficits less than 3 percent of GDP, with a public debt under 60 percent of GDP. Many established members and aspirants alike flunked the tests after they joined the EMU, setting a pernicious precedent for the future GIIPS countries.

Was this wise? Few pondered the precedent, focusing instead on first principles, but here too there were grounds for caution. The theory of optimal currency areas clearly implied that monetary union was not a one-way street. Its merit depended on various trade-offs. Milton Friedman observed that nations can deal more deftly with disorders if they have their own currency, allowing them to vary prices and wages, but this requires them to accept high costs of doing business across national boundaries. Consequently, monetary unions are attractive where the volume of intraregional trade and labor mobility is high but are unattractive otherwise. The supranational fiscal regime likewise is a matter of concern. If it is strong and tasked to assist members confronted with deficient aggregate effective demand, the risk members incur in surrendering the monetary option is partly compensated by pledges of supranational fiscal aid. If it is weak, nations place all their eggs in the supranational monetary basket, with no recourse other than accepting painful deflationary adjustments in order to regain competitiveness.

The United States provides a good example of an optimal currency area. It has a high volume of intranational trade (McKinnon 1963). American labor is mobile (Mundell 1961), and Washington has the muscle effectively to use fiscal power in alleviating distress in vulnerable states (Kenen 1967). Also, the Federal Reserve has the authority

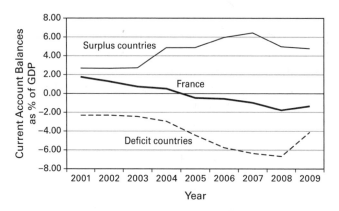

Figure 4.1
Divergences Within the EMU

to act as a "lender of last resort" if Washington's fiscal policy is insufficient.[9]

The EMU by contrast is a dubious candidate for an optimal currency area because although it too trades intensively within the region, national work restrictions greatly impair intra-European labor mobility, and supranational fiscal power is feeble because rich members don't want to assume heavy financing burdens during turbulent times. The obverse also is true. Countries such as Sweden and Norway that shunned the euro are thriving and appear to have benefited by retaining their monetary option.[10] Figure 4.1 describes current account imbalances within the euro system, which were in the process of becoming wider in the wake of the euro crisis.

Robert Mundell and Marcus Fleming have succinctly formulated the problem bedeviling optimal currency unions,[11] particularly supranational ones in the form of a two-not-three tri-lemma.[12] Countries seeking to form a monetary union can enjoy only two out of three desirable policy goals: (1) free international capital flows (connected with optimal fiscal policy); (2) potent monetary policy to stabilize output, employment, inflation, and financial markets; and (3) exchange rate stability. The United States picked free capital mobility and monetary independence, letting its foreign exchange rate float. China decided to retain its monetary independence and control its exchange rate, abandoning free capital flows, while the European Union has selected a third way. It mimicked the United States at the supranational level, accepting floating exchange rates for the euro, but at the national level it failed to complement the choice with a supportive fiscal regime for distressed economies and friction-free labor mobility, leaving vulnerable nations like the GIIPS countries in a lurch. When times are bad, the euro appreciates as investors shift to what they perceive as a German safe haven thus reducing GIIPS export competitiveness, while idle labor in the periphery is prevented from migrating. What works for America doesn't work for the EU because of supranationality, the omitted variable in optimal monetary union discourse.[13] The tri-lemma solution for the GIIPS countries is three bads: no independent monetary policy, no independent exchange rate policy, and fiscal paralysis (due to excessive debt), while Germany and other current account surplus members retain free capital flows, a supranational monetary policy tailored to its needs, and an appreciating currency of its desire.

4.3   Heavy Borrowers: Individual Experiences

The GIIPS countries are not entirely straitjacketed. They can extricate themselves from their plight with a "real depreciation" or "internal devaluation," but this is little consolation because it places an immense burden on prices, wages, and productivity growth in an adverse financial environment.[14]

Superior German productivity growth, moreover, makes a bad situation for the GIIPS countries even worse.

Figure 4.2 reveals that GIIPS unit labor costs rose steadily in the period 2001–2010, while German unit labor costs fell reciprocally. Ceteris paribus, the incentive for Germany to outsource and invest in GIIPS countries diminished at the same time that foreigners were coaxed into diverting their purchases of EU exports from the GIIPS countries to Germany. Given the EMU's supranational straitjacket, there doesn't appear to any compelling reason to anticipate a swift reversal of the ill fortune of the GIIPS countries. A utopian welfare-state vision intended to ameliorate transnational income inequality thus may perversely aggravate the problem.

Needless to say, this outcome was unintended and indeed would not have occurred if GIIPS countries were virtuous Germans. They would not have assumed unmanageable debt obligations, and EU fiscal policy and monetary, and foreign exchange rate policies would have been appropriate for them. These requirements however underscore two fundamental defects in the EMU supranationalism. First, the systems architecture is too rigid. A meritorious regime should provide

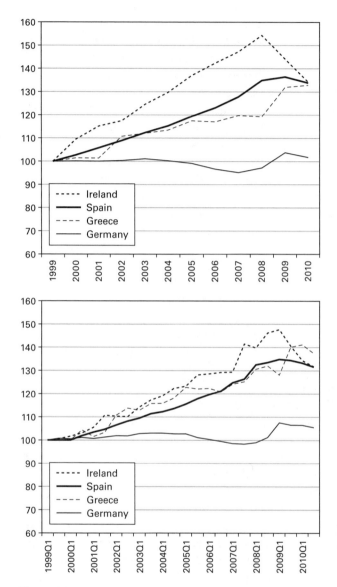

Figure 4.2
Unit Labor Costs and Exports

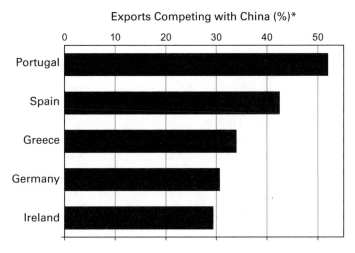

*Based on 72 industries, average 2005–2008.

Figure 4.2
(*Continued*)

good solutions across a wide spectrum of initial conditions. For the moment at least, the EMU has not devised the supplementary internal mechanisms needed to achieve efficient outcomes for all its members. Second, EU social democratic culture fostered values that enticed the GIIPS countries to overextend themselves. They may well have done so on their own volition, but this doesn't change the fact that the Schuman ethos abetted their delinquency by encouraging them to believe in miracles and eternal free rides.

The weak link in Schuman's social democratic utopianism is a predilection for egalitarian outcomes combined with an ambivalent attitude toward equal effort and value added. European Union leaders were pleased that the EMU enhanced the GIIPS countries' creditworthiness in private investors' eyes and welcomed outsourcing from the wealthy core to the periphery. They were delighted that Germany, France, Britain, and others shared in the windfall gains generated by these capital flows and the GIIPS countries' excess sovereign borrowing. This enthusiasm was tempered by the declining unit labor productivity and exorbitant social spending of the GIIPS countries, but not enough to outweigh the satisfaction derived from narrowing the intraunion per capita income gap. Just as each EMU member state dislikes but tolerates the "euro-sclerosis" fostered by equalizing outcomes, the European Council and Parliament refrained from engaging the GIIPS countries on the issue. Moreover, by raising the prospect of "haircuts" (debt forgiveness), they telegraphed the message that financial indiscipline and extravagant social programming ultimately may prove to be winning strategies. A culture that is ambivalent to moral hazard is unintentionally apt to encourage it, adding to the distress caused by the system's faulty supranational architecture.

Speculative bubbles like the one sparked by the EMU's contradictory welfare state political goals often end in crises. Investors panic when they discover that sand castles are crumbling, and debts may never be fully repaid even if they are restructured. This is what has been transpiring in fits and starts since autumn 2010. Ireland was the first victim. Its toxic debt had been accumulating for a decade fueled by Irish bank borrowing in the international wholesale market to finance a property development bubble. Ireland's bank assets were at the time a multiple of its GDP by a factor of 4 or 5. When real estate crashed, private bank balance sheets melted down, panicking the government into plugging the hole with a €50 billion commitment, equivalent to a third of Ireland's GDP. Ireland's government finances were overwhelmed in 2010 when its government bailed out the country's banks but did not impose losses on their bondholders. Ireland has put up with an extraordinary amount of pain as it tries through austerity policy to correct for the triple disaster of an extreme housing bubble, unsustainable public spending, and a banking collapse, but with support from the EMU member states. This dubious Irish pledge was swiftly followed in 2008 by an equally ill-advised 100 percent guarantee of all bank deposits and most debt. The ECB joined the party allocating a quarter of its euro-zone lending to Irish banks by September–October 2010, all to no avail. Ireland ultimately managed to staunch runs on its private banks by borrowing approximately $145 billion (70 percent of GDP), but this raised its government debt to GDP ratio to stratospheric Greek levels, effectively bankrupting the nation. The Irish government saved its banks and their creditors by forcing the Irish people to shoulder an unbearable burden. A 10 percent drop in GDP slashed jobs, driving the unemployment rate to 14 percent.

Spain's experience followed a similar script, but its real estate bubble that began in 1985 was homegrown, with the government providing incentives for owning rather than renting, including 40- and even 50-year mortgages. After Spain adopted the euro, speculation accelerated, driven by huge capital inflows until 2008, when the global financial crisis took the wind out of the real estate market's sails, throwing the country into deep recession. The national budget plummeted into deficit: It was 9.2 percent in 2010, and, even if pared, the debt to GDP ratio is expected to rise to 90 percent. On balance, Spain appears stronger than other GIIPS countries because of its relatively well regulated banking industry. However, Madrid is now in the thick of it. Further deterioration in housing prices in adverse times could threaten mortgage-dependent private bank solvency and intensify the decline in housing demand because under Spanish law, evicted owners remain liable for their mortgage debt. A $120 billion bailout of its banks appears to have backfired. Because the rules of the rescue funds preclude direct equity injection into Spanish banks, and the rescue funds must be funneled via loans to the Spanish government, they pile up more debt onto the Spanish government, dragging it a step closer to a full sovereign bankruptcy. Private capital inflows have dried up completely.

Greece's version of the supranational EMU melodrama has a different plot. The principle culprit in Hellas was unrestrained government welfare expenditures financed with overseas borrowing. Greek governments customarily have run large public deficits to fund government sector jobs, pensions, and other social benefits since democracy was restored in 1974. Its debt to GDP ratio has exceeded 100 percent since 1993. The burden was softened before 2001 by drachma devaluation, but this option was foreclosed in 2001 when Greece adopted the euro. At first this didn't seem to matter because euro accession allowed Athens to finance debt on favorable terms, an advantage leveraged by persistently falsifying official data on the country's financial condition.[15] The chickens, however, finally came home to roost. On April 27, 2010, the Greek debt rating was cut to "junk" status by Standard & Poors. The ECB has tried to help by suspending its prohibition on buying junk collateral, but the situation continues deteriorating despite new austerity measures approved by parliament in July 2011 in part because the fear of default raises the possibility of interest and principal costs that cannot be paid.

The best current estimates of the GIIPS countries' budgetary deficits and cumulative debt forecast that Greece's debt to GDP ratio will reach 180 in 2014; Ireland's plight will be nearly as dire with a debt to GDP ratio of 145, followed by Portugal at 135 and Spain 90. Figure 4.3 describes the path over time of government debt and the GDP growth in the GIIPS countries.

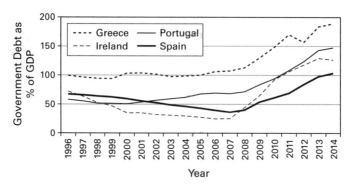

Figure Above Bar Shows % of GDP

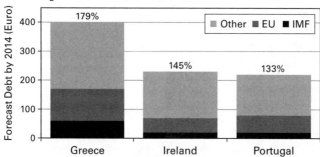

GDP Falls in Crisis-Hit Countries

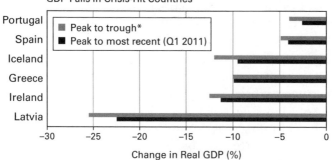

*Peaks in 2007/2008; troughs in 2009/2010

Figure 4.3
Government Debt and GDP Growth

Obviously, while Europe's sovereign debt crisis can go from bad to worse as Germany and France permit, the longer the GIIPS debt problem is left unattended, the more dire the consequences will be.

The maxim that the rich should pay at the supranational level means that the ECB, perhaps supplemented with new institutions, will grudgingly provide loans to prevent the GIIPS countries from defaulting on their sovereign debt. They also could provide "solidarity" grants by analogy with foreign catastrophe aid. If these tactics prove insufficient, wealthy EMU members such as Germany and France can consent to partial "haircuts." This could be done in diverse ways, but the details aren't matters of high principle. What matters is that creditors will be transformed into limited liability partners sharing the cost of past transgressions so that debtors can have a fresh start without being formally cast into permanent default.

4.4   The Role of the European Central Bank

Recently, Paul De Grauwe (2011) called for the ECB to be even more determined, serving as lender of last resort both to euro-zone member banks and those facing sovereign debt crises, stressing how easily liquidity crises can degenerate into system-wide insolvency. The lender-of-last-resort capability is what the U.S. Federal Reserve System is empowered with in the U.S. single-currency area. De Grauwe's argument is that sovereign debt in a single-currency area is denominated in "foreign" money (money that cannot be issued by the governor of the individual member central bank), because the individual central bank cannot perform as "lender of last resort" by printing money. Only the ECB can do it, and this requires complex coordination with other ECB governors and with governments. Therefore, he argues that it is wrong to restrict ECB monetary policy to inflation fighting, ignoring the contagion of sovereign debt crises spreading from one country to another as systemic financial risks develop. Inflation fighting he insists, contrary to Goodfriend's advice (Goodfriend 2011), must be integrated with a war against insolvency because the catastrophic potential of illiquidity-bred insolvency dominates the moral hazard risk.[16]

De Grauwe doesn't downplay the moral hazard problem, but claims reassuringly that it can be managed by imposing rules that constrain government debt issuance. He is right in principle but glosses the problem of supranationality. The sovereign debt crisis besetting the EMU today hasn't arisen because the European Council encouraged the GIIPS countries to misbehave or because the Germans are fixated on inflation fighting. It erupted because the GIIPS countries refused to listen, and the rich members of the EMU refused to transfer income to the poor members. The EMU cannot compel them to desist regardless of whether the ECB adopts a conservative or liberal monetary regime.[17] Yet in summer 2012, the ECB pledged to do "whatever it takes" to preserve the euro. Indeed, financial market conditions in the euro zone improved markedly as a result.

Protecting the people means placing a floor on the reduction of public spending in deficit countries. Schuman and others may have equated the notion with full employment and high aggregate economic activity, but, idle chatter aside, modern social democracies place much less weight on providing jobs and realizing production potential than on preserving government programs. Consequently, solving the debt crisis isn't a matter of economically optimal debt but of politically appropriate levels of excessive sovereign borrowing, matched by extreme difficulty of income transfers among EMU member state taxpayers.

Thus, it is unlikely that the European Union will easily confront a moment of truth in the foreseeable future when members seriously contemplate secession. At the same time, it is highly unlikely that the rich EMU member states will foot the bill necessary to do a workable debt restructuring. Winners in the daily trench wars (as distinct from attaining the competitive ideal) such as Germany, which enjoys current account surpluses, high national savings, rising productivity, and moderate per capita GDP growth, risk losing more than they gain from exiting the EMU, even if they have to pay for partial haircuts. Germany still carries the baggage of distrust from the Nazi era and is able to pursue its business and foreign policy agenda much more effectively under EMU cover than if it tried to obtain similar concessions by other means. The French value the EMU relationship for other reasons, but, like Germany, France is nowhere near the threshold of secession.

The EMU's bailout of Greece on July 21, 2011, confirms this surmise. The euro-zone countries and the International Monetary Fund (IMF) gave Greece a second bailout worth €109 billion ($155 billion), on top of the €110 billion granted a year previously. Banks and other private investors will add €50 billion ($71 billion) more to the rescue package until 2014 by either rolling over Greek bonds that they hold, swapping them for new ones with lower interest rates, or selling the bonds back to Greece cheaply. The deal involving private creditors may well be deemed a "selective default" by rating agencies, making Greece the first euro country ever to be in default, but this isn't expected to have drastic consequences given the other positive aspects of the rescue package. To dampen adverse effects, the euro zone will back with guarantees the new Greek bonds issued to banks. This is essential because Greek banks use Greek government debt as collateral for emergency support from the ECB. Those bonds would no longer qualify as collateral if hit with a default rating, meaning Greek banks would lose ECB support and quickly collapse. Bond rollovers, or swaps, were supposed to give Greece more time to recover and cut approximately 21 percent of its future debt burden.[18] Authorities agreed to provide the new euro-zone rescue loans to Greece at a 3.5 percent interest rate, with maturities between 15 and 30 years, plus an additional 10-year grace period. Moreover, EU bailout overseers were given the power to intervene in countries before they are beset with full-blown crises, an institutional reform opposed by Germany.

Nonetheless, this judgment should not be construed to mean that a default, should it occur, would be innocuous. The inflexibility of the EMU's supranational architecture raises the specter of hyper-deleveraging. For example, if the EMU's latest rescue plan for Greece proves inadequate and its sovereign debt goes into full default despite euro-zone guarantees, Greek bank lending capacity will plummet placing extraordinary downward pressure on wages, prices, and aggregate effective demand because Athens doesn't control its interest rate (equivalently, its money supply) or foreign exchange rate. Argentina's experience in 2001 under less rigid conditions suggests that EU supranationality could make GIIPS countries' pain and suffering a protracted ordeal.[19] Therefore, it can be reasonably concluded that the political and economic benefits of EU supranationality as they are currently constituted are asymmetric. GIIPS countries for their part regret having to pay the piper (creditors, reduced government spending, depression, and mass unemployment), but the political and economic benefits of EMU membership still lopsidedly exceed costs, even in a worst-case scenario where defaults trigger a decade of suffering. They might contemplate exiting the EMU in order to increase the number of instruments for dealing with problems largely of their own making, but they still value the EMU's benefits: enhanced creditworthiness and the possibility of compassionate transfers when the going gets tough. Moreover, rich members seeking to rid themselves of noisome GIIPS countries cannot compel them to exit the EMU by treaty, and practical difficulties will likely dissuade GIIPS countries from attempting to resurrect national currencies on their own.

The same principles apply for new entrants. Costs and benefits of EU (but not similarly to the EMU) accession will depend on each individual case more than generic economic considerations. It follows directly not only that talk of EMU and/or EU dissolution is premature, but also that EU enlargement, considered the partnership's greatest foreign policy success, remains on track. Croatia is acceding, Montenegro and Macedonia are official candidates, and negotiations are in process for Turkey and Iceland. Preliminary discussions have been conducted with Russia.

4.5   Political Union, Fiscal Union, and Bank Union

Obstfeld (2013) proposes a new fiscal tri-lemma for currency unions: one cannot simultaneously maintain all three of (1) cross-border financial integration, (2) financial stability, and (3) national fiscal independence. For example, if countries forgo the options of financial repression and capital controls, they simply cannot credibly stabilize their financial systems without external fiscal support, either directly (from partner country treasuries) or indirectly (through monetary financing from the union-wide central bank). That is, a country that adheres to fiscal independence will likely sacrifice financial integration as well as stability.[20]

The EU and the euro zone (EZ) tomorrow will not be radically different than they are today: a loose political and fiscal union. Members will try to find better cooperative supranational solutions to the micro, macro, and financial problems besetting them including fiscal reform, but this won't be easy on macroeconomic grounds and will be even more complicated if the fiscal regime mutualizes micropolicy.

In the simplest case, fiscal union might merely provide increasing liquidity to cash-strapped GIIPS countries, but if this fails to make them solvent, member debts can be consolidated with the EZ or EU assuming partial or full responsibility.[21]

This would relieve the GIIPS countries' debt burden. However, it would also spark a new wave of deficit spending unless repayments were complemented with mutualized political control over excess spending. Fiscal union without fiscal discipline is conceivable but not viable unless Germany can be cajoled into indulging the GIIPS countries, come what may. Germany, the largest creditor in the EMU, can be bent, but the German people will not write blank checks.[22] Sooner or later, the GIIPS countries will be compelled to bear the consequences of their actions individually or mutually outside or within a fiscal union. This includes the possibility that the GIIPS countries will exert self-restraint and voluntarily repay their own debts. Fiscal union isn't a panacea: It is just a policy tool that can be used if profligate governments are unwilling to allow others to compel them to be disciplined when they otherwise refuse to voluntarily curtail excess spending, within either a supranational or federative setting.

Sims (2012) asserts that the design of the EMU misses three important aspects of central banking: absence of a fiat-money lender of last resort so that the combination of a treasury that can issue fiat-currency debt and a central bank that can conduct open market operations provides a unique lender of last resort.

Thomas Sargent made this the central point of his Nobel address after establishing that the EU would probably have been wiser to start with a fiscal union before adding a monetary union following the American historical precedent.[23] He concluded that the EU might have been better advised to model its supranationality compatibly with the American historical sequence rather than vice versa, but counseled that this alone wouldn't have been sufficient to shield the GIIPS countries from the consequences of their folly. What goes up must come down. If nations collectively overspend under any combined fiscal-monetary union, they will bear an inflation tax compounded perhaps by defaults and involuntary unemployment. Sargent's postulate deserves attention because it cuts to the chase. Some EU factions take the position that the GIIPS crisis can be resolved and supranationality burnished by institutional reform alone, but this stance is myopic. The root of the EU and EZ woes is political and requires a political epiphany.

In the absence of bank union, bank failures link circularly to sovereign debt defaults. This feedback loop is a potential source for a panic-based contagion across heavy borrower members. Bank union means (1) a single-supervisor, common rescue fund that can be used directly to recapitalize troubled banks, a common deposit insurance authority, and a bank-resolution authority.

4.6   Secular Stagnation

Despite significant efforts to liberalize the economies of individual EU member states and increase competitiveness across the common

market, the counterimpulse to overprogram, overmandate, overregu-
late, and overtax and overtransfer has caused regional per capital GDP
to persistently decelerate for nearly four decades in what should otherwise have been a favorable growth environment. Some of the problem
is attributable to the particularities of EU supranationality, but just as
the formality of fiscal union won't necessarily transform "naughty"
GIIPS countries into "frugal" ones, any fiscal union likely to be unani-
mously approved won't cure euro-sclerosis.[24]

Banks and governments in the euro zone face a similar problem: the
unbalanced maturity structure of assets and liabilities. This unbalanced
maturity structure makes both banks and governments vulnerable to
movements of market distrust. The consequent liquidity crisis can
degenerate into solvency crisis. Policy reactions in the euro zone tilt
toward austerity, which retards growth (figure 4.4).[25]

In the fourth quarter of 2012, euro zone GDP dropped at an annual-
ized rate of 2.3 percent, the fastest pace since the height of the world

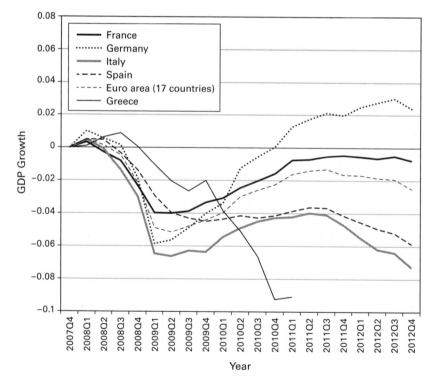

Figure 4.4
$u(r_1)$ GDP Growth in the Euro Zone

recession in early 2009. Over 2012, GDP fell by 0.6 percent. The reason is that everyone is cutting back at the same time. The slump in the GIIPS economies spilled over to the block's core economy of Germany and France.

4.7 Euro-Zone Institutions

The substantive issue moving forward therefore is whether members are sufficiently dissatisfied with muddling through that they are willing to reform or ditch supranationality. Inertia favors doing nothing fundamental. Resistance to replacing member governance with unified federal rule is likely to be insurmountable now that the bloom is off the rose, while German and French authorities will be charier than ever of ceding ultimate control over the purse to supranational bodies. The EMU's inflexible supranational architecture is the patchwork result of contradictory goals and political interests and pure institutional design. Any changes made therefore only are apt to improve flexibility at the margin rather than functioning as a viable surrogate for a unified state. As such, reform may deter or mitigate crises in some instances, but wouldn't prevent them. Politics has been in command from the beginning and continues to take precedence over economic potential and performance.

In a redesign of the EMU, consider a European-wide bank deposit insurance and single bank-regulation authority as a means to prevent a European financial contagion that is spreading across the Southern European countries. A banking union can be created only with greater political integration. From the Dutch and German point of view, it is politically difficult and unfair to their taxpayers to underwrite the banks of the Southern European countries using their own money to pay for generous social benefits that are more generous than those existing in their own countries. In a political union, the Netherlands and Germany, being the source for the money transfer, will also have a say in leveling the generosity of social benefits across Europe, which can make it politically feasible to help sustain the European bank union.[26]

The EU has wrought substantial political benefits including the democratization of new members and avoidance of major intra-European war, but the EMU architecture is comparatively economically inefficient, bubble prone, and unusually subject to systemic risk. This package may be good enough for supporters of the welfare state, but emulators should weigh the evidence more judiciously. A greater political union is a key to the preservation of the European Monetary Union.

4.8   Concluding Remarks

Michael Bordo and Harold James (2013) compare the European Monetary Union with another international monetary regime, the gold standard. The EMU is a monetary union with the ECB at its apex; the gold standard had no such institution.

Common to both systems, countries face the international finance tri-lemma: the impossibility of concomitant fixed rates, free movement of capital, and an independent monetary policy. This means that when currencies are locked and capital can flow freely, countries surrender their ability to conduct their own monetary policy. Start with monetary independence. By throwing away the key of exchange rates, countries must alter their relative domestic prices and wages when they become misaligned. In its heyday, before World War I, the gold standard worked well. It generated pressures on both surplus and deficit countries when they respectively gained or lost competitiveness. States with surpluses acquired gold, pushing up the money supply, raising prices, and making them less competitive. States with deficits lost gold, which caused the money supply to shrink, pushing prices down, and sharpening their edge against rivals.

But the euro resembles the flawed interwar version of the gold standard rather than the classical pre-war model. After the gold standard was restored in the 1920s, central banks in surplus states such as France (which had rejoined it at an undervalued exchange rate) sterilized the monetary effects of gold inflows so that prices did not rise. That put all the pressure to adjust on countries such as Britain, which rejoined the gold standard in 1925 at an overvalued rate. A similarly harsh deflationary process is now under way in peripheral euro-zone countries such as Greece. Their adjustment would be much less draconian if the core states were prepared to tolerate considerably higher inflation than the euro-zone average. But Germany fiercely resists this.[27]

A stable and sustainable supranational economic regime requires an economic union combining both a monetary, banking, and fiscal union. Monetary union allows members to reap the benefits of a common currency and interest and exchange rates. Fiscal union permits central authorities effectively to coordinate deficit spending and finance across the community. There is no need to choose between them. They are mutually compatible, but to prevent financial instabilities, it is better to proceed by introducing fiscal union first and monetary and banking union later in accordance with the American example (fiscal union 1790; monetary union 1913). Although an effective fiscal regime shouldn't cause macroeconomic disorder, a well-functioning monetary union may unintentionally trigger severe macroeconomic disequilibrium by abetting euro-zone GIIPS-like speculative investment and overconsumption. When the bubble bursts and government budgets deteriorate, there is no institutional mechanism for intergovernment spending and revenue allocations. Had a political consensus for fiscal union existed within Europe in the 1990s, the EU project might well have proceeded in reverse order starting with fiscal and ending with monetary union (Sargent 2012). The result in all likelihood would have been better. But there was no political mandate, and EU leaders decided to push forward with monetary union despite the U.S. precedent.

II   Elements of the Theory of Financial Crises

In this part, we review the elements of three branches of the theoretical literature on financial crises. The first branch deals with banking crises, originating from coordination failure among bank creditors and depositors. The second branch deals with frictions in credit and interbank markets due to problems of moral hazard and adverse selection. The third branch deals with bubbles and crashes.

Financial trade and monetary systems are designed to improve the efficiency of real activity and resource allocation. The European Monetary Union, like many monetary arrangements in the past, was created to facilitate free trade and financial transactions between European countries and also between Europe and other parts of the world. Banking systems and other financial intermediaries are built to improve the transfer of capital from savers to investors in production capacity. Asset markets, to the extent that they are not disturbed by financial crises, enable risk sharing among investors encouraging more efficient production. A financial crisis marks the disruption of these normal functions of financial and monetary systems, thereby hurting the efficient functioning of the real economy.

One problem is that of a *coordination failure*. In the context of banking crises, this leads to bank runs, which stand at the root of the fragility of banking systems. Bank runs are generated by *strategic complementarities* among investors. When more depositors withdraw their money from the bank, the bank is more likely to fail, and so other depositors have a stronger incentive to withdraw. Coordination failures also stand behind many currency crises. When the central bank tries to maintain a fixed exchange rate regime, it might decide to abandon it under pressure from foreign exchange agents. Then, speculators again find themselves in a coordination problem, where they attack the regime if and only if they believe others will do so. In such coordination failures, the event of a banking crisis, a currency crisis, is then a self-fulfilling belief. Likewise, coordination failure also stands behind debt crises. The borrowers (either corporations or governments) may decide to default under pressure from some creditors. Then, other creditors are having a coordination problem, when they liquidate if and only if they believe others will liquidate their claims. Consequently, a debt crisis becomes a self-fulfilling expectation.

Another common problem in financial systems, which I review here, is that of adverse incentives. Models of credit frictions are based on a principal-agent setting where the borrower has the ability to divert resources for private use at the expense of the creditor. Hence, for credit to flow efficiently from the creditor to the borrower, it is crucial that the borrower maintains "skin in the game"; that is, he has enough at stake in the success of the project and so does not have a strong incentive to divert resources. This creates a limit on credit, and it can be amplified when economic conditions worsen when this limit tightens up. Hence, the financial friction has a real effect, hurting the investment opportunities of potential borrowers. A similar *moral hazard* problem can lead to bubbles in asset prices, as investors, who borrow to buy assets, benefit from the upside and have limited exposure to the downside risk, and so bid the price of the asset up. This also has real implications as they borrow excessively and invest in overly risky projects.

As described in chapters 3 and 4, recent years have been characterized by great turmoil in the world's financial markets: starting from the collapse of housing prices in the United States, followed by the meltdown of leading financial institutions in the United States and Europe, and then the ongoing challenge to the European Monetary Union. These events exhibit ingredients from all types of financial crises in recent history: banking crises, currency crises, credit frictions, market freezes, and the bursting of asset bubbles. In this chapter and the next two chapters, I provide a review of the analytical underpinnings of these types of crises and the way they explain recent events.[1]

All these elements have played an important role in the causes and manifestations of the crisis events of the past years. A main cause of the global crisis was the bubble in housing prices. This bubble was driven to a large extent by excessive and unregulated credit provided to households for the purpose of buying houses. A moral hazard problem was clearly at play, as households were not bearing the full downside risk, and nor were lenders, who securitized the loans shedding the risk to the financial market at large. Then, the collapse of house prices ignited the problems in the financial system, and these problems were aggravated by the contagion, as many financial institutions were invested in such securities or in other institutions that were invested in such securities, and so on.

The coordination problems leading to bank runs and related phenomena were also exhibited very vividly. A "textbook" type of a bank run was seen in the United Kingdom for Northern Rock Bank, where investors were lining up in the street to withdraw money from their accounts. But, the system as a whole saw many other examples of runs. The monetary authority failed to recognize the risk of contagion of bank runs, citing "moral hazard" if the central bank becomes too generous. The central bank was slow to extend assistance to the rest of the banking system, except at penal rates. By the time the Bank of England reversed course, credit markets had all begun to seize up. The U.S. repo market, where investment banks finance themselves on a very short-term basis, had dried up in 2008, leading to the failure of financial institutions such as Bear Stearns and Lehman Brothers. This was to a large extent a coordination failure among key providers of capital in this market, who refused to roll over credit, expecting a failure of the borrower due to the refusal of other key lenders to roll over credit. This is similar to the models of bank runs due to coordination problems that we analyze. In the money-market-funds industry, there were also runs, as investors realized that the funds did not have enough resources to pay the promised amounts to all of them.

The ongoing crisis in the European Monetary Union is an illustration of the basic models of currency crises. In the basis of the theory of currency crises lies the famous international financial tri-lemma, according to which a country can choose two but not three of the following three goals: free international capital flows; reliance on monetary policy to stabilize the economy; and benefit from the stability of the exchange rate and the reduction it brings in the transaction costs of doing international business, trade, and investment. Countries in the euro zone now realize that in their attempt to achieve the first and third goals, they have given up on the second goal, and so have limited ability to absorb the shocks in economic activity and sustain their national debts, partly brought about by the global meltdown. Coordination problems among investors and currency speculators aggravate this situation, as in the models of currency crises that we analyze.

The credit freeze that followed the financial meltdown of 2008 and the freeze in the interbank markets are both manifestations of the amplification of economic shocks due to the frictions in credit provision, as understood from principal-agent models we review here. As economic conditions deteriorated, borrowers found themselves undercapitalized, and therefore with less "skin in the game," and so lenders refused to provide credit to them, as doing so would lead borrowers to divert cash and take excessive risk. This, in turn, worsened the economic condition of borrowers, amplifying the initial shock. Similarly, the increase in asymmetric information following the collapse of Lehman Brothers in 2008 contributed to a market freeze where creditors and borrowers were reluctant to trade financial assets with each other because of the heightened uncertainty about the value of the financial assets they trade.

5 Analytics of Financial Fragility of Banks

Depository institutions, including banks, investment banks, hedge funds, and so forth, are inherently unstable because they have a mismatch in maturity between the term structure of assets and liabilities. In particular, they typically finance long-term investments with short-term deposits. This exposes banks to the risk of bank runs: When many depositors demand their money in the short term, banks will have to liquidate long-term investments at a loss, leading to their failure.

Diamond and Dybvig (1983)[1] provide a framework for coherent analysis of this phenomenon. In the model, agents may suffer idiosyncratic short-term liquidity needs. Without banks, they would not be able to enjoy the fruits of long-term investments. By offering demand-deposit contracts, banks enable short-term consumers to enjoy those fruits. Banks rely on the fact that only a forecastable fraction of agents will need to consume early, and thus offer a deposit contract that allows a transfer of consumption from the long-term (patient) consumers to the short-term (impatient) consumers. This contract improves expected welfare as long as agents demand early withdrawal only if they genuinely need to consume (at the point the deposit is made) in the short term. Banks thereby enable risk sharing between the depositors who do not know in advance whether they will be in future liquidity needs or not. But, the contract may also lead to a catastrophic bank run, where all depositors demand early withdrawal and the bank collapses. This is rational expectations equilibrium, as under the belief that the bank is going to collapse, the rational behavior is indeed to run on the bank.[2]

5.1 Fragility of the Liabilities Side of the Bank's Balance Sheet

The Diamond-Dybvig economy is described as follows: There are three periods (0, 1, 2), one good, and a continuum [0, 1] of agents.[3] Each agent is born in period 0 with an endowment of one unit. Consumption occurs only in period 1 or 2 (c_1 and c_2 denote an agent's consumption levels). Viewed at period 0, each agent can turn into one of two types: With probability λ the agent is impatient, and with probability $1 - \lambda$ she is patient. Agents' types are i.i.d.[4] Agents learn their types (which are their private information) at the beginning of period 1. Impatient agents can consume only in period 1. They obtain utility of $u(c_1)$. Patient agents can consume at either period; their utility is $u(c_1 + c_2)$. Function u is twice continuously differentiable, increasing, and for any $c \geq 1$ has a relative risk-aversion coefficient, $-cu''(c)/u'(c)$, greater than 1. Without loss of generality, we assume that $u(0) = 0$.[5]

Agents have access to a productive technology that yields a higher expected return in the long run. For each unit of input in period 0, the technology generates one unit of output if liquidated in period 1. If liquidated in period 2, the technology yields R units of output with probability $p(\theta)$, or 0 units with probability $1 - p(\theta)$. Here, the fundamental θ is the state of the economy. It is drawn from a uniform distribution on $[0, 1]$ and is known to bank depositors at the time that they make a choice whether or not to withdraw money from the bank in period 1.

We assume that $p(\theta)$ is strictly increasing in θ. It also satisfies $E_\theta[p(\theta)]u(R) > u(1)$, so that for patient agents, the expected long-run return is superior to the short-run return.

5.2   Risk Sharing via Maturity Transformation

In financial autarky, impatient agents consume one unit in period 1, whereas patient agents consume R units in period 2 with probability $p(\theta)$. Because of the high coefficient of risk aversion, a transfer of consumption from patient agents to impatient ones could be beneficial, ex ante, to all agents, although it would necessitate the early liquidation of long-term investments. A social planner who can verify agents' types, once realized, would set the period 1 consumption level c_1 for the impatient agents. The aggregate amount of the endowment left to the patient consumer is $1 - \lambda c_1$ and the per capita endowment is $(1 - \lambda c_1)/(1 - \lambda)$. So the all-informed central planner will maximize the consumer ex ante (expected) welfare, $\lambda u(c_1) + (1 - \lambda)u\left(\frac{1-\lambda c_1}{1-\lambda} R\right)E_\theta[p(\theta)]$. Here, λc_1 units of investment are liquidated in period 1 to satisfy the consumption needs of impatient agents. As a result, in period 2, each of the patient agents consumes $\frac{1-\lambda c_1}{1-\lambda} R$ with probability $p(\theta)$.

Denote the first-best period 1 consumption that maximizes this ex ante expected welfare c_1^{FB}. The condition equates the benefit and cost from the early liquidation of the marginal unit of investment. It can be shown that $c_1^{FB} > 1$; that is, the consumption available in period 1 to impatient consumers exceeds the endowment (i.e., what they could consume in autarky). Hence, at the first-best allocation, there is risk sharing, which is achieved via maturity transformation: a transfer of wealth from individuals who are not struck by liquidity shocks, the patient ones, to individuals who are struck by liquidity shocks, the impatient ones. The individual, ex ante, pays insurance against the contingency that she will be hit by liquidity shocks.

5.3 Panic-Based Equilibrium

Assume that the economy has a banking sector with free entry and that all banks have access to the same investment technology. Unlike the central all-informed planner, banks cannot verify the depositor's type, once realized. Because banks make no profits due to perfect competition, they offer the same contract as the one that would be offered by the representative bank. Perfect competition implies that the deposit contact must maximize the ex ante welfare of agents. Table 5.1 describes ex post payments to depositors, where n is the number of agents who withdraw their money in the first period. Suppose the bank sets the payoff to early withdrawal r_1 at the first-best level of consumption, c_1^{FB}. If only impatient agents demand early withdrawal, the expected utility of patient agents is $E_\theta[p(\theta)] \cdot u\left(\frac{1-\lambda r_1}{1-\lambda} R\right)$. As long as this is more than the utility from withdrawing early $u(r_1)$, there is equilibrium in which, indeed, only impatient agents demand early withdrawal. In this

Table 5.1
Period 1 Payments to Depositors

Period	$n < 1/r_1$	
1	r_1	$\begin{cases} r_1 & \text{prob} & \dfrac{1}{nr_1} \\ 0 & \text{prob} & 1-\dfrac{1}{nr_1} \end{cases}$
2	$\begin{cases} \dfrac{(1-nr_1)}{1-n}R & \text{prob} & p(\theta) \\ 0 & \text{prob} & 1-p(\theta) \end{cases}$	0

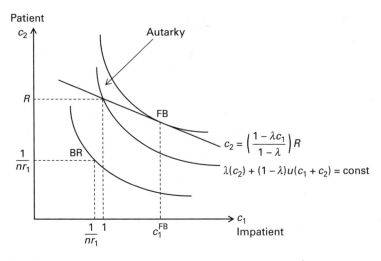

Figure 5.1
Autarkic, First-Best, and Bank-Run Equilibria

equilibrium, the first-best allocation is obtained. However, as Diamond and Dybvig point out, the demand-deposit contract makes the bank vulnerable to runs.

Indeed, there is a second equilibrium in which *all* agents demand early withdrawal. When they do so, period 1 payment is r_1 with probability $1/r_1$, and period 2 payment is 0, so that it is indeed optimal for all agents to demand early withdrawal. But in the event of bank runs, there should be some first-come, first-served rule for payments. Because with $r_1 = c_1^{FB} > 1$ not everyone can get $r_1 = c_1^{FB}$, late comers will get nothing; on average, depositors get 1 only. This equilibrium is evidently inferior to the autarkic regime.

Figure 5.1 assumes $p(\theta) = 1$. It illustrates the welfare ranking across different allocations: (i) autarky equilibrium, (ii) first-best equilibrium, and (iii) bank-run equilibrium. There is a clear welfare ranking: first-best equilibrium is superior to an autarky, and an autarky is superior to equilibrium with bank runs.

5.4 Heterogeneous Signals

Goldstein and Pauzner (2005) extend the model described above to situations where there is no common knowledge about the shock to the fundamental. The extension is in the spirit of the global-games literature, pioneered by Carlsson and van Damme (1993) and first applied

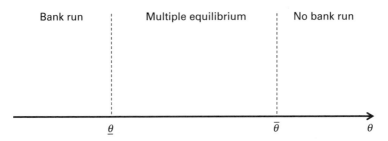

Figure 5.2
Bank Runs with Common Knowledge: Tripartite Classification of the Fundamentals

to currency attacks by Morris and Shin (1998). They demonstrate how a bank-run model generates a unique equilibrium.

Let us start with a benchmark where there is common knowledge about the fundamental θ. Then the possible equilibrium outcomes depend on which one of three regions the fundamental θ is in. This is depicted in figure 5.2. Below a threshold $\underline{\theta}$, there is a unique equilibrium where all depositors—patient and impatient—run on the bank and demand early withdrawal. Here, the fundamentals are so low that the bank will fail no matter what other depositors do, and hence each depositor undoubtedly finds it profitable to withdraw. Above a threshold $\bar{\theta}$, there is a unique equilibrium where patient depositors do not withdraw. Here, the fundamentals are so high that the bank can survive and pay its liabilities even if all depositors demand early withdrawal. Hence, they choose not to withdraw. Between $\underline{\theta}$ and $\bar{\theta}$, there are multiple equilibria. Either everyone runs and the bank fails or only impatient agents withdraw and the bank remains solvent. There are strategic complementarities, as depositors benefit from the run if and only if other depositors run, and hence there are two possible equilibria.

Now let us introduce some noise in speculators' information about the *fundamental* θ, such that every depositor gets a signal composed of the true fundamental θ plus an i.i.d. noise. The existence of noisy signals dramatically changes the predictions of the model, even if the noise is very small. The signal is received at the time when period 1 decisions about whether or not to withdraw deposits are made. The new predictions are depicted in figure 5.3. Now, the intermediate region between $\underline{\theta}$ and $\bar{\theta}$ is split into two subregions: below θ^*, a run occurs and the bank fails, while above it, there is no run.[6]

This result can be best understood by applying the logic of a backward induction. Because of the noise in patient depositors' information

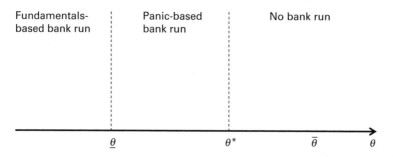

Figure 5.3
Equilibrium Outcomes in a Bank-Run Model with Non-Common Knowledge

about θ, their decisions about whether to withdraw no longer depend only on the information conveyed by the signal about the fundamental but also on what the signal conveys about other depositors' signals. Hence, between $\underline{\theta}$ and $\overline{\theta}$, depositors can no longer perfectly coordinate on any of the outcomes (run or not run), as their actions now depend on what they think other depositors will do at other signals. Hence, a depositor observing a signal slightly below $\overline{\theta}$ knows that many other depositors may have observed signals above $\overline{\theta}$ and chose not to run. Taking this into account, she chooses not to run. Then, knowing that depositors with signals just below $\overline{\theta}$ are not running on the bank, and applying the same logic, depositors with even lower signals will also choose not to run. This logic can be repeated again and again, establishing a boundary well below $\overline{\theta}$, above which depositors do not run on the bank. The same logic can then be repeated from the other direction, establishing a boundary well above $\underline{\theta}$, below which depositors do run on the bank. The mathematical proof shows that the two boundaries coincide at a unique θ^*, such that all depositors run below θ^* and do not run above θ^*.

As figure 5.3 shows, in the range between $\underline{\theta}$ and $\overline{\theta}$, the level of the fundamental now perfectly predicts whether or not a crisis occurs. In particular, a crisis surely occurs below the cutoff point, θ^*. We refer to crises in this range as *panic-based* because a crisis in this range is not necessitated by the fundamentals; it occurs because agents think it will occur, and in that sense it is self-fulfilling. However, the occurrence of a self-fulfilling crisis here is uniquely pinned down by the fundamentals. So, in this sense, the panic-based approach and the *fundamental-based* approach are not inconsistent with each other. The occurrence of a crisis is pinned down by fundamentals, but crises are self-fulfilling as they would not have occurred if agents did not expect them to occur. The key is that the fundamentals uniquely determine agents' expectations about whether a crisis will occur, and in that, they indirectly determine whether a crisis occurs. Agents' self-fulfilling beliefs amplify the effect of fundamentals on the economy. Similarly, between θ^* and $\bar{\theta}$, even though the fundamental could support a crisis, it does not occur, as agents' expectations are coordinated on the no-crisis outcome.

Knowing when runs occur, one can compute their probability and relate it to the terms of the banking contract. Goldstein and Pauzner (2005) show that when banks offer more risk sharing, they become more vulnerable to runs. That is, the threshold θ^*, below which a run happens, is an increasing function of the short-term payment offered to depositors r_1. (Note that the lower threshold $\underline{\theta}$ below which running is a dominant strategy is also an increasing function of r_1.) However, even when this destabilizing effect is taken into account, banks still increase welfare by offering demand-deposit contracts (provided that the range of fundamentals where liquidation is efficient is not too large). Characterizing the short-term payment in the banking contract chosen by banks taking into account the probability of a run, Goldstein and Pauzner show that this payment does not exploit all possible gains from risk sharing, as doing so would result in too many bank runs. Still, in equilibrium, panic-based runs occur, resulting from coordination failures among bank depositors. This leaves room for government policy to improve overall welfare.

5.5 Policy Implications

One of the basic policy remedies to reduce the loss from panic-based runs is introduction of deposit insurance by the government. This idea goes back to Diamond and Dybvig (1983), where the government promises to collect taxes and provide liquidity (bailout) to the bank in case the bank faces financial distress (i.e., when the number of agents demanding early withdrawal n exceeds the number of impatient agents λ).

In the context of the model described earlier, with deposit insurance patient agents know that if they wait they will receive the promised return independently of the number of agents who run. Hence, panic-based runs are prevented: patient agents withdraw their deposits only when this is their dominant action; that is, when θ is below $\underline{\theta}(r_1)$ [rather than below the higher threshold $\theta^*(r_1)$]. Extending the context of the above model, Keister (2012) has highlighted another benefit of deposit insurance: it helps provide a better allocation of resources by equating the marginal utility those agents derive from private consumption and public-good consumption. That is, when bank runs occur, private consumption decreases, generating a gap between the marginal utility of private consumption and that of public-good consumption, so with bailouts, the government can reduce the public good and increase private consumption to correct the distortion.

However, deposit insurance also has a drawback, as it creates moral hazard: When the bank designs the optimal contract, it does not internalize the cost of the taxes that might be required to pay the insurance. Thus, the bank has an incentive to overexploit the deposit insurance by setting r_1 higher than the socially optimal level. This drawback of deposit insurance is consistent with the critique made by Calomiris (1990) that "today's financial intermediaries can maintain higher leverage and attract depositors more easily by offering higher rates of return with virtually no risk of default." In the context of the model, this is costly as it increases the lower threshold $\underline{\theta}(r_1)$, below which crises occur without a coordination failure.[7]

5.6 Fragility of the Asset Side of the Bank's Balance Sheet

Banks provide a risk-sharing service through maturity transformation. A key consideration of the rules of the game concerning liquidity support to banks is the dynamic inconsistency of the monetary authorities. Ex post reactions of authorities do not necessarily coincide with announced ex ante rules. If ex ante constraints on financial agents are not strong enough, the understanding that the government will not let the economy collapse will lead to self-fulfilling equilibrium. A collective moral hazard was analyzed by Schneider and Tornell (2004) and Farhi and Tirole (2012). Private leverage choices of banks depend on the anticipated interest policy reaction to economy-wide maturity mismatch. When making decisions on refinancing of long-term projects, bankers put at risk bank-industry stakeholders: industrial companies that depend on bank loans for their financing, and consumers that depend on loan refinancing to hold onto their assets. Farhi and Tirole (2012) model of the possibility of multiple equilibria illustrates that banks' leverage decisions are strategic complements. Each bank's leverage decision has an effect on the other banks through the policy reaction function in the event of a crisis. In essence, excessive credit boom and deterioration of lending standards in the run-up to the financial crisis has been blamed on the expectation of government bailouts.

5.6.1 Banking Entrepreneurs

There are three periods, $t = 0, 1, 2$. Banking entrepreneurs have utility function $u = c_0 + c_1 + c_2$, where c_t is their date-t consumption. They are protected by limited liability, and their only endowment is their wealth A at date 0. Their technology set exhibits constant returns to scale. At date 0, they choose their investment scale i and a level of short-term debt (see later). At date 1, a safe cash flow πi accrues, which can be used to pay back the short-term debt. Uncertainty bears on the investment project: It is intact with probability, α, and distressed with probability $1 - \alpha$. Whether the project is intact or distressed depends on the realization of an aggregate shock—akin to a "crisis." In other words, the shocks impacting the different banking entrepreneurs are perfectly correlated.

If the project is intact, the investment delivers at date 1; it then yields, besides the safe cash flow πi, a payoff of $\rho_1 i$, of which only $\rho_0 i$ is pledgeable to lenders. Because the entrepreneur is indispensable, incentives to counter moral hazard require a positive "agency wedge," $\rho_1 - \rho_0$. If the project is distressed, the project yields no payoff at date 1, except for the safe cash flow πi. It yields a payoff at date 2 if fresh resource j is reinvested. The project can be downsized at the refinancing stage to any level $j \leq i$. It then delivers at date 2 a payoff of $\rho_1 i$, of which $\rho_0 i$ is pledgeable to lenders. The core model is a maturity mismatch issue where long-term projects require occasional refinancing. The banking entrepreneur has to compromise between the initial investment, of size i, with its corresponding leverage, and refinancing of the investment at a reduced scale j, in case of crisis. The bank's raising of initial scale i requires loading up on short-term debt and exhausting its own reserves of pledgeable income. This in turn forces the bank to downsize and de-leverage in the event of a crisis. Conversely, limiting the amount of short-term debt to mitigate maturity mismatch requires reducing the initial scale i.

The interest rate, a policy tool, is a key determinant of the collateral value of a project. It plays an important role in determining the initial investment scale i as well as the reinvestment scale j. Extended debt guarantees by the government that lower the interest rate R paid by the banking entrepreneur are essentially a subsidy to the borrowing institution. The subsidy is paid by the taxpayer, who ends up bearing the risk of the debt. In sum, the gross rate of interest is equal to 1 between dates 0 and 1. Between dates 1 and 2, the interest rate is equal to 1, the equilibrium rate from the consumer Euler equation, in the absence of a crisis, and to $R \leq 1$ otherwise. That is, R refers to the interest rate between dates 1 and 2 if there is a crisis.

The bank issues state-contingent short-term debt. It is always optimal for a bank to be able to set short-term debt in event of no crisis equal to πi. We denote di (where $d \leq \pi$) the amount of short-term debt in the event of a crisis. The excess $xi = (\pi - d)i$ of the safe cash flow πi over debt payments di represents cash available at date 1 in the event of a crisis (x is the analog of a liquidity ratio). We assume that any potential surplus of cash over liquidity needs for reinvestment—$\max[(\pi - d)i -j(1 - \rho_0/R), 0]$—is consumed by banking entrepreneurs.

At date 1, in the adverse state, the bank can issue new securities against the date 2 pledgeable income $\rho_0 j$, and so its continuation $j \in [0, i]$ must satisfy

$$j \leq (\pi - d)i + \rho_0 j / R$$

yielding continuation scale

$$j = \min\left[\frac{x}{1-(\rho_0 / R)}, 1\right]i.$$

This formula captures the fact that lower interest rates facilitate refinancing.

The bank needs to raise $i - A$ from lenders at date 0. Because the bank returns $di + (\pi - d)i + \rho_0 i$ to these lenders in the good state and only di in the bad state, its borrowing capacity at date 0 is given by $i - A = \alpha(\pi i + \rho_0 i) + (1 - \alpha)di$; that is,

$$i = \frac{A}{1 - \pi - \alpha\rho_0 + (1 - \alpha)x}.$$

The banking entrepreneur therefore maximizes

$$(\rho_1 - \rho_0)\left[\alpha i + (1 - \alpha)j\right] = \rho(\rho_1 - \rho_0)\left[\frac{\alpha + \dfrac{(1-\alpha)x}{1-\dfrac{\rho_0}{R}}}{1 - \pi - \alpha\rho_0 + (1-\alpha)x}\right]A,$$

where its control variables are

$d \in [\pi - (1 - \rho_0/R), \pi]$ or equivalently $x \in (0, 1 - \rho_0/R)$.

5.6.2 Rest of the Economy

Consumers born at date $t \in \{0, 1\}$ consume at date $t + 1$, so their utility is $u_t = c_{t+1}$. They are endowed with a large amount of resources (savings) s when born.

A short-term *storage technology* yields 1 in the next period for 1 invested today. In particular, the natural rate of interest (the marginal rate of transformation) between dates 1 and 2 is $R = 1$. For the date 1 interest rate is $R \neq 1$. Throughout the paper, we assume that s is large enough to finance all the necessary investments in the projects of banking entrepreneurs at each date t. As a result, consumers always invest a fraction of their savings in the short-term storage technology.

The storage technology must be taxed at rate $1 - R$ to induce the consumer not to invest all her resources in the storage technology rather than refinancing the bank's investment in the event of a crisis. The proceeds are rebated lump-sum to consumers at date 2. Taxing the short-term storage technology and rebating the proceeds lump-sum to consumers is essentially equivalent to subsidizing investment in the banks and financing this subsidy by a lump-sum tax on consumers.

The set of feasible interest rates is $[\rho_0, 1]$. There exists a distortion or deadweight loss, analogous to fixed costs $L(R) \geq 0$ when the interest rate R diverges from its natural rate, 1. $L(1) = L'(1) = 0$, and L is decreasing on $[\rho_0, 1]$.

Suppose that date 0 investment is equal to i and that banks hoard liquidity x and so can salvage $j = xi/(1 - \rho_0/R)$ in case of crisis. Then

(i) if there is a crisis at date 1, date 1 consumer welfare is $V = -L(R) - (1 - R)\rho_0 j/R$;
(ii) if there is no crisis at date 1, date 1 consumer welfare is $V = -L(1) = 0$.

In (i), the second term in the equation stands for the implicit subsidy from savers to borrowing banks. Indeed, date 1 consumers' return on their savings $\bar{s}$ is $R\bar{s} + (1 - R)(\bar{s} - \rho_0 j/R)$ (the last term representing the lump-sum rebate on the $\bar{s} - (\rho_0 j/R)$ invested in the storage technology), or $\bar{s} - (1 - R)\rho_0 j/R$. We can ignore the welfare of date 0 consumers because they have constant utility $u_0 = s$, regardless of the interest policy.

The deadweight loss function L can also be interpreted as a reduced form of a more standard distortion associated with conventional monetary policy, as emphasized in the New Keynesian literature (see part IV of this book). Here I have in mind not a short-term intervention, but a prolonged reduction of interest rates (a year to several years; think of Japan). Even though our model is entirely without money balances, sticky prices, or imperfect competition, it captures a key feature of monetary policy in New Keynesian models routinely used to discuss and model monetary policy. In New Keynesian models, the nominal interest rate is controlled by the central bank. Prices adjust only gradually according to the New Keynesian Phillips curve, and the central bank can therefore control the real interest rate. The real interest rate regulates aggregate demand through a version of the consumer Euler equation—the dynamic IS curve. Without additional frictions, the central bank can achieve the allocation of the flexible price economy by setting nominal interest rates so that the real interest rate equals the "natural" interest rate. Deviating from this rule introduces variations in the output gap together with distortions by generating dispersion in relative prices. To the extent that these effects enter welfare separately and additively from the effects of interest rates on banks' balance sheets—arguably a strong assumption—our loss function $L(R)$ can be interpreted as a reduced form for the loss function associated with a real interest rate below the natural interest rate in the New Keynesian model. Under this interpretation, monetary policy works both through the usual New Keynesian channel and through its effects on banks via a version of the "credit channel."

5.6.3   Welfare Analysis

At date 1, the central bank's objective function is a weighted average W of consumer welfare V and continuation scale j ($j = I$ if there is no crisis): $W = V + \beta j$. At date 0, the central bank's objective function is the expectation of its date 1 objective function.

The second term βj has this interpretation. Imagine that, say, three categories of banking stakeholders benefit from the banks' ability to continue. First, the banking entrepreneurs themselves. Second, the larger is j, the better off are their borrowers. Third, the workers working in banks and industrial companies; to the extent that they are better off employed (e.g., they receive an efficiency wage) and that preserved employment is related to j, then workers' welfare grows with j.

We will analyze two situations: one where the central bank can commit at date 0 to a specific contingent policy at date 1, and the (probably more likely) alternative where the central bank lacks commitment and instead determines its policy at $t = 1$ with no regard for previous commitments. In both cases, banking entrepreneurs and consumers form expectations regarding the interest rate $R \in [\rho_0, 1]$ that will be set if a crisis occurs.

No Commitment Equilibria At date 0, lenders and the banks form an expectation $R^* \in [\rho_0, 1]$ for the interest rate that the government will set in the event of a crisis. Based on this expectation, the representative bank invests $i(R^*)$ and hoards liquidity $x^* = 1 - (\rho_0/R^*)$ to be reinvested in the event of date 1 crisis. The reinvestment scale is determined by

$$j = \frac{x^*}{1 - \frac{\rho_0}{R}} i(R^*) = \frac{1 - \left(\frac{\rho_0}{R^*}\right)}{1 - \frac{\rho_0}{R}} i(R^*).$$

The government sets $R^{nc} \in R(R^{nc})$ so as to maximize the ex post welfare, which is given by

$$W^{\text{ex post}}(R; R^*) = -L(R) + \frac{\left[\beta - \frac{(1-R)\rho_0}{R}\right]\left(1 - \frac{\rho_0}{R^*}\right)}{1 - \frac{\rho_0}{R}} i(R^*).$$

The condition for R^{nc} to be an equilibrium is given by

$$\frac{w\rho_0}{1 - \frac{\rho_0}{R}}\left(\frac{1}{R^{nc}} - \frac{1}{R}\right) i(R^{nc}) \geq L(R^{nc}) - L(R) \text{ for all } R \in [R^{nc}, 1].$$

The left-hand side represents the cost in terms of lower investment scale of setting a higher interest rate $R > R^{nc}$. The right-hand side represents the gain in terms of lower interest rate distortion of setting such rate.

With this condition there exist multiple equilibria: $R^{nc} = 1$ and $R^{nc} = \rho_0$ are equilibria of the non-commitment policy regime.

This means that the banking entrepreneurs' leverage decisions generate strategic complementarity. Strategic complementarity results from the interactions of three components in a Farhi-Tirole mechanism:

a bank's imperfect pledgeability; the government's untargeted instrument of policy; and time inconsistency on the side of policy makers.

5.7 Policy Implications

The Volcker rule, which separates proprietary trading from insured banks, the Dodd-Frank Act, which made changes in the American financial regulatory environment that affect all federal financial regulatory agencies and almost every part of the nation's financial services industry, and the "Basel III," a comprehensive set of reform measures developed by the Basel Committee on Banking Supervision to strengthen the regulation, supervision, and risk management of the banking sector, are all examples of ways to manage and regulate the fragile financial intermediation institutions.

The framework developed earlier enables one to compare the benefits and costs of deposit insurance and provide policy recommendations regarding the optimal design of this insurance. Here, we only used the framework to highlight the trade-off, but more research is needed to provide more precise policy recommendations along these lines.

5.8 Pricing Liquidity

In traditional asset pricing models based on perfect markets, agents are able to raise funds on the capital market up to the level of their expected income. But with liquidity constraints, financial assets that can serve as a cushion to liquidity shocks command a liquidity premium. Bengt Holmstrom and Jean Tirole (2001) developed a stylized, liquidity-based asset-pricing model that has implications for monetary and exchange rate policies. They note that in the standard consumption-based models, asset prices are driven entirely by the consumer's intertemporal marginal rates of substitution (IMRS), and only real allocations matter. The net supply of financial assets is irrelevant.

Holmstrom and Tirole's (2001) model works as follows. There are three periods, $t = 0, 1, 2$, one good, and a continuum of mass 1 of identical entrepreneurs, each with one project. Entrepreneurs are risk neutral and have a zero discount rate. They have no endowment. In period 0, they get their finance from consumers (investors) to spend on set-up cost, I, of the project. In period 1, the project generates a random verifiable income, x. The distribution of the continuous variable x, identical for all projects (aggregate uncertainty) on the support $[0,\infty)$, is $G(x)$, with a mean greater than I.

Based on his income x, in period 1 the entrepreneur has an opportunity to invest for his private benefit an amount y. The entrepreneur is risk averse with respect to the reinvestment level y. Reinvestment generates a private payoff in period 2:

$$by - \frac{y^2}{2}, \quad b \geq 1.$$

The first-best reinvestment level is

$$y^{FB} = b - 1 > 0.$$

Period 1 payoff from the original investment, x, is however pledgeable. But, period 2 payoff of the reinvestment is not pledgeable, and this is the source of market imperfection.

There is one safe and liquid asset. There are $\bar{L}$ units of the liquid asset, each yielding in period 1 one unit of the good, in every state. The price of the liquid asset is denoted by q.

Consumers (investors) are risk neutral with a zero rate of discount. Their utility function is

$$u = c_0 + c_1 + c_2.$$

Because consumers buy any asset with positive expected rate of return, the market price of the liquid asset, q, must be greater than or equal to 1. Consumer income is not pledgeable; consumers cannot borrow against their future income. Thus, they cannot short sell the liquid asset, and with sufficient strong demand for the asset by the entrepreneurs, $q > 1$.

A contract between consumers (investors) and entrepreneurs specifies L units of the liquid asset, purchased in period 0 by the entrepreneur, a level $y(x)$ that he can reinvest in period 1, and an amount $t(x)$ to be paid out to the entrepreneur in period 1. The balance of income in period 1 is paid back to consumers (investors):

$$x + L - y(x) - t(x).$$

Because consumers (investors) cannot commit to pay out of their own income in period 1, the contract must satisfy the following liquidity constraints:

$$y(x) + t(x) \leq x + l, \tag{5.1}$$

for all x. The expectation in period 0 from the contract to guarantee consumers a positive expected return out of period 1 reimbursements, is

$$E_0[x - I - y(x) - t(x) - (q - 1)L] \geq 0. \tag{5.2}$$

Evidently, with competitive markets, constraint (5.2) holds with equality.

An optimal contract will maximize the expected sum of the entrepreneur's payoffs,

$$E_0 \left[by(x) - \frac{y(x)^2}{2} + t(x) \right],$$

subject to constraints (5.1) and (5.2).

Letting μ denote the shadow price of constraint (5.2), the optimization problem can be restated as:

$$\max_{(y(.),\, L)} \left(E_0 \left\{ by(x) - \frac{y(x)^2}{2} + t(x) + \mu[x - I - y(x) - t(x) - (q - 1)L] \right\} \right),$$

subject to constraint (5.1).

For fixed L, the solution to the unconstrained program is $y^* = b - \mu$, and the solution to the liquidity-constrained program is therefore

$$y(x) = \min[y^*, x + L].$$

The entrepreneur is liquidity constrained in the low-income states, $x < y^* - L$. In all these states, he does not pay back to consumers (investors). In the unconstrained states,

$$x > y^* - L,$$

returns on the original investment are sufficiently large so that he can reach the desired reinvestment level y^*, and he does pay back to the consumers (investors) nonnegative sums.

The Lagrange multiplier, μ, must be greater than or equal to 1 or else the solution to the unconstrained program will not pay consumers (investors) anything in period 1; violating constraint (5.2).[8]

The focus of the exercise is the period 0 choice of liquidity and the pricing of the liquid asset. Accordingly, L is chosen to maximize:

$$\int_0^{y^* - L} \left[b(x + L) - \frac{(x + L)^2}{2} - \mu(I + qL) \right] g(x) dx$$

$$+ \int_{y^* - L}^{\infty} \left\{ by^* - \frac{y^{*2}}{2} - \mu[I + y^* + (q - 1)L] - x \right\} g(x) dx.$$

The first-order condition is

$$q-1= \int_0^{y^*-L} \left[\frac{b-(x+L)}{\mu}-1\right]g(x)dx.$$ (5.3)

Define

$$m(x)= \begin{cases} \frac{b-(x+L)}{\mu}, \text{ if} \\ \quad x\leq y^*-L \\ 0, \text{ if} \\ \quad x>y^*-L \end{cases}$$

as the marginal value of liquidity service. Then,

$$q =1+ E_0[m(x)].$$

The liquidity premium is equal to the expected marginal value of liquidity services.[9] In liquidity shortage states,

$$x\leq y^*-L,$$

an extra unit of the liquid asset allows the entrepreneur to increase the reinvestment, in period 1, by one unit, and the private benefit by

$$b-(x+L).$$

This marginal private benefit, expressed in monetary terms, is equal to

$$\frac{b-(x+L)}{\mu}.$$

The increase in reinvestment has a monetary cost equal to 1.

An equilibrium consists of a pair of period 0 prices $[q,\mu]$ and optimal-contract quantities $(L,y(.))$, such that $t(x) = 0$ for all x, the expected rate-of-return constraint (5.2) holds with equality, and the asset-pricing equation (5.3) holds with $q > 1$, with liquid-asset market clearing condition, $L=\bar{L}$.

Equation (5.3) implies that the liquid asset commands a liquidity premium. Treasuries and high-rated bonds offer better insurance against liquidity shortages than stocks. When there is a high probability of a liquidity shortage, such as during the 2008 liquidity crisis, the option-like liquidity service is "in the money," and the liquid asset price will command a sizeable liquidity premium. Furthermore, the value of the marginal liquidity service $m(.)$, and the price of the liquid asset, are monotonically decreasing in the aggregate supply of the liquid asset, $\bar{L}$.

5.9   Concluding Remarks

The main reason for concern with banking crises is that they spread across banks leading many to fail at the same time, hence creating systemic risk. There is a large literature on contagion of banking crises, highlighting the different sources for spillovers and coordination among banks. Allen and Gale (2000b) show how contagion arises due to bank interlinkages. Banks facing idiosyncratic liquidity needs insure each other and so provide efficient risk sharing. However, this creates links across banks, leading to spillover of shocks and contagion of crises. Dasgupta (2004) extends Allen and Gale's model using the global-games framework described earlier, analyzing the optimal insurance contracts among banks and taking into account their undesirable implications for contagion. In Goldstein and Pauzner (2004), contagion is generated because a common pool of investors invest in different banks. The failure of one bank leads investors to lose wealth and become more risk averse, and so they are more likely to run on the other bank.

Another source of systemic risk is the "too-big-to-fail" problem. Banks that become too big pose a big threat on the economy in case they fail, and so governments will be willing to provide a bailout to prevent this from happening. This in turn generates disincentives such that the bank will take on excessive risk knowing that the consequences will be borne by the taxpayer.

6 Analytics of Credit Frictions and Market Freezes

6.1 Moral Hazard

In this chapter, we review models that analyze frictions in loans extended by financial institutions and other lenders.[1] Broadly speaking, these are models of credit frictions and market freezes. This literature highlights two key problems that create frictions in the flow of credit from lenders to borrowers. When these frictions strengthen, a financial crisis ensues that can even lead to a complete freeze. One problem is that of moral hazard. If a borrower has the ability to divert resources at the expense of the creditor, then creditors will be reluctant to lend to borrowers. Hence, for credit to flow efficiently from the creditor to the borrower, it is crucial that the borrower maintains "skin in the game"; that is, that he has enough at stake in the success of the project and so does not have a strong incentive to divert resources. This creates a limit on credit, and it can be amplified when economic conditions worsen, leading to a crisis. Another problem is that of adverse selection. In the presence of asymmetric information between lenders and borrowers or between buyers and sellers, credit and trade flows might freeze. Again, this may lead to a crisis if asymmetric information is very extreme.

In the above models of financial institution failures, the returns on assets and loans held by the bank were assumed to be exogenous, and the focus was on the behavior of depositors. The next group of models focuses on the credit market, where firms and entrepreneurs borrow from financial institutions in order to finance their investments. Stiglitz and Weiss (1981) provide a basic rationale for the presence of frictions in the credit market. When lending to a firm, a bank needs to make sure that the firm has a large enough incentive to preserve (or improve) the quality of the investment and repay the loan. A direct implication

Table 6.1
Private Benefits and Probabilities

	Project		
Parameter	Good	Bad (Low Private Benefit)	Bad (High Private Benefit)
Private benefit	0	b	B
Probability of success	p_H	p_L	p_L

is that for the bank to lend to the firm, the firm has to have a large enough stake in the investment or it has to be able to secure the loan with collateral. These considerations limit the amount of credit available to firms. They can lead to amplification of shocks to fundamentals and ultimately to financial crises.

Holmstrom and Tirole (1997) provide a canonical representation of this mechanism. In their model, there is a continuum of entrepreneurs, with access to the same investment technology and different amounts of capital A. The distribution of assets across entrepreneurs is described by the cumulative distribution function $G(A)$. The investment required is I, so an entrepreneur needs to raise $I - A$ from outside investors. The return is either 0 or R, and the probability depends on the type of project that the entrepreneur chooses. The possible projects are described in table 6.1.

If the entrepreneur chooses a good project, the probability of a high return is higher than if he chooses a bad project: $p_H > p_L$. However, the entrepreneur may choose a bad project to enjoy nonpecuniary private benefit. The private benefit is either b or B, where $B > b$, so if unconstrained, the entrepreneur will always choose a bad project with high private benefit over a bad project with low private benefit.

The rate of return demanded by outside investors is denoted by γ, which can be either fixed or coming from an upward-sloping supply function $S(\gamma)$. The assumption is that only the good project is viable:

$$p_H R - \gamma I > 0 > p_L R - \gamma I + B.$$

That is, investing in the bad project generates a negative total surplus. Hence, for outside investors to put money in the firm, it is essential to make sure that the entrepreneur undertakes the good project. The incentive of the entrepreneur to choose the good project will depend on how much "skin in the game" he has. That is, the entrepreneur will need to keep enough ownership of the project so that he has a monetary incentive to make the "right" decision. A key implication is that it would be easier to provide external finance to entrepreneurs with large assets A, as they are more likely to internalize the monetary benefit and choose the good project rather than enjoy the nonpecuniary benefits of the bad project.

Consider a contract where the entrepreneur invests A, and the outside investor puts in $I - A$. Clearly, no one will receive any payment if the project fails and yields zero. The key is to determine how the entrepreneur and the outside investor split the return of the project in case it succeeds, yielding R. In general, one can denote the payment to the entrepreneur as R_f and the payment to the outside investor as R_u, such that $R_f + R_u = R$.

A necessary condition for outside investors to be willing to provide financing to the entrepreneur is that the entrepreneur has an incentive to choose the good project; that is, he benefits more from taking the good project than from taking the bad project. This implies:

$$p_H R_f \geq p_L R_f + B.$$

Denoting $p = p_H - p_L$ we get the incentive compatibility constraint:

$$R_f \geq B / \Delta p.$$

This implies that the maximum amount that can be promised to the outside investors—the pledgeable expected income—is

$$p_H (R - B / \Delta p).$$

Hence, to satisfy the participation constraint of the outside investors (i.e., to make sure that they get a high enough expected income to at least break even), we need

$$\gamma (I - A) \leq p_H (R - B / \Delta p).$$

This puts an endogenous financing constraint on the entrepreneur, which depends on how much internal capital A he has. Defining the threshold $\bar{A}(\gamma)$ as

$$\bar{A}(\gamma) = I - p_H / \gamma (R - B / \Delta p),$$

we get that only entrepreneurs with capital at or above $\bar{A}(\gamma)$ can raise external capital and invest in their projects. This is the classic credit-rationing result going back to Stiglitz and Weiss (1981). The entrepreneur cannot get unlimited amounts of capital, as he needs to maintain a high enough stake in the project so that outside investors are willing to participate.

Holmstrom and Tirole go on to introduce financial intermediaries, who have the ability to monitor entrepreneurs.[2] The monitoring technology available to financial intermediaries is assumed to prevent the entrepreneur from taking a bad project with high nonpecuniary private benefit B, thereby reducing the opportunity cost of the entrepreneur from B to b. Monitoring yields a private cost of c to the financial intermediary. Financial intermediaries themselves need to have an incentive to pay the monitoring cost and make sure entrepreneurs are prevented from enjoying high private benefits B. Hence, they need to put in their own capital, and the amount of intermediary capital K_m is going to be a key parameter.

An intermediary can help relax the financing constraint of the entrepreneur by monitoring him and reducing his incentive to take the bad project. Hence, even entrepreneurs with a level of capital lower than the threshold $\bar{A}(\gamma)$ will be able to get financing assisted by the intermediaries. Denoting the return required by the intermediaries as β, where β is determined in equilibrium and is decreasing in the supply of capital K_m that is available in the financial intermediary sector, the threshold $\underline{A}(\gamma, \beta)$ of the entrepreneur's capital A above which the entrepreneur can raise capital via financial intermediaries and invest is

$$\underline{A}(\gamma, \beta) = I - I_m(\beta) - p_H / [R - (b + c) / \Delta p].$$

Hence, in equilibrium, we get the following graphical description of which entrepreneurs will be financed and invest, depending on how much capital they have, as depicted in figure 6.1.

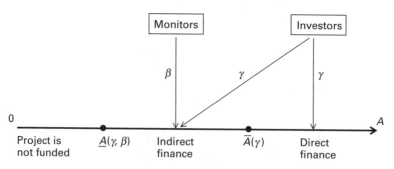

Figure 6.1
Investment Finance: Direct and Indirect

We can see that entrepreneurs with little capital [below $\underline{A}(\gamma, \beta)$] cannot get financed and do not invest in their projects; those with an intermediate level of capital [between $\underline{A}(\gamma, \beta)$ and $\bar{A}(\gamma)$] can get financed only with the monitoring by the financial intermediary sector; and those with a high level of capital [above $\bar{A}(\gamma)$] can get financed by the outside investors even without monitoring.

In this model, a negative aggregate shock in the economy, shifting the distribution of capital $G(A)$ to the left (i.e., such that entrepreneurs have less capital on average), will be amplified, as entrepreneurs having less wealth will face stricter financial constraints and will be less likely to raise external financing. Hence, there is an accelerator effect, whereby shocks to the economy are amplified. Another form of accelerator effect in this model operates via the financial intermediary sector, as a decrease in the capital K_m of the financial intermediary sector will also have an adverse effect on the real economy. This is because it leads to an increase in the equilibrium return β demanded by financial intermediaries and to an increase in the threshold $\underline{A}(\gamma, \beta)$, above which middle-size entrepreneurs can get financed and invest. Hence, a decrease in financial intermediary capital will lead to contraction in real investment, specifically of middle-size firms.

Holmstrom and Tirole (1998) study a similar setup and develop the implications for government policy. Recall that entrepreneurs need to keep sufficient ownership in the firms that they run (R_f needs to be sufficiently high), so that they take the good project rather than the bad project. This limits their ability to offer sufficient return to outside investors (R_u is limited), and so in case of an adverse liquidity shock, they are limited in how much capital they can raise to keep running their projects and prevent welfare-reducing bankruptcy. This creates an incentive for holding liquid securities ex ante, so that they can use them when they are hit by adverse shocks and are financially constrained. Holmstrom and Tirole (1998) show that, in case of aggregate uncertainty, the government can improve overall welfare by issuing government debt and supplementing the supply of liquid securities in the economy.

Similar financial accelerators have been discussed in macroeconomic setups, showing how shocks to asset values can be amplified and become persistent in equilibrium. Bernanke and Gertler (1989) provide the first financial-accelerator model, emphasizing that financial frictions amplify adverse shocks and that they are persistent. That is, a temporary shock depresses not only current but also future economic activity. Kiyotaki and Moore (1997) identify an important dynamic feedback mechanism. The cutback of investment in the future will reduce the asset price of future periods, and, because this asset-price decline is anticipated, it will be immediately reflected in a fall in the current asset price. This lowers the current collateral value of assets, reducing firms' debt capacity even further. Hence, demand for these assets falls and price declines further, eroding productive agents' net worth in turn, and so on. These models are reviewed in chapter 13.

More recent work builds on Kiyotaki and Moore's (1997) analysis of credit constraints. Kocherlakota (2000) stresses that credit cycles are asymmetric; sharp downturns are followed by slow recoveries. Eisfeldt and Rampini (2006) develop a model where credit constraints are more binding in recessions in order to match the empirical regularity that capital reallocation is lower in downturns than in booms. Iacoviello (2005) evaluates the quantitative relevance of the Kiyotaki-Moore mechanism in a setting with nominal mortgage debt using real estate as collateral. Caballero and Krishnamurthy (2001) and Mendoza (2010) study sudden stops—a dry-up of international capital inflows.

In Kiyotaki and Moore's analysis, credit is limited by the expected price of the collateral in the next period. In the analyses by Geanako-plos (1997, 2003) and Brunnermeier and Pedersen (2009), borrowing capacity is limited by greater future price volatility. In the analysis by Brunnermeier and Sannikov (2010), more productive entrepreneurs are concerned about hitting their solvency constraint in the future and consequently do not fully exploit their debt capacity. As volatility rises, they cut back on borrowing by selling assets. This depresses prices further, leading to rich volatility dynamics.

6.2   Asymmetric Information

A major friction in the operation of financial markets is the presence of asymmetric information. The basic insight goes back to the model of Akerlof (1970). If sellers have private information about the quality of the assets, buyers will be reluctant to buy the assets from them because they realize that the sale represents negative information about the asset. In extreme situations, when the only motivation to trade is based on information, this leads to a market freeze: no transactions will happen in equilibrium. Pagano (1989) and Dow (2004) show that coordination problems among uninformed traders can arise due to the asymmetric information described above. Uninformed traders have stronger incentive to participate in the market if they know that there are more uninformed traders there, as then they are exposed to a lesser adverse selection problem. These coordination problems can lead to sharp changes in market depth, resembling what we see in a financial crisis. Recently, Morris and Shin (2012) show that the amplification becomes even more severe when traders have different information about the extent of the adverse selection problem (i.e., about how many informed traders are present). This leads to a contagious process, by which very small changes can lead to a market freeze.

7 Analytics of Asset Bubbles

Two prominent views about financial markets have been established in the history of economic thought. First, the view promoted by Hayek (1945) is that financial markets aggregate information and thus track fundamental developments in the economy. Second, the view promoted by Keynes (1936) is that financial markets are like a beauty contest, where participants just try to guess the views of other participants.[1] Characterizing financial speculation, Keynes says, is like "anticipating what average opinion expects the average opinion to be." According to Keynes, this feature of the financial market leads to bubbles, crashes, and generally poor connection with economic fundamentals. Hence, such forces may be able to account for financial market crashes such as in 1929 and 1987.

Several models capture this higher-order-belief aspect of financial markets. As shown by Allen, Morris, and Shin (2006) and Bacchetta and van Wincoop (2006), speculators care about other speculators' expectations about asset fundamentals more than about the fundamentals themselves, and this might lead to large deviations of prices from fundamentals. As shown by Abreu and Brunnermeier (2003), financial market speculators know that a bubble exists, but not when it will burst. Speculators then have an incentive to ride on the bubble before it bursts, thus adding more fuel to it.[2]

Market crashes have also been explained in the literature as a result of speculators' need to sell an asset when its price drops below a certain threshold (see Gennotte and Leland 1990; Bernardo and Welch 2004; Morris and Shin 2004; Brunnermeier and Pedersen 2009). This may happen due to a margin constraint, for example, that results from an underlying agency problem. In that, this mechanism echoes the credit cycles due to collateral constraints found in Kiyotaki and Moore (1997).[3] Market segmentation has also been perceived to contribute to crashes.

As shown by Allen and Gale (1994), speculators choose ex ante where to invest and cannot easily switch later. This implies that a group of similar investors ends up holding an asset, and when they are hit by a shock, there is no natural buyer, and so the price crashes. It should be noted that the deviation of asset prices from fundamental values that happens in all these models is also related to the literature on limits to arbitrage (see, e.g., De Long, Shleifer, Summers, and Waldman 1990; Shleifer and Vishny 1997).

Swings in market prices may also come as a result of the feedback effect that financial markets have on the real economy. This may happen even under Hayek's (1945) view of the world, and in fact particularly due to this view of the world. That is, if asset prices aggregate useful information about fundamentals, agents in the real side of the economy (e.g., providers of capital, firm managers, policy makers, etc.) will learn from market prices and use the information in their real decisions. This will generate a feedback effect from asset prices to firms' investments and cash flows. In such a framework, changes in asset prices may become self-fulfilling and give rise to wide swings in asset prices (and in real values). Goldstein and Guembel (2008) provide such a model, where short selling by market speculators reduces market prices and leads to the cancellation of real investments due to the perception of underlying negative information. This leads to decline in firm values and hence enables short sellers to profit on their trades. Ozdenoren and Yuan (2008) also study a model of feedback effects that generate high volatility, although without endogenizing the source of the feedback.

7.1 Risk-Shifting Bubbles

A model of bubbles that links bubbles to financial crises is provided by Allen and Gale (2000a). Their model is motivated by the empirical literature (e.g., Kaminsky and Reinhart 1999) documenting that financial crises are often preceded by credit expansions and increases in asset-market prices. A leading example at the time was the events prior to the collapse of the bubble in Japan in 1990. Clearly, this has been a major feature in the 2008 global financial crisis, which was preceded by credit expansions and real estate bubbles.

In the model, Allen and Gale consider an economy where a continuum of risk-neutral investors has access to two types of projects—a safe project and a risky project—but has no capital. Therefore, investors need to borrow from banks in order to invest. Banks have total capital at the amount of B and do not have access to the investments on their own or any alternative use for the capital.

Investors choose the amount X_S to invest in the safe asset and the amount X_R to invest in the risky asset. A critical assumption is that banks cannot observe the types of investments made by investors. The return on the safe asset is determined endogenously in equilibrium and is denoted by r. This asset can be thought of as investment in bonds issued by the corporate sector, and the return r is then equal to the marginal productivity of the capital lent to the corporate sector,

$$r = f'(X_S),$$

where $f(X_S)$ is a standard production function with diminishing marginal productivity of capital. The safe asset has infinite supply.

The return on the risky asset is denoted by R, which is a random variable with a continuous positive density $h(R)$ on the support $[0, R_{MAX}]$ and a mean $\bar{R}$. This asset can be interpreted as real estate or some other risky asset out there in the economy. It has a limited supply of 1. Investors bear a nonpecuniary increasing and convex cost $c(X_R)$ when investing in the risky asset.

Investors and banks are restricted to use of debt contracts with a fixed interest rate. It is shown in the paper that the interest rate on loans from the banks has to be equal to the endogenously determined return on the safe asset: r. The total amount borrowed is $X_S + PX_R$, where P is the endogenously determined price of the risky asset.

The main result in the paper is that the price P of the risky asset will be higher than the fundamental value of this asset (i.e., there is a bubble in the risky-asset market). This is due to the fact that investors, benefiting from limited liability, enjoy the upside of this asset and do not lose that much from the downside (i.e., when they default). Hence, they excessively bid up the price of the risky asset. This is the well-known asset-substitution or risk-shifting phenomenon. Banks, in turn, cannot observe the misbehavior of the investors and settle for a lower return (which is still above their alternative return from holding onto their funds).

To see this, note that investors break even on their investment in the safe asset, and their profit is only driven by their expected return from the risky asset, given the limited liability. Hence, they set the quantity X_R of the risky asset to maximize

$$\max_{X_R \geq 0} \int_{rP}^{R_{MAX}} (RX_R - rPX_R)h(R)dR - c(X_R).$$

That is, their profit is the return from the risky asset RX_R minus the borrowing cost rPX_R, as long as the return is higher than the borrowing cost, and minus the nonpecuniary cost $c(X_R)$. Note that r serves as a lower bound on losses. The limited liability makes for one-sided riskiness, which is the root of risk shifting. The other equilibrium conditions are the market-clearing condition in the market for the risky asset and the market-clearing condition in the credit market:

$$X_R = 1;$$

$$X_S + P = B.$$

Recalling that $r = f'(X_S)$, we have four equations that determine the equilibrium variables X_R, X_S, r, and P.

We can see that the subject of investigation P is determined such that investors are indifferent about investing in the marginal unit of the risky asset (but make a profit on their overall investment in the risky asset). The fact that they enjoy from the upside and have limited loss on the downside from this investment implies that the price that makes them marginally indifferent has to rise. Allen and Gale (2000a) show that the price rises above the fundamental value, where the fundamental value is defined as an equilibrium price that investors will be willing to pay without the possibility of risk shifting, as if banks can observe what they do; that is, it is given by

$$\max_{(X_S, X_R) \geq 0} \int_{0}^{R_{MAX}} (rX_S + RX_R)h(R)dR - c(X_R)$$

s.t. $X_S + PX_R = B.$

The first-order conditions for the maximization problem along with the market-clearing equation $X_R = 1$ enable us to solve for the price of the risky asset. Here, the investors get the value of the asset without shifting risk and thus enjoy the upside and bear the cost of the downside. Therefore, they break even.

Notably, Allen and Gale (2000a) show that the bubble will be bigger when the risky asset is more risky (i.e., when there is more room for risk shifting) and when there is more credit available in the economy. This corresponds very well to the historical events mentioned earlier as the motivation for the paper, as well as to the recent crisis.

The bubble reflects overinvestment in risky assets stemming from lack of transparency and expansionary credit policy. This is costly to the real side of the economy because the risky assets fail too often and lead to costly waste of resources. Policy makers can address these situations by keeping credit under control and requiring transparency in real investments so that they are not overly shifted to the risky assets. In a recent paper, Barlevy (2008) extends the model to add the possibility of speculative bubbles (i.e., when agents buy assets for the possibility of reselling the later on) and provides a comprehensive policy analysis in this setting.

7.2   Leverage Bubbles

A central problem in the credit market is that lenders are reluctant to make loans because they cannot easily determine whether a prospective borrower has resources to repay the loan. If the loan is made, the lender is concerned whether the borrower will engage in risky behavior that could lower the probability that the loan will be repaid. Collateral reduces this information asymmetry problem because good collateral (i.e., assets that are easily valued and easy to take control of) significantly decreases the losses to the lender if the borrower defaults on the loan. Good collateral also reduces the moral hazard problem because the borrower is reluctant to engage in excessively risky behavior because now he or she has something to lose.

Asset bubbles often are based on inconsistent and diverging views about the future. Geanakoplos (2003, 2010) and Fostel and Geanakoplos (2012) developed an analytical framework with heterogeneous beliefs to study the dynamics of collateral values and market values that produce credit cycles. The framework features risky and safe assets. Agents are heterogeneous, with a continuum of subjective probabilities concerning the driving forces behind the fundamentals of the risky-asset returns. Agents with more optimistic beliefs about the risky asset would naturally like to acquire as much as they can of the risky asset, but they are also credit constrained by the market value of the collateral. They can use the risky asset in their endowments as collateral to raise debt financing from the less optimistic agents. In equilibrium, the credit market and asset market boom together. On the one hand, a higher collateral value allows the optimistic buyer to obtain financing at a lower cost. This tends to bid up the risky-asset price. On the other hand, a higher risky-asset price increases this asset collateral value. But,

Table 7.1
Assets' State-Dependent Returns

	Good X	Good Y
State U	1	1
State D	1	$0 < R < 1$

a sizeable bad shock to the fundamental driving force of the risky-asset returns wipes out the boom period–optimistic asset owners, who have used maximum debt in terms of the riskless debt to finance their insolvent asset position. The shock shifts down the degree of optimism among the remaining investors and generates a crash in the risky-asset market value. That is, credit and asset market prices crash together after the bad shock.

The model benchmark model assumes a two-period model, with $t = 0, 1$, and two goods: Y and X. In period 1, asset returns realize, and consumption of good X takes place. Period 1 consists of two states: U (up) and D (down). In period 0, investors trade in assets (consumption does not take place in period 0). The two assets that are traded in period 0 are cash, X, with return $X_U = X_D = 1$ unit of the consumption good in each state; and Y, a risky asset, with return $Y_U = 1$, $Y_D = R < 1$ unit of the consumption good (good Y serves as an investment good). Asset returns are described in table 7.1.

Investors are identical except for their probability beliefs. Probability beliefs are uniformly distributed on a continuum $[0, 1]$. All investors have the same endowments: 1 unit of X and 1 unit of Y in period 0. They are all risk neutral.

The expected (linear) utility of investor h is

$$U^h(x_U, x_D) = q_U^h x_U + q_D^h x_D, \quad h \in [0, 1],$$

where q_U^h and q_D^h are the probabilities of state U and state D, respectively. Because in the D-state the return R is less than 1, a higher h denotes more *optimism*.

7.2.1 Complete Markets

As a benchmark, we begin by describing the equilibrium where markets are complete. As usual, two securities, with independent return structure, are necessary in order to complete the market in a two-stage model: an Arrow-U security, which pays 1 unit of X in the U state, or

0 otherwise, and an Arrow-D security, which pays 1 unit of X in the D state, or 0 otherwise. There exists a marginal investor h_1, who equates the marginal rate of substitution between consumption of good X in state U and consumption of good X in state D to the relative price of good X in state U, in terms of units of good X in state D:

$$\frac{P_U}{P_D} = \frac{q_U^{h_1}}{1 - q_U^{h_1}}. \tag{7.1}$$

(Recall that due to the assumption of a risk-neutrality state, the contingent marginal utility is unity.)

The marginal buyer, h_1 (who is indifferent between buying Arrow-U or Arrow-D securities at the equilibrium relative price) sets, in effect, the equilibrium relative price of the state-contingent goods. Any investor h, $h > h_1$, will buy all he can afford of only the Arrow-U securities; whereas any investor h, $h < h_1$, will buy all he can afford of only the Arrow-D securities.[4]

We now consider how the identity of the marginal buyer h_1 is endogenously determined in equilibrium.

Aggregate consumption in state U is 2 units of good X and in state D is $1 + R$ units of good X. The uniform distribution of investor types implies that the fraction of the investor population $1 - h_1$, the optimists, will buy what they can afford of the Arrow-U securities, and the fraction of the investor population h_1 will buy all they can afford of the Arrow-D securities. Aggregate revenue from sales of the Arrow-U security is then equal to

$$(1+1)\frac{P_U}{P_D},$$

whereas aggregate expenditure of good X by the buyers of type h, $h > h_1$, is

$$(1 - h_1)\left[2\frac{P_U}{P_D} + (1+R)\right].$$

Equating aggregate sales and aggregate expenditures yields

$$2\frac{P_U}{P_D} = (1 - h_1)\left[2\frac{P_U}{P_D} + (1+R)\right]. \tag{7.2}$$

Equation (7.2), given equation (7.1), determines the identity of the marginal buyer h_1 in the complete-market equilibrium.

In analyzing the complete-markets Arrow-security economy, however, we gloss over the question why borrowers have an incentive to voluntarily keep in period 1 the promises made in period 0. To ensure repayments, security contracts must involve a *collateral*, and this is absent in the Arrow-security economy.

7.2.2 Collateral Contracts

To understand the role of collateral contracts, we start with an economy in which such contracts are not available and promises cannot be kept because in such a *no-leverage* economy, there is no incentive to keep any promise. That is, investors can only trade long in their security endowments, X and Y. Under the assumption of strict monotonicity in the continuous identity index of agent h, of the probability of the good state, q_U^h, there will be again a unique marginal buyer, h_1^{NL}, who will be indifferent between buying and selling the risky security Y.

The relative price is determined by

$$\left(\frac{P_Y}{P_X}\right)^{NL} = q_U^{NL} + q_D^{NL} R. \tag{7.3}$$

That is, the relative price of the risky asset is set equal to the expected return on the asset by the marginal buyer. All investors with

$$h > h^{NL}$$

buy all they can afford of the Y security, and all investors with

$$h < h^{NL}$$

buy all they can afford of the X security.

Let $p^{NL} = (P_Y/P_X)^{NL}$. The aggregate value from sales of the Y asset is $1 \cdot p^{NL}$, whereas aggregate expenditure (endowment of X plus revenues from asset sales) on the risky asset is $(1 - h^{NL})(p^{NL} + 1)$. In equilibrium we have

$$p^{NL} = (1 - h^{NL})(p^{NL} + 1). \tag{7.4}$$

This equation determines the identity of the marginal buyer in the no-leverage economy.

In a *leverage* economy, where investors are allowed to borrow, they can buy more of the risky asset, Y, compared to the situation in the *no-leverage* economy because they can borrow in X and spend more on Y. Investors are able to issue a noncontingent *promise*, using the Y asset as *collateral in the amount of R*. Thus, the lender will get a *safe* return, independent of whether state U or state D occurs. Thus, the equilibrium interest rate on a loan is zero. This zero interest rate makes the marginal buyer indifferent between lending and borrowing in equilibrium. Investors trade in noncontingent *collateral contracts* in period 0. A generic financial contract (A, C) consists of both a *promise*, $A = (A_U, A_D)$, and collateral, $C \in \{X, Y\}$. The creditor has the right to seize as much of the collateral, but no more, if the borrower breaches the promise. The contract therefore delivers to the creditor $\min(A_U, C_U)$ in state U or $\min(A_D, C_D)$ in state D. Every contract is collateralized by either 1 unit of X or 1 unit of Y. Although many potential contracts are priced in equilibrium, the only contract that is actively traded is a *max min contract*, which corresponds to the zero-risk rule. That is, there will be no actual default in equilibrium using this contract because the borrower has a proper incentive to repay her debt fully. Specifically in the current model, a loan of R units of good X, in period 0, will have a payoff to the lender of R units of good X in each state, U and D. For a loan of the amount R, the collateral of R units will secure the payments of R units in both the down and the up states.

As before, there will be a marginal buyer, h_1^L, who is indifferent between buying and selling the Y security. All the optimistic investors will buy all they can afford of the risky good, Y, by selling both their endowment of cash, X, and borrow by using Y as collateral (see table 7.2).

Table 7.2
Security Trade Pattern

	Complete-Markets Economy	No-Leverage Economy	Leverage Economy
Marginal buyer	h_1	h_1^{NL}	h_1^L
Optimists	Sell the Arrow-D security and buy the Arrow-U security	Sell the X asset and hold only the risky Y asset	Buy the risky Y asset and borrow in terms of the safe X security; place a collateral in terms of the Y asset
Pessimists	Sell the Arrow-U security and buy the Arrow-D security	Sell the Y asset and hold only the safe X asset	Sell the risky Y asset and lend in terms of the safe X security

The marginal buyer of security Y, who is indifferent between buying X or Y, equates the marginal rate of substitution between holding security X and Y to the relative price of security Y:

$$P^L = q_U^L + q_D^L R. \tag{7.5}$$

That is, the relative price of the risky asset is equal to the expected return on the asset by the marginal buyer. [Note that although condition (7.5) for the leverage economy is the similar to condition (7.3) for the non-leverage economy, the subjective probabilities are different because the identity of the marginal buyer is different.]

All investors with

$$h > h^L$$

buy all they can afford of the Y security while borrowing in X and placing a collateral in Y. All investors with $h < h^L$ sell their endowment Y security and lend by using their X security.

Aggregate value of sales of the Y asset are given by $p^L \cdot 1$. Aggregate expenditure on the Y asset is given by $(1 - h)(1 + p) + R$. The first term is total income (endowment of X plus revenue from the Y asset sales) of buyers with $h < h^L$.

The second term is borrowing at a zero safe interest rate. The marginal buyer is indifferent between borrowing and lending. The optimists will have incentive to borrow because they place higher-probability weight on state U than the marginal buyer, so that they expect a net gain from investing in the risky asset financed by the borrowed money. The pessimists have incentive to lend for the opposite reason. Equating value of sales and expenditures, we get

$$p^L = (1 - h^L)(p^L + 1) + R. \tag{7.6}$$

Equation (7.6), given equation (7.5), determines the identity of the marginal buyer in the leverage economy.

Comparing the two-equation system, which determines p and the identity of the marginal buyer, equations (7.3)–(7.4) and equations (7.5)–(7.6), in the no-leverage and the leverage economies, respectively, one can show the following:

1. In the no-leverage economy, the marginal investor has a higher $h, h \in [0,1]$, than that of the marginal buyer in the leverage economy; that is, $h_1^L < h_1^{NL}$.

2. In the no-leverage economy, the relative price of the risky asset is lower than in the leverage economy; that is, $p^{NL} < p^L$.

In other words, the proportion of *optimists* in the population is larger in the leverage economy than in the no-leverage economy; leading to the *overpricing* of the risky asset in the leverage economy equilibrium.

Now consider how the security market equilibrium changes over time. Suppose markets open in period 1. If a good outcome occurs, the expectations of the optimists have been validated, and they can continue to keep the collateral and enjoy the high consumption in period 1. If, however, a bad outcome happens to occur, optimists surrender the collateral and will not be able to access the market any more. Opening the market after the realization of a bad outcome in period 1 implies then that the identity of the marginal buyer changes and h^L shifts up over time. As a result, p^L shifts down and the leverage bubble bursts. The Fostel-Geanakoplos model captures key effects of shifts in market optimism on leverage bubbles.

7.3 Concluding Remarks

Another stream of the literature (e.g., Samuelson 1958; Tirole 1985; Martin and Ventura 2012) addresses rational asset-pricing bubbles in the framework of the overlapping-generations model. Rational bubbles may crowd out productive capital accumulation by lowering the demand for capital, on one hand, but, on the other hand, they may relax credit constraints by appreciating the collateral value, thereby raising credit and investment in capacity.

Recently, Gali (2013) replaced the infinite-horizon model in the Dynamic Stochastic General Equilibrium (DSGE) framework with an overlapping-generations model to introduce rational asset-pricing bubbles into a macroeconomic framework. Introduction of nominal rigidities (in the form of prices that are set in advance) enables the central bank to influence the real interest rate and the size of the bubble. Monetary policy can strike a balance between stabilization of the bubble and stabilization of aggregate demand. But with rational asset-pricing bubbles, monetary policy cannot affect the conditions of the existence of the bubble.

However, the limitation of the literature on rational asset-pricing bubbles, when applied to data, lies in the requirement that market agent expectations are perfectly coordinated on the bubble. The bubble phenomenon disappears with deviation from this knife-edged assumption. Recall that an important element in the 2008 global crisis was the excessive leverage in the housing market, followed by the collapse of housing prices. In this chapter, we describe a unique mechanism whereby the leverage-based bubbles are driven by excessive optimism. The bubble bursts when the optimists default on their debt and pessimism prevails. This analytical framework is developed in the papers of Geanakoplos and Zame (1997), Geanakoplos (2010), and Fostel and Geanakoplos (2012).

III   Exchange Rates and Capital Flows

Governments try to maintain certain financial and monetary arrangements, most notably a fixed exchange rate regime. Their goal is to stabilize the economy. At times, these arrangements become unstable and collapse leading to financial crises. This strand of the literature analyzes currency crises characterized by a speculative attack on a fixed exchange rate regime.

The best way to understand the origins of currency crises is to think about the basic tri-lemma in international finance. A tri-lemma, as Mankiw (2010) recently wrote in the context of the 2010 euro crisis, is a situation in which someone faces a choice among three options, each of which comes with some inevitable problems. In international finance, the tri-lemma stems from the fact that, in almost every country, economic policy makers would like to achieve the following goals: First, make the country's economy open to international capital flows, because by doing so, policy makers of a country enable foreign investors to diversify their portfolios overseas and achieve risk sharing. The country also benefits from the expertise brought to the country by foreign investors. Second, use monetary policy as a tool to help stabilize inflation, output, and the financial sector in the economy. This is achieved as the central bank can increase the money supply and reduce interest rates when the economy is depressed and reduce money growth and raise interest rates when it is overheated. Moreover, the central bank can serve as a lender of last resort in case of financial panic. Third, maintain stability in the exchange rate. This is because a volatile exchange rate, at times driven by speculation, can be a source of broader financial volatility and makes it harder for households and businesses to trade in the world economy and for investors to plan for the future.

The problem, however, is that a country can only achieve two of these three goals. In order to maintain a fixed exchange rate and capital mobility, the central bank loses its ability to control the interest rate or equivalently the monetary base—its policy instruments—as the interest rate becomes anchored to the world interest rate by the interest rate parity, and the monetary base is automatically adjusted. This is the case of individual members of the European Monetary Union. In order to keep control over the interest rate or equivalently the money supply, the central bank has to let the exchange rate float freely, as in the case of the United States. If the central bank wishes to maintain both exchange rate stability and control over the monetary policy, the only way to do it is by imposing capital controls, as in the case of China.

8 Analytics of Currency Crises

Currency crises[1] occur when a country is trying to maintain a fixed exchange rate regime with capital mobility but faces conflicting policy needs (such as fiscal imbalances or a fragile financial sector) that need to be resolved by independent monetary policy and thus effectively shift the regime from the first goal of the tri-lemma to the second goal.[2]

8.1 First-Generation Models

The gold standard and the 1944 Bretton Woods system (which established the International Monetary Fund [IMF] and the World Bank Group) fixed and adjustable peg exchange rate mechanisms are no longer with us, being replaced in the early 1970s by flexible exchange rates. The branch of models, the so-called first-generation models of currency attacks, was motivated by a series of events where fixed exchange rate regimes collapsed after speculative attacks; for example, the early 1970s breakdown of the Bretton Woods global system. The first-generation models locate the causes of currency crises in unsustainable government policies. Consequently, pegged exchange rates are subject to a fatal attack by investors.

The first paper in the first-generation crisis literature is Krugman (1979).[3] He describes a government attempting to maintain a fixed exchange rate regime, but it is subject to a constant loss of reserves, due to the need to monetize persistent government budget deficits. These two features of the policy are inconsistent with each other and lead to an eventual attack on the international reserves of the central bank, which culminates in the collapse of the fixed exchange rate regime.

Flood and Garber (1984) extended and clarified the basic mechanism, suggested by Krugman (1979), generating the formulation of lack of control by the monetary and fiscal authorities that undermines the fixed exchange rate system that has been widely used since then.

Let us provide a simple description of this model. Recall that the asset side of the central bank's balance sheet at time t is composed of domestic assets, $B_{H,t}$, and the domestic-currency value of foreign assets, $S_t B_{F,t}$, where S_t denotes the exchange rate (i.e., the value of foreign currency in terms of domestic currency). The total assets have to equal the total liabilities of the central bank, which are, by definition, the monetary base, denoted by M_t.

Because of fiscal imbalances, the central bank's domestic assets grow at a fixed and exogenous rate:

$$\frac{B_{H,t} - B_{H,t-1}}{B_{H,t-1}} = \mu.$$

Because of perfect capital mobility, the domestic interest rate is determined through the interest rate parity, as follows:

$$1 + i_t = \left(1 + i_t^*\right)\frac{S_{t+1}}{S_t},$$

where i_t denotes the domestic interest rate at time t, and i_t^* denotes the foreign interest rate at time t. Finally, the supply of money (i.e., the monetary base) has to be equal to the demand for money, which is denoted as $L(i_t)$, a decreasing function of the domestic interest rate.

The inconsistency between a fixed exchange rate regime, $S_t = S_{t+1} = \bar{S}$, with capital mobility and the fiscal imbalances is due to the fact that domestic assets of the central bank keep growing, but total central bank assets cannot change because the monetary base is pinned down by the public-at-large demand for money, $L(i_t^*)$, which is anchored by the foreign interest rate. Hence, the obligation of the central bank to keep financing the fiscal needs puts downward pressure on the domestic interest rate, which in turn puts upward pressure on the exchange rate. To prevent depreciation, the central bank has to intervene by reducing the inventory of foreign reserves. Overall, $\bar{S}B_{F,t}$ decreases by the same amount as $B_{H,t}$ increases, so the monetary base remains the same.

The problem is that this process cannot continue forever, as the reserves of foreign currency must have a lower bound. Eventually, the central bank will have to abandon the solution of the tri-lemma through a fixed exchange rate regime and perfect capital mobility for a solution of the tri-lemma through a flexible exchange rate, with stabilizing mon-

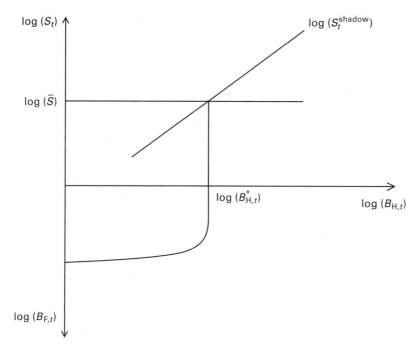

Figure 8.1
Exchange Rate and Foreign Reserves

etary policy (i.e., flexible monetary base or equivalently domestic interest rate) and perfect capital mobility.

The question is as follows: What is the critical level of domestic assets $B_{H,t}$ and the corresponding period of time T at which the fixed exchange rate regime collapses? As pointed out by Flood and Garber (1984), this happens when the shadow exchange rate—defined as the flexible exchange rate under the assumption that the central bank's foreign reserves reached their lower bound while the central bank keeps increasing the domestic assets to accommodate the fiscal needs— is equal to the pegged exchange rate. This is depicted in figure 8.1.

The figure describes the critical value of central bank domestic assets where foreign assets are suddenly depleted and a switch to a fully flexible exchange rate regime occurs.

8.2   Second-Generation Models

After the collapse of the Exchange Rate Mechanism (ERM) in the early 1990s in Europe (which was characterized by the trade-off between recessed activity level, while the exchange rate is stable, and recovering activity, while the exchange rate is volatile), the so-called first-generation model of currency regime switch did not seem relevant. The ERM crisis in Europe then led to the development of the so-called second-generation model of currency attacks, pioneered by Obstfeld (1994, 1996).

A basic idea here is that the government's policy is not described as just being on "automatic pilot," like in Krugman (1979) above, but rather that the government is setting the policy endogenously, trying to maximize a well-specified objective function. But the problem is that the government is not able to commit fully to a given policy ahead of time.

In this group of models, there are usually self-fulfilling multiple equilibria, where an expectation of a collapse of the fixed exchange rate regime by market participants leads the government to choose to abandon the fixed exchange rate regime. This is related to the Diamond and Dybvig (1983) model of bank runs, discussed in chapter 4, creating a link between these two branches of the literature.

Obstfeld (1996) discusses various mechanisms that can create the multiplicity of equilibria in a currency-crisis model. Let us describe one of them, inspired by Barro and Gordon (1983). Suppose that the government minimizes a loss function of the following type:

$$(y - y^*)^2 + \beta \varepsilon^2 + cI_{\varepsilon \neq 0}.$$

Here, y is the level of output, y^* is the target level of output, ε is the rate of depreciation, which in the model is equal to the inflation rate, and $I_{\varepsilon \neq 0}$ is an index function with value 0 if $\varepsilon = 0$ or value 1 otherwise. Hence, the interpretation is that the government maintains a fixed exchange rate regime or abandons the regime altogether.

Deviating from the fixed exchange rate regime has two costs. The first is captured by the index function in the third term in the expression above, which says that there is a fixed cost in case the government depreciates the currency. The second is captured by the second term in the expression above, saying that there are costs to the economy in case of inflation. But, there is also a benefit: The government wishes to reduce deviations from the target output, and increasing the depreciation rate above the expected level serves to boost output, via the Phillips curve. This can be seen in the following expression, specifying how output is determined:

$$y = \bar{y} + \alpha(\varepsilon - \varepsilon^e) - u.$$

Here, $\bar{y}$ is the natural output ($\bar{y} < y^*$; i.e., the government sets an ambitious output target level to overcome distortions in the economy), u is a random shock, and ε^e is the expected level of depreciation/inflation that is set endogenously in the model by wage setters based on rational expectations. The idea is that an unexpected inflationary shock boosts output by reducing real wages and increasing production.

Importantly, the government cannot commit to a fixed exchange rate. Otherwise, it would achieve a minimum value of the loss function by committing to $\varepsilon = 0$. However, in the absence of ability to make such commitment, a sizable shock u will lead the government to depreciate and achieve the increase in output bearing the loss of credibility. Going back to the tri-lemma discussed earlier, a fixed exchange rate regime prevents the government from using monetary policy to boost output, and a large enough shock will cause the government to deviate from the fixed exchange rate regime.

It can be shown that the above model generates a multiplicity of equilibria. The rationale is as follows: If wage setters coordinate on a high level of expected depreciation/inflation, then the government will validate this expectation with its policy by depreciating more often. If wage setters coordinate on a low level of expected depreciation, then the government will have a weaker incentive to deviate from the fixed exchange rate regime. Hence, depreciation becomes a self-fulfilling expectation.

Similarly, one can describe mechanisms where speculators may force the government to abandon an existing fixed exchange rate regime by attacking its reserves and making the maintenance of the regime too costly. If many speculators attack, the government will lose many reserves and will be more likely to abandon the regime. A self-fulfilling speculative attack is profitable only if many speculators join it. Consequently, there is one equilibrium with a speculative attack and a collapse of the regime, and there is another equilibrium where these things do not happen.[4] Similarly, speculators can attack government bonds demanding higher rates due to expected sovereign debt default, creating an incentive for the central bank to abandon a currency regime and reduce the value of the debt. As argued by De Grauwe (2011), the problem can become more severe for countries that participate in a currency union, as their governments do not have the monetary tools to reduce the cost of the debt.

As we discussed in the previous section, having a model of multiple equilibria creates an obstacle for policy analysis. Morris and Shin (1998) were the first to tackle the problem of multiplicity in the second-generation models of speculative attacks. They first expressed this model in an explicit market framework, where speculators are players having to make a decision whether to attack the currency or not. Then, using the global-game methodology, pioneered by Carlsson and van Damme (1993), they were able to derive a unique equilibrium, where the fundamentals of the economy uniquely determine whether a crisis occurs or not. This is important because it enables one to ask questions as to the effect of policy tools on the probability of a currency attack.[5] The global-game methodology, relying on heterogeneous information across speculators, also brought to the forefront the issue of information in currency-attack episodes, leading to analysis of the effect that transparency, signaling, and learning can have on such episodes (e.g., Angeletos, Hellwig, and Pavan 2006).

8.3   Third-Generation Models of Currency Crises

The Asian financial crisis that erupted in 1997 was a money and credit implosion induced by foreign capital flight. It began as a run on Asian banks by foreign short-term depositors and expanded into an assault on government foreign currency reserves, sending shock waves as far as the shores of Russia and of Argentina. Banks were decimated by acute insolvency. They did not have the cash on hand to cover mass withdrawals of short-term deposits because these funds had been lent long, sparking asset fire sales, slashed capitalizations, and credit and money contractions, which in turn triggered widespread business failures, depressions, and mass unemployment. The world economy has witnessed the interplay between currency and banking crises, sometimes referred to as the *twin crises*, and balance of payments crises caused by currency mismatch in the balance sheet of the private sector.[6] Such crises include those in Mexico, Brazil, Argentina, and Chile in 1982, Sweden and Finland in 1991, Mexico again in 1995, Thailand, Malaysia, Indonesia, and Korea in 1997–1998, Argentina again in 2002, and the 2010–2013 episodes in Iceland, Ireland, Greece, Portugal, Spain, Italy, and Cyprus. The foundation for the crisis was laid by a massive inflow of foreign investment into the country. Capital inflows were followed by a sudden rush out and run on the banks. These financial crises exhibited a combination of the collapse of fixed exchange rate regimes, capital flows, financial institutions, and credit (see also chapter 2).[7]

There are many theories of what caused the East Asian crisis. Potential explanations include panic-stricken investors (Radelet and Sachs

1998), corrupt corporate government practices (Krugman 1998b), moral hazard and other policy distortions (Dooley and Shin (2000), and inadequate financial infrastructure (Rajan and Zingales 1998a, 1998b).

While the traditional literature on currency crises focused on the government alone (reviewed in sections 8.1 and 8.2), in section 8.3 we review third-generation models of currency crises, which essentially connect models of banking crises and credit frictions (reviewed in chapters 5 and 6, respectively) with models of currency crises. Such models were motivated by the East Asian crises of the late 1990s, where financial institutions and exchange rate regimes collapsed together, demonstrating the linkages between governments and financial institutions that can expose the system to further fragility. This is again relevant for the current situation in Europe, as banks and governments are intertwined, and the fragility of the system depends to a large extent on the connections between them.

One basic mechanism outlined in third-generation models is where unhedged foreign currency liabilities play the key role in causing and transmitting crises. One of the first models to capture this joint problem was presented in Krugman (1999). In his model, firms suffer from a currency mismatch between their assets and liabilities: their assets are denominated in domestic goods, and their liabilities are denominated in foreign goods. Then, real exchange rate depreciation increases the value of liabilities relative to assets, leading to deterioration in firms' balance sheets. Because of credit frictions as in Holmstrom and Tirole (1997), described in chapter 6, this deterioration in firms' balance sheets implies that they can borrow less and invest less. The novelty in Krugman (1999) is that the decrease in investment validates the depreciation in general equilibrium. This is because the decreased investment by foreigners in the domestic market implies that there will be a decrease in demand for local goods relative to foreign goods (the *transfer problem* in international trade), leading to real depreciation. Hence, the system has multiple equilibria with high economic activity, appreciated exchange rate, and strong balance sheets in one equilibrium, and low economic activity, depreciated exchange rate, and weak balance sheets in the other equilibrium. Other models that extended and continued this line of research include those of Aghion, Bacchetta, and Banerjee (2001), Caballero and Krishnamurthy (2001), and Schneider and Tornell (2004). The model of the latter authors fully endogenizes the currency mismatch between firms' assets and liabilities.

A different line of research links currency problems with the bank runs described in chapter 5. Chang and Velasco (2001) and Goldstein (2005) model the vicious circle between bank runs and speculative attacks on the currency. On the one hand, the expected collapse of the currency worsens banks' prospects, as they have foreign liabilities and domestic assets, and thus generates bank runs. On the other hand, the collapse of the banks leads to capital outflows that deplete the reserves of the government, encouraging speculative attacks against the currency. Accounting for the circular relationship between currency crises and banking crises complicates policy analysis. For example, a lender-of-last-resort policy or other expansionary policy during a banking crisis might backfire as it depletes the reserves available to the government, making a currency crisis more likely, which in turn might further hurt the banking sector that is exposed to a currency mismatch.

8.4   Contagion of Currency Crises

The European Monetary Union (EMU) is a dubious candidate for an optimal currency area (see chapter 3), because although it too trades intensively within the region, national work restrictions greatly impair intra-European labor mobility, and supranational fiscal power is feeble because rich members don't want to assume heavy financing burdens during turbulent times. The obverse also is true. Countries such as Sweden and Norway that shunned the euro are thriving and appear to have benefited by retaining their monetary option. One of the major issues in the ongoing euro-zone crisis is the contagion across the heavy borrowing members of the EMU.

   The forceful transmission of crises across countries generated a large literature on international financial contagion. Kaminsky, Reinhart, and Vegh (2003) provide a nice review of the theories behind such contagion.[8] They define contagion as an immediate reaction in one country to a crisis in another country. There are several theories that link such contagion to fundamental explanations. The clearest one would be that there is common information about the different countries, and so the collapse in one country leads investors to withdraw out of other countries. Calvo and Mendoza (2000) present a model where contagion is a result of learning from the events in one country about the fundamentals in another country. They argue that such learning is likely to occur when there is vast diversification of portfolios, as then the cost of gathering information about each country in the portfolio becomes prohibitively large, encouraging investors to herd.

Another explanation is based on trade links (see, e.g., Gerlach and Smets 1995). If two countries compete in export markets, the devaluation of one country's currency hurts the competitiveness of the other country, leading the other country to devalue its currency as well. A third explanation is the presence of financial links between the countries. As shown by Kodres and Pritsker (2002), investors optimize the allocation of their portfolios. A crisis-caused decrease in the share of their portfolios held in one country leads them to rebalance their portfolios by reducing their holding in another country. This causes co-movement in prices. As shown by Allen and Gale (2000b), different regions insure each other against excessive liquidity shocks, but this implies that a shock in one region is transmitted to the other region via the insurance linkage.

Empirical evidence has followed the above theories of contagion. The common-information explanation has vast support in the data. Several of the clearest examples of contagion involve countries that appear very similar. Examples include the contagion that spread across East Asia in the late 1990s and the one in Latin America in the early 1980s. A vast empirical literature provides evidence that trade links can account for contagion to some extent. These include Eichengreen, Rose, and Wyplosz (1996) and Glick and Rose (1999). Others have shown that financial linkages are also empirically important in explaining contagion. For example, Kaminsky, Lyons, and Schmukler (2004) have shown that U.S.-based mutual funds contribute to contagion by selling shares in one country when prices of shares decrease in another country. Caramazza, Ricci, and Salgado (2004), Kaminsky and Reinhart (2000), and Van Rijckeghem and Weder (2003) all show similar results for common commercial banks.

8.5 Single-Currency-Area Crises

The 2000s saw remarkable worldwide growth in capital flows and banking activity, domestically and across national borders. It was especially strong within Europe, in part due to the increasing (and policy-driven) integration of the euro zone.

Banks and governments face a similar problem, unbalanced maturity of assets and liabilities, thus making both banks and governments vulnerable to movements of distrust. The distrust will lead to liquidity crises and can generate solvency crises. When banks collapse, sovereign debt is in trouble. The need to have a government budget as a shock absorber is based on Keynes' savings paradox: When after a crash the private sector has to reduce debt, it does two things, it tries to save more, and it sells assets. The private sector can only save more if governments borrow more (i.e., higher budget deficit). If government also tries to save more, attempts to save more by the private sector are self-defeating, and the economy is pulled into a deflationary spiral. These stabilizing features are relatively well organized at the national level (e.g., United States, United Kingdom, France, Germany), but not at the international level, nor at the level of a monetary union, such as the euro zone. For a number of European countries, however, the creation of a monetary union undermined the ability of individual member governments credibly to backstop their national banking systems through purely fiscal means.

Within the euro zone, national banking systems are if anything more interdependent than they are outside of the euro zone, yet the key functions of bank regulation and resolution and of fiscal policy remain national even in the absence of national discretion with respect to potential need of last-resort lending. These features magnify private- and public-sector financial fragility within the euro zone.

In this context, Obstfeld (2013) proposes a new policy tri-lemma for currency unions such as the euro zone: A country cannot simultaneously maintain all three of

1. full cross-border financial integration;
2. financial stability;
3. national fiscal independence.

Supposing that countries forgo the options of financial repression and capital controls (goal 1), they cannot credibly stabilize their financial systems (goal 2). If the single-currency area has reached a sufficient degree of financial integration, these countries cannot achieve financial stability without external fiscal support, either directly (from partner country treasuries) or indirectly (through monetary financing from the union-wide central bank); thus sacrificing goal 3. Alternatively, a country that is reliant mainly on its own fiscal resources (goal 3) will likely sacrifice financial integration in order to achieve financial stability, as is true in the euro area today, because markets will then assess financial risks along national lines.

Alternatively, voluntary withdrawal from the single financial market might allow a country with limited fiscal space to control and insulate its financial sector enough to minimize its fragility.

9   Foreign Investment: Information Asymmetry

Economists tend to favor capital mobility across national borders as it allows capital to seek the highest rate of return adjusted for risk. Unrestricted capital flows further offer several advantages.

First, international capital flows allow international risk sharing and indirectly, through a general equilibrium channel, enhance more efficient allocation of capital and labor across the various sectors of the economy. The risk-sharing role of capital flows is highlighted by Helpman and Razin (1978). Their model predicts that international trade in stocks provides a risk-sharing role that allows factor allocations across the various productive sectors of the economy to restore the country's comparative advantage.[1]

Second, international equity and bond flows have a global insurance element. Let a country engage in international trade in equities, A, with rate of return, r^A, and bonds, L, with a rate of return r^L. The net external asset law of motion is

$$NA_{t+1} = (1 + r^A_{t+1})A_t - (1 + r^L_{t+1})L_t + Y_t - C_t,$$

where NA, Y, and C denote net external assets, GDP, and consumption, respectively.

Let r stand for the risk-free rate: the Euler conditions are

$$(1 + r_{t+1})E_t \left[\frac{\beta u'(C_{t+1})}{u'(C_t)} \right] = E_t \left[\frac{\beta u'(C_{t+1})}{u'(C_t)} \right](1 + r^A_{t+1}) = E_t \left[\frac{\beta u'(C_{t+1})}{u'(C_t)} \right](1 + r^L_{t+1}) = 1,$$

where E is expectations operator and u is the utility function of the representative individual.

Multiplying the net external asset rule of motion by the Euler conditions, and taking expected values, yields

$$E_t\left[\frac{\beta u'(C_{t+1})}{u'(C_t)}\text{NA}_{t+1}\right] = A_t - L_t + \frac{Y_t - C_t}{1 + r_t}.$$

This implies that in expectation, the net external asset low of motion becomes

$$E_t(\text{NA}_{t+1}) = (1 + r_t)\text{NA}_t + Y_t - C_t - (1 + r_t)\text{COV}\left[\frac{\beta u'(C_{t+1})}{u'(C_t)}, \text{NA}_{t+1}\right],$$

where COV denotes covariance.

This means that if the net external position co-moves negatively with the stochastic discount factor (which decreases when the marginal utility of consumption is high), the country serves as a global insurer. The country gains by the ability to increase the expected return on its net external asset position above the risk-free rate.

Alternatively, by having a net external position that co-moves positively with the stochastic discount factor (which falls when the marginal utility of consumption is high), the country is able to lower the expected return on its net external asset position above the risk-free rate. In this case, the country benefits from having been effectively insured by the rest of the world.[2]

These benefits from the global capital market integration, however, are based on a frictionless framework. With information and credit frictions, global capital integration need not always be beneficial. As Rey (2013) observes, "periods of low risk are associated with a build-up of a global financial cycle: more capital inflows and outflows, more credit creation, more leverage and higher asset price inflation." The credit bubble is often a prelude to global crises, as the world witnessed in 2008.

This chapter and subsequent chapters deal with how international capital markets perform under contract and information frictions.

9.1   International Debt Contracts Under Limited Enforcement

Domestic and foreign investors may differ in their information sets regarding future domestic and foreign stock returns with no information frictions. This may lead to home bias in the domestic country portfolio, which has important implications for the efficiency of domestic saving and investment.

Debt flows remain the dominant form of flows to developing economies, although their relative importance has declined over time.[3] The empirical literature on financial globalization documents a systematic empirical link between exposure to debt flows and the likelihood and severity of financial crises. Rodrik and Velasco (1999) find that countries with a larger short-term debt stock than reserves are more likely to experience a financial flows reversal. Tong and Wei (2011) find that a large pre-crisis exposure to non–foreign direct investment (non-FDI) capital inflows tends to be associated with a more severe credit crunch during the crisis. However, debt flows can be beneficial in certain circumstances. A country that has no access to equity or foreign direct investment (FDI) inflows might still be able to benefit from debt inflows to finance illiquid investments (Diamond and Rajan 2001).[4]

Tong and Wei (2011) argue that sudden reversals of capital flows are more likely to occur among countries that rely relatively more on portfolio debt flows, including bank loans, and less on FDI. Moreover, short-term bank loans to developing countries tend to increase during booms and rapidly decrease during economic slowdowns. Claessens, Dooley, and Warner (1995) find that long-term debt flows are often as volatile as short-term flows. The pro-cyclicality and high volatility of debt flows can lead to inefficient capital allocation and generate moral hazard. McKinnon and Pill (1996) show that financial liberalization without adequate supervision can result in overborrowing by banks. Furthermore, banks may expose their balance sheets to currency risk if the taking of speculative open positions in foreign exchange is permitted.

With access to complete international credit markets, an economy would be able to borrow to finance a stable level of consumption and investment. However, in reality, countries often experience capital outflows in very-low-income periods. Eaton and Gersovitz (1981) pioneered the stream of the literature dealing with incomplete international credit markets and the risk of debt repudiation. International lenders cannot fully seize collateral from another country when it refuses to honor its debt obligations. Intertemporal sanctions arise because of a threat of cutoff from future borrowing if a country defaults. As shown by Eaton and Gersovitz (1981), the level of debt is the minimum of the economy's credit demands and the constraints on credit imposed by the lenders. Borrowing occurs in periods of relatively low income and must be fully repaid in the following period. Failure to repay prevents borrowing in a subsequent period. Bulow and Rogoff (1989) demonstrate that international lending must be supported by the direct sanctions available to creditors and cannot be supported by a country's "reputation for repayment." Aguiar and Gopinath (2006) demonstrate how countries default in bad times to smooth consumption. Building on the intertemporal approach, Atkeson (1991) studies explicitly models of moral hazard and the enforcement problem. The introduction of moral hazard due to asymmetric information between the borrower and the lender explains why the occurrence of especially low output realizations prompts international lenders to enforce repayment of the debt by the borrower. Tsyrenikov (2007) shows that capital outflows in the lowest-output state are quantitatively significant when limited enforcement becomes a problem, as is typical in the case of international debt contracts.

The literature so far is unable fully to account why sovereign default does occur and why international lenders extend credit to bad borrowers as much as they do.

The theoretical literature on international debt often makes strong assumptions about creditor behavior. Bulow and Rogoff (1989) invoke the premise that countries that default do not suffer from a substantially higher cost of borrowing after the debt crisis. They regain access to the international credit markets soon after they default on their debt. A new study by Cruces and Trebesch (2013), which extends the work of Sturzenegger and Zettelmeyer (2006), finds that default episodes with large "haircuts" to creditors are associated with (1) high future sovereign spreads and (2) long periods of market exclusion.

9.2   Foreign Direct Investment: Benchmark Case

Consider a small, capital-importing country, referred to as a home country. There are N, ex ante identical, risk-neutral domestic firms. There are two time periods. Each firm chooses capital input K in the first period. In the second period, the output is equal to $F(K)(1 + \varepsilon)$, where $F(K)$ is a standard production function exhibiting diminishing marginal productivity of capital, and ε is a random productivity factor. The productivity factor ε is independent across firms; it has zero mean and is bounded below by -1. The cumulative distribution function of the productivity shock ε is $\Phi(\cdot)$. The domestic interest rate is denoted by r and the foreign interest rate by r^*.

A representative foreign direct investor buys a domestic firm before the investment decision is made. The foreign direct investors and domestic direct investors are equally informed.[5] Let the capital stock K^* be imported from the foreign country and the corresponding output level be $F(K^*)(1 + \varepsilon)$. The number of firms bought by foreign investors is denoted by J. The market value of the firm that is sold to the foreign direct investor is then given by

$$V^* = \frac{F(K^*)}{1+r^*} - K^*.$$

The aggregate quantity of inward foreign direct investment is

$$\text{FDI} = J(K^* + V^*).$$

In equilibrium (with positive number of firms owned by both domestic and foreign investors), we must have

$$V^* = V,$$

where

$$V = \frac{F(K)}{1+r} - K.$$

The optimal level of capital investment K^* and K should satisfy

$$F'(K^*) = 1 + r^*$$

$$F'(K) = 1 + r.$$

When FDI investors have access to the domestic debt market, then

$$r = r^*.$$

We get

$$F'(K^*) = 1 + r^* = F'(K) = 1 + r.$$

These equalities mean that allocation of capital in the global capital markets is efficient. Unlike the cases of foreign portfolio investment and foreign debt investment, the asymmetric information problems are alleviated due to the actual exercise of management and control in the case of FDI.

9.3   Debt-Financed Foreign Investment

Let the domestic investors be informed and the foreign investors uninformed.

Consider again a continuum of domestic firms, indexed by ε. The mean value of the productivity level is

$$E(\varepsilon) = \int_{-1}^{\bar{\varepsilon}} \varepsilon F(\varepsilon) = 0,$$

where $F(\varepsilon)$ is the density function of ε.

Each ε-firm can invest I in either a "good" project, yielding

$R(1 + \varepsilon)$, with probability p^H, or 0, with probability $1 - p^H$,

or in a "bad" project, yielding

$R(1 + \varepsilon)$, with probability p^L, or 0, with probability $1 - p^L$,

and extra *private* benefit B, as in Holmstrom and Tirole (1997); see chapter 6.[6]

To induce the ε-firms to invest only in the good project, the domestic bank requires minimum equity of $\underline{A}(\varepsilon)$ (recall that loans are granted after the realization of ε). The cutoff equity $\overline{A}(\varepsilon)$ is

$$\overline{A}(\varepsilon) = I - \frac{p^H}{1+R}\left[R(1+\varepsilon) - \frac{B}{\Delta p}\right], \tag{9.1}$$

where $\Delta p = p^H - p^L$ measures the riskiness of investment,[7] I is a discrete investment, and R is the rate of return required by domestic investors.

Firms are owned by domestic residents, who are informed about ε. Let $V(\varepsilon)$ be the market value of the ε-firm to its original (domestic) owner:

$$V(\varepsilon) = \frac{p^H}{1+R}\left\{R(1+\varepsilon) - \left[I - \overline{A}(\varepsilon)\right]\right\} - \overline{A}(\varepsilon).$$

Uninformed foreign investors (who do not observe ε) buy the low-end of the ε distribution. This low-end is below a cutoff ε (denoted ε_0), which is defined by

$$V(\varepsilon_0) = \frac{p^H R(1+\varepsilon) - p^H\left[I - \dfrac{\int_{-1}^{\varepsilon_0}\overline{A}(\varepsilon)F'(\varepsilon)d\varepsilon}{F(\varepsilon_0)}\right]}{1+R*} - \frac{\int_{-1}^{\varepsilon_0}\overline{A}(\varepsilon)F'(\varepsilon)d\varepsilon}{F(\varepsilon_0)}, \tag{9.2}$$

where $R*$ is the rate of return required by foreign investors ($R > R*$).

Equation (9.2) implies that if the private benefit B increases, then the threshold $\overline{A}(\varepsilon)$ also increases,

$$\frac{d\varepsilon_0}{dB} < 0.$$

From equations (9.1)–(9.2), ε_0 falls if B goes up.

This implies that when the private benefit rises, foreign investment falls. Equation (9.2) implies that if the difference between the probability of the investment project's success and its probability of failure increases, then the threshold ε_0 falls:

$$\frac{d\varepsilon_0}{d\Delta p} < 0.$$

This implies that inward foreign investment declines as riskiness in the host country rises (i.e., the difference between the investment project's probabilities of success and failure widens).

The model can be extended, as in section 6.1, to include financial intermediaries that have access to a monitory technology. A negative aggregate shock in the host economy will tighten the foreign investors' financial constraints. Thus, they will be less likely to raise external financing and invest abroad. Hence, there is an accelerator effect, whereby shocks to the host economy are amplified and reverse the inflow of foreign investment.

Appendix: Pecking Order of Foreign Investment

This appendix[8] evaluates the efficiency of equilibrium, under asymmetric information between foreign and domestic investors, for two types of international investment: foreign portfolio investment (FPI), foreign debt investment (DEBT), and foreign direct investment (FDI).

As in section 9.2, consider a small, capital-importing country, referred to as a home country. There are N, ex ante identical, risk-neutral domestic firms. There are two time periods. Each firm chooses capital input K in the first period. In the second period, the output is equal to $F(K)$ $(1 + \varepsilon)$, where $F(K)$ is a standard production function exhibiting diminishing marginal productivity of capital, and ε is a random productivity factor. The productivity factor ε is independent across firms; it has zero mean and is bounded below by -1. The cumulative distribution function of the productivity shock ε is $\Phi(\cdot)$. The domestic interest rate is denoted by r and the foreign interest rate by r^*.

9.A1   Foreign Debt Investment
Investment decisions through debt finance are made by firms before ε is observed. Given its investment decision (K) at a stage where uncertainty is unresolved, a firm may choose to default on its debt if

$F(K)(1 + \varepsilon)$ is smaller than $K(1 + r)$. Therefore, firms with productivity $\varepsilon > \varepsilon_0$ will fully repay their nonrecourse loans, where ε_0 is a threshold level of ε, such that $F(K)(1 + \varepsilon_0) = K(1 + r)$. So, the fraction of solvent firms is $N[1 - \Phi(\varepsilon_0)]$.

Assume that domestic firms are better informed than the foreign lenders. They are able to observe productivity ε before making their loan decisions. Thus, domestic lenders will extend loans only to firms with productivity $\varepsilon > \varepsilon_0$. In contrast, foreign lenders will advance loans to all firms because they do not observe ε at this stage. Denote the fraction of solvent firms financed by foreign lenders by β. Therefore, the expected payoff of foreign lenders is given by

$$\text{Payoff} = \beta N[1 - \Phi(\varepsilon_0)]K(1 + r) + N\Phi(\varepsilon_0)F(K)(1 + e^-),$$

where

$$e^- = E(\varepsilon / \varepsilon \leq \varepsilon_0).$$

The amount of loans given by foreign lenders is given by

$$\text{Loan} = \{\beta N[1 - \Phi(\varepsilon_0)] + N\Phi(\varepsilon_0)\}K.$$

The expected value of the representative firm is

$$V = F(K) - \{[1 - \Phi(\varepsilon_0)]K(1 + r) + \Phi(\varepsilon_0)F(K)(1 + e^-)\}. \tag{9.A1}$$

Accordingly, the value maximizing level of K is such that

$$F'(K) = [1 - \Phi(\varepsilon_0)]K(1 + r) / [1 - \Phi(\varepsilon_0)(1 + e^-)], \tag{9.A2}$$

implying that

$$F'(K) < 1 + r, \tag{9.A3}$$

due to the possibility of default. The above inequality epitomizes an oversaving inefficiency: Equilibrium saving (which is equal to the stock of capital) is larger than what domestic savers are willing to pay for in terms of forgone current consumption.

The expected payoff of the foreign lender should be equal to the capital income on loans, which implies that $r^* < r$, and

$$F'(K) > 1 + r^*. \tag{9.A4}$$

This indicates aggregate production inefficiency, so that the economy can marginally gain from an additional debt-financed increase in the stock of domestic capital.

9.A2   Foreign Portfolio Investment

As before, all firms choose investment level K in the first period before the random productivity factor ε is observed. All firms are originally owned by domestic investors, who equity finance their capital investment. Foreign investors do not observe the productivity ε when they purchase shares in existing firms. Therefore, they offer to buy at the same price all firms with low and high productivity. The price therefore reflects the average productivity of the firms that foreigners invest in. As a result, there is a threshold level of productivity ε_0 such that initial owners of firms whose productivity is above ε_0 will not be willing to sell at that price.

The value of the representative firm is equal to $F(K)(1 + \varepsilon)$. Thus, the threshold productivity ε_0 is defined by

$$F(K)(1 + e^-) / (1 + r^*) = F(K)(1 + \varepsilon_0) / (1 + r). \tag{9.A5}$$

If foreigners have positive holdings in domestic firms, then it is necessary that $r^* < r$.

Then, the amount of foreign portfolio investment is given by

$$\text{FPI} = N\Phi(\varepsilon_0)F(K)(1 + e^-) / (1 + r^*). \tag{9.A6}$$

The firm's expected market value net of the original capital investment is

$$V = \Phi(\varepsilon_0)F(K)(1 + e^-) / (1 + r^*) + [1 - \Phi(\varepsilon_0)][F(K)(1 + e^+)] / (1 + r) - K. \tag{9.A7}$$

Maximizing this expression with respect to K yields the following first-order condition:

$$\Phi(\varepsilon_0)F'(K)(1 + e^-) / (1 + r^*) + [1 - \Phi(\varepsilon_0)][F'(K)(1 + e^+)] / (1 + r) - 1 = 0. \tag{9.A8}$$

Because the firm knows, when making its capital investment decision, that it will be sold at a premium if faced with low-productivity events, it tends to overinvest relative to the rate of return to domestic investors and underinvest relative to the rate of return to foreign investors,

$$(1 + r^*) < F'(K) < (1 + r). \tag{9.A9}$$

As in the case with debt flows, the information asymmetry between domestic and foreign investors creates inefficiencies such as oversaving by domestic investors and underinvestment by foreigners that reduce the gains from international capital flows.

10   Foreign Investment: Liquidity Shocks

Emerging economies typically have countercyclical current accounts and experience large capital outflows during crises. The theoretical literature argues that financial crises lead to an exit of foreign investors even if there are no shocks to fundamentals. The following papers link financial crises and liquidity through models of self-fulfilling investor runs: Chang and Velasco (2001) place international illiquidity at the center of financial crises. They argue that a small shock may result in financial distress, leading to costly asset liquidation, a liquidity crunch, and a large drop in asset prices. Caballero and Krishnamurthy (2001) argue that during a crisis, self-fulfilling fears of insufficient collateral may trigger a capital outflow.

However, financial crises may be associated with an outflow of foreign portfolio investment (FPI) and a simultaneous inflow of foreign direct investment (FDI). This behavior reflects the *fire-sale FDI* phenomenon where domestic companies and assets are acquired by foreign investors at fire-sale prices. Krugman (2000) notes that the Asian financial crisis was accompanied by a wave of inward direct investment. Furthermore, Aguiar and Gopinath (2005) analyze data on mergers and acquisitions in East Asia between 1996 and 1998 and find that the liquidity crisis is associated with an inflow of FDI. Moreover, Acharya, Shin, and Yorulmazer (2011) observe that FDI inflows during financial crises are associated with acquisitions of controlling stakes. Baker, Foley, and Wurgler (2004) argue that FDI inflows may also reflect arbitrage activity by multinationals as well as the purchase of undervalued host country assets. The term *sudden stop* was coined by Calvo (1998) in consideration of episodes of balance-of-payment crises of developing countries.

10.1   Efficiency-Liquidity Trade-offs

This section presents a model developed by Goldstein and Razin (2006) of international capital flow reversals driven by a liquidity shortage.

Consider a small economy faced by a continuum [0, 1] of foreign investors. Each foreign investor has an opportunity to invest in one investment project. Foreign investment can occur in one of two forms: either as a direct investment or as a portfolio investment. A direct investor effectively acts like a manager, whereas in the case of a portfolio investment, the project is managed by an outsider.

There are three periods of time: 0, 1, and 2. In period 0, each investor decides whether to make a direct investment or a portfolio investment. In period 2, the project matures. The net cash flow from the project is given by

$$R(K,\varepsilon) = (1+\varepsilon)K - \left(\frac{1}{2}\right)AK^2, \tag{10.1}$$

where ε is an idiosyncratic random productivity factor, which is independently realized for each project in period 1, and K is the level of capital input invested in the project in period 1, after the realization of ε. The parameter A reflects production costs, and R is the payoff for the project. The productivity shock ε is distributed between -1 and 1 with mean 0 with the cumulative distribution function, $\Phi(\cdot)$, and the density function is $f(\cdot) = \Phi'(\cdot)$. Investors choose the form of investment that maximizes (ex ante) expected payoff.

In period 1, after the realization of the productivity shock, the manager of the project observes ε. Thus, if the investor owns the project as a direct investment, she observes ε, and chooses K, so as to maximize the net cash flow: $K^d(\varepsilon) = (1+\varepsilon)/A$.

Therefore, the ex ante expected net cash flow from a direct investment, if held until maturity, is

$$EV_d = \frac{E[(1+\varepsilon)^2]}{2A}, \tag{10.2}$$

where E is the expectation operator and V is the present value of a mature project. In the case of a portfolio investment, the owner has an arm's-length relationship with the manager, and thus she cannot observe ε. In this case, the owner maximizes the expected return absent any information on the realization of ε; and decisions are based on the ex ante zero mean. Thus, the manager will be instructed to choose $K^P = K^d(0) = (1/A)$. Then, the ex ante expected payoff from a portfolio investment, if held until maturity, is

$$EV_p = 1/(2A). \tag{10.3}$$

Comparing (10.2) with (10.3), we see that if the project is held until maturity, it yields a higher payoff as a direct investment than as a portfolio investment. This reflects the efficiency that results from a hands-on management style in the case of a direct investment.

There are also costs for FDI investment, however. First, an FDI investor has to incur a fixed cost in order to acquire the expertise to manage the project directly. We denote this cost, which is exogenously given in the model, by C. Second, there is an endogenous cost arising from the possibility of liquidity shocks occurring in period 1. There is a discount when selling a project managed as direct investment due to information asymmetries, as demonstrated below.

In period 1, before the value of ε is observed, the owner of the project might get a liquidity shock. With the realization of a liquidity shock, the investor is forced to sell the project in period 1. This feature of the model is similar to the preference-shock assumption made by Diamond and Dybvig: An investor who is subject to a liquidity shock derives her utility only from period 1 consumption. If, however, she is not subject to a liquidity shock, she derives her utility from period 2 consumption. We denote by λ the probability of a liquidity shock. We assume that there are two types of foreign investors. In particular, half of the investors will need to sell with probability λ_H and half with probability λ_L such that $1 > \lambda_H > (1/2) > \lambda_L > 0$, and $\lambda_H + \lambda_L = 1$.

Investors know ex ante whether they are of a λ_H type or a λ_L type, and this is their private information. In addition to liquidity-based sales, there is a possibility that an investor will liquidate a project in period 1 if she observes a low realization of ε. Then the price that buyers are willing to pay for a direct investment that is being sold in period 1 is

$$P_D = \frac{1}{2A} \frac{(1-\lambda_D)\int_{-1}^{\varepsilon_D}(1+\varepsilon)^2 f(\varepsilon)d\varepsilon + \lambda_D}{(1-\lambda_D)\Phi(\varepsilon_D)+\lambda_D}. \tag{10.4}$$

Here, ε_D is a threshold level of ε, set by the direct investor; below which the direct investor is selling the project without being forced to do so by a liquidity shock; λ_D is the probability, as perceived by the market, that an FDI investor gets a liquidity shock. In equation (10.4), it is assumed that if the project is sold because of a liquidity shock, that is, before the initial owner observes ε, the value of ε is not recorded by the firms before the sale. Therefore, the buyer does not know the value of ε. However, if the project is sold for low-profitability reasons, the new owner will know the value of ε after the sale. The threshold $\underline{\varepsilon}_D$ is determined in equilibrium. The initial owner sets the threshold level $\underline{\varepsilon}_D$, such that given the price P_D, when observing $\underline{\varepsilon}_D$, an investor is indifferent between selling and not selling the project in absence of a liquidity shock. Thus,

$$P_D = \frac{(1+\underline{\varepsilon}_D)^2}{2A}.$$
(10.5)

Equations (10.4) and (10.5) together determine P_D and $\underline{\varepsilon}_D$ as functions of the *market-perceived* probability of sale due to the liquidity shock (λ_D). We denote these functions as $\underline{\varepsilon}_D(\lambda_D)$ and $P_D(\lambda_D)$.

When a portfolio investor sells the projects in period 1, everybody knows she does it because of a liquidity shock. Thus, the price of the project is given by

$$P_P = \frac{1}{2A}.$$
(10.6)

Comparing the price of FDI, which is determined by equations (10.4) and (10.5), with the price of FPI, which is determined by equation (10.6), we see that the resale price of a direct investment in period 1 is always lower than the resale price of a portfolio investment in that period. The intuition is that if a direct investor prematurely sells the investment project, the market price must reflect the possibility that the sale originates from inside information on low prospects of this investment project. This constitutes the second (liquidity) cost of FDI.

Based on our analysis, we can write the ex ante expected net cash flow from FDI:

$$EV_D(\lambda_i,\lambda_D,A,C)$$

$$= \left\{ (1-\lambda_i)\left([1+\underline{\varepsilon}_D(\lambda_D)]^2\,\Phi[\underline{\varepsilon}_D(\lambda_D)] + \int_{\underline{\varepsilon}_D(\lambda_D)}^{1} \frac{(1+\varepsilon)^2}{2A}f(\varepsilon)d\varepsilon \right) + \lambda_i\frac{[1+\underline{\varepsilon}_D(\lambda_D)]^2}{2A} \right\} - C.$$
(10.7)

The ex ante expected net cash flow from FPI is simply

$$EV_p(A) = \frac{1}{2}A .$$ (10.8)

Then, the difference between the expected value of FDI and the expected value of FPI is

$$\text{Diff}(\lambda_i, \lambda_D, A, C) \equiv EV_D(\lambda_i, \lambda_D, A, C) - EV_p(A).$$ (10.9)

Clearly, investors will choose FDI (FPI) when $\text{Diff}(\lambda_i, \lambda_D, A, C) > 0$ (< 0) and will be indifferent between the two (i.e., may choose either FDI or FPI) when $\text{Diff}(\lambda_i, \lambda_D, A, C) = 0$.

To complete the description of the equilibrium, it remains to be specified how λ_D, the market-perceived probability that an FDI investor will get a liquidity shock, is determined. Assuming that rational expectations hold in equilibrium, λ_D has to be consistent with the equilibrium choice of the two types of investors between FDI and FPI, such that

$$\lambda_D = (\lambda_H \lambda_{H,FDI} + \lambda_L \lambda_{L,FDI}) / (\lambda_{H,FDI} + \lambda_{L,FDI}),$$ (10.10)

where $\lambda_{H,FDI}$ is the proportion of λ_H investors (H investors) who choose FDI in equilibrium, and $\lambda_{L,FDI}$ is the proportion of λ_L investors (L investors) who choose FDI in equilibrium.

Five possible cases can potentially be observed in equilibrium. Case 1: All investors choose FDI. Case 2: L investors choose FDI; H investors split between FDI and FPI. Case 3: L investors choose FDI; H investors choose FPI. Case 4: λ_L investors split between FDI and FPI; H investors choose FPI. Case 5: All investors choose FPI. Equilibrium outcomes depend on production cost A and liquidity preferences (λ_L, λ_H).

As the production cost A increases, we are more likely to observe FPI and less likely to observe FDI in equilibrium. As the difference in liquidity needs of the two types of investors widens, we are more likely to see a separating equilibrium, where different types of investors choose different forms of investment.

10.2   Welfare Implications

We start with the *source* country investors where the liquidity shocks take place. We note that under case 3, H investors choose FPI and gain an expected payoff of $1/2A$. Similarly, under case 2, these investors are indifferent between FDI and FPI, and thus also gain an expected payoff of $1/2A$. Under case 1, however, they choose FDI and gain an expected payoff greater than $1/2A$. By the revealed preferences argument, the H investors chose the FDI type of foreign investment rather than FPI, from which they get $1/2A$. Evidently, the H investors are better off under case 1 because they benefit from the higher efficiency of FDI than that of FPI. Other equilibria occur because of a *coordination failure*: H investors choose not to invest in FDI because they believe H will not invest in FDI, and thus will reduce the expected payoff from this type of investment.

As for L investors, in all three equilibria they choose FDI. We know that the L investors are better off in case 1. The reason is that under case 1, all the H investors choose direct investments, and thus the price of direct investments in period 1 is higher.

Now turn to the residents of the *host* country. In it there is a continuum [0, 1] of local residents; each one holds an investment project in period 0. At this time, they sell the projects to the foreign investors. The welfare analysis from the point of view of the local residents boils down to analyzing the price that they get for their projects in period 0. Recall that there are two types of foreign investors buying the investment projects from the residents of the host country: H investors and L investors. Competition among initial owners of the project, where the type of each foreign investor is not observable, implies that the price of projects in period 0 will be determined by the lowest between the H investor demand price and the L investor demand price. But the demand price of the L investors is always lower than that of the foreign investors. Thus, L investors capture some of the rent due to their ability to maintain the project for a long time, whereas H investors do not capture any rent. The price that local residents get for the projects in period 0 will then be $1/2A$ when either case 2 or case 3 is the realized equilibrium, and expected payoff from FDI investment is larger than $1/2A$ when case 1 is the realized equilibrium. When all three equilibria are likely, the domestic residents get higher prices when case 1 is the realized equilibrium. This suggests that the host country initial owners of the projects benefit from encouraging more foreign investments that are in the form of FDI.

10.3 Aggregate Liquidity Shocks

In section 10.2, we considered only idiosyncratic shocks. In this section, we formalize the occurrence of aggregate shocks, which trigger the idiosyncratic shocks. Suppose that an aggregate liquidity shock occurs in period 1 with probability q. Conditional on the realization of the aggregate liquidity shock, individual investors must sell their investments in period 1, with probabilities λ_L and λ_H.

This implies that as the probability of an aggregate liquidity shock q increases, there will be more FPI and less FDI in equilibrium. Thus, the ratio of FPI to FDI will increase. The intuition is that as the probability of an aggregate liquidity shock increases, agents know that they are more likely to sell the investment early, in which case they will get a low price because buyers do not know whether they sell because of an individual liquidity need or because of adverse information on the productivity of the investment. As a result, the attractiveness of FDI decreases.[1]

10.4   Concluding Remarks

The key mechanisms through which information frictions affect the composition and the volatility of international capital flows are market based. FDI investors get more efficient outcomes than FPI investors because the former have more direct control over management. Thus, they are able to make a better-informed decision of how to run the business. However, the better information mires FDI investors with the "lemons" problem: If the investors' liquidity dries up, forcing the investors to sell off foreign subsidiaries, market participants would not know whether the subsidiary is liquidated because of the investors' liquidity problems or because of bad inside information about the profitability of the subsidiary. Consequently, the market will place a discount on assets sold by an FDI investor, who has the inside information, unlike the FPI investor. Thus, the liquidated stock of an FDI investor is sold at a discount. High-liquidity-risk investors opt for FPI investment, whereas low-liquidity-risk investors opt for FDI investment. Market participants form expectations about the liquidity risk composition of FDI investors. The larger the share of high-liquidity-risk investors who select to be FDI investors, the higher will be the market-conceived probability of the liquidity shock that will force liquidation of FDI-owned subsidiaries. That is, such informational externality generates multiple equilibria in the world equilibrium allocation of capital. In this case, the volatility of foreign investment flows does not depend on the fragility of the economic fundamentals in the source and the host economies. It arises because of the information externality.

IV   The Emerging Macroeconomic Paradigm

Part IV of this book addresses key developments of the New Keynesian macroeconomic paradigm that took place after the 2008 crisis (see chapter 3). Pre-crisis models with frictionless credit were used to provide an analytical framework for the monetary and fiscal policies of the period known as the Great Moderation. More recent models provide an analytical framework for policy discussions in de-leveraging situations after the bust of a long-developing credit boom and where the interest rate is down to its lower bound. These are important features of the Great Recession, which followed the global financial crisis in 2008. Bank runs, which triggered the Great Recession, are now incorporated into dynamic, stochastic, general equilibrium macroeconomic models. The financial intermediaries occupy center stage, featuring financial-accelerator effects and bank runs, as in chapters 5 and 6. As shown by Diamond and Dybvig (1983), a bank run is possible if individual depositors have an incentive to withdraw deposits early because they believe that other households will also roll over their deposits. Bank runs can also be triggered by shocks to the real economy that give rise to severe deteriorations of macroeconomic conditions. Bank asset value falls short of liabilities, thus causing the economy-wide runs. Bank failures feed back into the macroeconomy because they undermine the transfer from household savings to efficient investment through financial intermediaries, causing a sharp decline in output.

11   The Benchmark Paradigm

When the possibility of market arbitrage exists, the interest rate on long-term nominal bonds depends on the expected future path of short-term interest rates.[1] Short-term interest rates, set by the central bank, determine the expected future path of inflation rates. Therefore, the central bank controls the expected path of the real interest rates; hence, it helps determine savings and investment. This mechanism is formally captured in dynamic, stochastic, general equilibrium (DSGE) models in the literature. These models were useful in understanding monetary policy during the Great Moderation era, which preceded the 2008 crisis. To set the stage for the analysis of the emerging new paradigm of macroeconomics in which financial frictions occupy the center stage, this chapter describes the pre-2008 crisis workhorse model of macroeconomists.

The benchmark model comprises three globalization features:

1. International labor mobility: both inward and outward movements of labor. The presumption is that labor flows tend to mitigate wage demands because they introduce a substitution between domestic and foreign labor.
2. International trade in goods. The presumption is that trade leads to specialization in domestic production and diversification in domestic consumption. Therefore, trade tends to weaken the link between domestic production and domestic consumption. As a result, the effect of the fluctuations of domestic production on inflation is also weakened by the presence of international trade in goods.
3. Financial integration with the rest of the world. International trade in financial assets allows households to smooth their consumption over time and over states of nature. Such consumption smoothing also mitigates the fluctuations in the representative household labor

supply. Smoothed fluctuations weaken the link between domestic output fluctuations and those associated with inflation.

The Great Moderation from 1985 to 2007 is the period where the Federal Reserve, central banks, and institutions of the European Union provided a broadly stable macroeconomic environment in which the private sector could make its economic decisions. In those 22 years, the rate of inflation rose above 5 percent for only 3 years and fell below 2 percent for only 2 years. GDP growth was relatively stable. A wave of globalization across emerging economies and developed economies took place.

Bean (2006) wrote about the Phillips curve in the era of globalization:

One of the most notable developments of the past decade or so has been the apparent flattening of the short-run trade-off between inflation and activity. The seventies were characterized by an almost vertical relationship in the United Kingdom, in which attempt to hold unemployment below its natural rate resulted in rising inflation. In the eighties, the downward sloping relationship reappears, as inflation was squeezed out of the system by the slack of the economy. However, since the early nineties, the relationship looks to have been rather flat. Three factors—increased specialization; the intensification of product market competition; and the impact of that intensified competition and migration on the behavior of wages—should all work to flatten the short-run trade-off between inflation and domestic activity.[2]

The reason why the New Keynesian framework is capable of generating a trade-off between inflation and economic activity is that producer-desired prices rise with the economy's output, when marginal costs slope upward due to diminishing returns to scale. Furthermore, because labor supply increases, workers experience increasing marginal disutility of labor. As a result, real-wage demands could rise. Increased wage demands put an upward pressure on the marginal cost, and consequently on the producer-desired prices. Thus, our analytical challenge is to find how trade in goods, financial openness, and migration affect economic output utilization and wage demands.

A massive globalization process has swept emerging markets in Latin America, the European transition economies, and the East Asian emerging economies in the past two decades. The 1992 single-market reform in Europe and the formation of the euro zone are remarkable episodes of globalization. Similarly, emerging markets, including China and India, became significantly more open.

Wynne and Kersting (2007) note that in the 1970s, more than three quarters of industrial countries had restrictions of some sort on international financial transactions. By the 2000s, none did. Likewise, restrictions on these transactions among emerging markets fell from 78 percent in the 1970s to 58 percent in the 2000s.

An important aspect of openness relates to labor flows. International migrants constituted 2.9 percent of the world population in the 2000s, up from 2.1 percent in 1975. In some countries, changes have been more dramatic. In Israel in the 1990s, there was a surge of immigrants of up to 17 percent of the population, and the central bank accomplished a sizable decline of inflation. It is possible that the two episodes are related.[3] In Spain in 1995, the percentages of foreigners in the population and in the labor force were, respectively, below 1 percent and below 0.5 percent. At the end of 2006, these rates were around 9 percent and 14 percent, respectively. The impact of the Spanish immigration boom on the Phillips curve has recently been addressed by Bentolila, Dolaldo, and Jimeno (2007).

During the Great Moderation, inflation around the world reduced substantially. The average annual inflation rate among developing countries was 41 percent in the early 1980s and came down to 13 percent toward the end of the 1990s. Global inflation in the 1990s dropped from 30 percent a year to about 4 percent a year.

Indeed, Rogoff (2003, 2004) observes that favorable factors have been helping to drive down global inflation in the past two decades. A hypothesis, which he put forth, is that "globalization—interacting with deregulation and privatization—has played a strong supporting role in the past decade's disinflation."[4]

Evidence of the effect of globalization on the Phillips curve includes the work of Loungani, Razin, and Yuen (2001), Razin and Loungani (2007), and Clarida (2008).[5] Previously, Romer (1993, 1998) and Lane (1997) showed that inflation and trade liberalization are negatively and significantly correlated in large (flexible exchange rate) OECD (Organisation for Economic Co-operation and Development) economies.

11.1 Analytical Framework

The analytical framework draws on the recent New Keynesian macroeconomics literature (see Woodford 2003). Following are the main features of the open-economy New Keynesian model:

The domestic economy produces a continuum of differentiated goods. Decisions of the representative household are governed by

Dixit-Stiglitz preferences (generating a fixed substitution elasticity). Purchasing power parity conditions prevail for the flexible price goods, and foreign firms' prices are taken as exogenous.

There is international trade in goods and financial assets and free international labor mobility. The representative-household utility is defined over consumption and leisure, as in the standard micro-based welfare analysis.

Labor supply is divided between domestic and foreign destinations. Exported labor receive a wage premium over unskilled foreign labor. Imported labor is unskilled, and native-born labor commands an endogenously determined skill premium.

Price updates are staggered (see Calvo 1983). Namely, producers update prices upon receiving a signal drawn from a stochastic distribution.

World prices are exogenous (i.e., a small open-economy assumption).

11.1.1 Representative Household

We assume that all goods are tradable. There is a continuum of goods, which is uniformly distributed over the unit interval, so that $j \in [0, 1]$. The utility function of the representative household is

$$\max E_0 \sum_{t=0}^{\infty} \beta^t \left\{ u(C_t; \xi_t) - \frac{1}{1+\phi} \int_0^1 \left[h_t^{\text{home}}(j) + \delta \cdot h_t^{\text{export}}(j) \right]^{1+\phi} \cdot dj + \Gamma\left(\frac{M_t}{P_t}; \xi_t\right) \right\},$$

$$(11.1)$$

where E is the expectations operator. The instantaneous utility function consists of a consumption composite, C_t, domestic labor supply, $h_t^{\text{home}}(j)$, exported labor supply, $h_t^{\text{export}}(j)$, and of real money balances, M_t/P_t (the ratio of money holdings, M_t, and the price level, P_t). We denote the discount factor by β and the labor disutility parameter by ϕ. The relative disutility of labor export in terms of domestic labor supply is indicated by the parameter $\delta > 1$.[6] The term ξ_t is a vector of preference shocks. The consumption composite, C_t, is a Dixit-Stiglitz composite of goods produced at home and imported goods:

$$C_t \equiv \left\{ \int_0^n [c_{\text{H},t}(j)]^{\frac{\theta-1}{\theta}} \cdot dj + \int_n^1 [c_{\text{W},t}(j)]^{\frac{\theta-1}{\theta}} \cdot dj \right\}^{\frac{\theta}{\theta-1}},$$

$$(11.2)$$

where n is the number of domestically produced goods in the consumption basket, and thus $1 - n$ can serve as a trade openness parameter. Subscripts H and W indicate home and foreign country variables, respectively. The variable $c_{i,t}(j)$ is the consumption level of good j, which is produced in country $i = $ H, W. The parameter $\theta > 1$ is the elasticity of substitution among different goods in the consumption composite. The budget constraint is

$$P_t C_t - P_t T_t + M_t + B_{H,t} + \varepsilon_t B_{W,t} - (1 + i_{H,t-1}) B_{H,t-1} - (1 + i_{W,t-1}) \varepsilon_t B_{W,t-1}$$

$$= M_{t-1} + \mu_t^H W_t^H \int_0^n h_t^{\text{home}}(j) \cdot dj + \varepsilon_t \cdot \mu_t^W W_t^W \int_n^1 h_t^{\text{export}}(j) \cdot dj + \int_0^1 D_t(j) dj,$$

(11.3)

where

$B_{H,t}$ = bond holdings at the beginning of date t (denominated in the domestic currency)

$B_{W,t}$ = bond holdings at the beginning of date t (denominated in the foreign currency)

M_t = domestic-money holdings at the end of period t

P_t = domestic consumer-price index.

W_t^H = wage rate of unskilled labor in the domestic market; expressed in terms of domestic currency

W_t^W = wage rate of unskilled labor in the foreign market, expressed in terms of foreign currency

μ_t^H = skill premium of native-born labor in the domestic labor market

μ_t^W = skill premium of native-born labor in the foreign labor market

$i_{H,t}$ = domestic currency–denominated interest rate

$i_{W,t}$ = foreign currency–denominated world interest rate

$D_t(j)$ = domestic j-firm's profits

ε_t = the exchange rate; the price of foreign currency in terms of domestic currency

T_t = domestic government lump-sum transfers

The Dixit-Stiglitz output composite is given by

$$Y_t \equiv \left\{ \int_0^1 [y_t(j)]^{\frac{\theta-1}{\theta}} \cdot dj \right\}^{\frac{\theta}{\theta-1}}.$$

11.1.2 Producers
Domestic firms produce with the aid of a decreasing return-to-scale production function by using native-born labor and immigrant labor:

$$y_t(j) = A_t \cdot \left[(1-\psi)^{\frac{v-1}{v}} \cdot h_t^{\text{home}}(j)^{\frac{1}{v}} + (\psi)^{\frac{v-1}{v}} \cdot h_t^{\text{import}}(j)^{\frac{1}{v}} \right]^{v\chi}, \tag{11.4}$$

where $y_t(j)$ is the output level of the j-firm, and A_t is an exogenous aggregate technology shock common to all firms. The elasticity of substitution between imported and native-born labor inputs is given by $v/v-1$, where $v > 1$, and the degree of returns to scale is given by $\chi < 1$. The variable $h_t^{\text{import}}(j)$ is the labor supply by immigrants employed by domestic firm j. We assume that native-born labor is skilled and immigrant labor is unskilled. (This captures labor market patterns in an industrialized economy.) Hence,

$$\psi \in \left[0, \frac{1}{2} \right].$$

It follows that the marginal productivity of domestic labor exceeds that of immigrant labor (for the same amount of labor input). Skill premium in the foreign market μ_t^W is exogenously determined, whereas skill premium in the domestic market μ_t^H is endogenously determined.

11.1.3   Domestic Labor Market

The assumption of a free migration of unskilled labor implies a world labor market arbitrage condition:

$$W_t^H = \varepsilon_t \cdot W_t^W.$$

The first-order conditions for the domestic household that allocates time between leisure, work in the domestic market, and work in the foreign market are

$$u_c(C_t; \xi_t) \cdot \frac{\mu_t^H \varepsilon_t W_t^W}{P_t} = \left[h_t^{\text{home}}(j) + \delta h_t^{\text{export}}(j) \right]^\phi, \tag{11.5}$$

$$u_c(C_t; \xi_t) \cdot \frac{\mu_t^W \varepsilon_t W_t^W}{P_t} = \delta \cdot \left[h_t^{\text{home}}(j) + \delta h_t^{\text{export}}(j) \right]^\phi. \tag{11.6}$$

Dividing equation (11.6) by equation (11.5) yields

$$\mu_t^H = \frac{\mu_t^W}{\delta}. \tag{11.7}$$

Because of free outward-migration flows, the equilibrium domestic skill premium is equal to the foreign skill premium adjusted by labor export utility costs. (Recall that δ denotes the relative disutility of labor export in terms of domestic labor supply.)

11.1.4 Marginal Cost
The real marginal cost function, in the presence of migration, is given by

$$mc_t(j) = z_t \cdot y_t(j)^{\frac{1-\chi}{\chi}}, \tag{11.8}$$

where the term $y_t(j)^{\frac{1-\chi}{\chi}}$ reflects the diminishing marginal productivity of labor. The term z_t is given by

$$z_t \equiv \frac{1}{\chi} \cdot \frac{1}{A_t^{\frac{1}{\chi}}} \cdot \frac{1}{\delta} \cdot \mu_t^W \cdot w_t^W \frac{1}{\left[(1-\psi)^{\frac{v-1}{v}} + \frac{\psi^{\frac{2v-1}{v}}}{(1-\psi)} \left(\frac{\mu_t^W}{\delta} \right)^{\frac{1}{v-1}} \right]^v},$$

where the real wage, w_t^W, in the foreign market is defined by

$$w_t^W \equiv \frac{\varepsilon_t \cdot W_t^W}{P_t}.$$

Thus, the exogenously determined z_t consists of a combination of parameters associated with technology and preferences, productivity shock, foreign-market skill premium, and the labor wage in the foreign market.

If the labor market is open to out-migration but closed to in-migration, the marginal cost function still takes the form of equation (11.8); in this case, however, the exogenous term z_t will be replaced by

$$z_t^{\text{out}} \equiv \frac{1}{\chi} \cdot \frac{1}{A_t^{\frac{1}{\chi}}} \cdot \frac{1}{\delta} \cdot \mu_t^W \cdot w_t^W \frac{1}{\left[(1-\psi)^{\frac{(v-1)}{v}} \right]^v}.$$

It can be verified that $z_t^{\text{out}} > z_t$. That is, in-migration exerts a lowering cost effect akin to technological progress.

To see the effect of the in-migration and out-migration on the marginal cost, we can compare equation (11.8) with the corresponding expression for the marginal cost function with no migration, as follows:

$$mc_t^{\text{closed}}(j) = z_t^{\text{closed}} \cdot \frac{1}{u_c(Y_t)} \cdot y_t(j)^{\frac{1+\phi-\chi}{\chi}}, \tag{11.9}$$

where

$$z_t^{\text{closed}} \equiv \frac{1}{\chi} \cdot \frac{1}{A_t^{\frac{1+\phi}{\chi}}} \cdot \frac{(1+\phi)}{(1-\psi)^{(\nu-1)(1+\phi)}},$$

and u_c denotes the marginal utility of consumption.

The output elasticity is equal to $(1 - \chi)/\chi$ in equation (11.8), while the corresponding elasticity is equal to $(1 + \phi - \chi)/\chi$ in equation (11.9). This means that in the presence of out-migration, which tends to make the labor supply faced by domestic producers more flexible, the output elasticity of the marginal cost decreases.

When the labor market is closed to out-migration, wage demands faced by domestic producers are upward sloping, both under in-migration and under a completely closed labor market. However, when the labor market is open to in-migration, domestic producers face an expanded labor supply: in addition to the skilled native-born labor supply (with upward-sloping wage demand), they also face a complementary unskilled foreign labor supply (with exogenously determined wage demand). That means that in-migration acts essentially like a domestic productivity shock.

To summarize, outward migration reduces the output elasticity of the marginal cost, whereas inward migration essentially works like a positive domestic productivity shock that lowers marginal costs.

11.2 Aggregate Supply

11.2.1 Perfect Mobility: Goods, Capital, and Labor
When there is perfect mobility of goods, then domestic producers specialize, and $n < 1$. That is, the number of domestically produced goods, n, falls short of the number of consumer goods, 1. Perfect mobility of capital implies perfect consumption smoothing; that is, $\hat{C}_t = \hat{C}_t^N$. The superscript N indicates the perfect price flexibility case.

The approximated aggregate supply curve is derived from the log linearization of the aggregate supply equations around a purely deterministic steady state.

The "hat" ($\wedge$) denotes the proportional deviation from the purely deterministic steady state, and the superscript N denotes the "natural" value of real variables; that is, the value of a variable that would have prevailed under completely flexible prices.

For the case of perfect mobility of labor, capital, and goods, the approximate aggregate supply curve is given by

$$\hat{\pi}_t = \kappa \cdot \left[\frac{\omega_p \cdot n}{1 + \omega_p \theta} \cdot x_t + \frac{\omega_p \cdot (1-n)}{1 + \omega_p \theta} \cdot \left(\hat{Y}_t^F - \hat{Y}_t^N \right) + \frac{1}{1 + \omega_p \theta} \cdot \hat{w}_t^W + \frac{(1-n)}{n} \cdot \hat{q}_t \right]$$

$$+ \frac{(1-n)}{n} \cdot \left(\hat{q}_t - \hat{q}_{t-1} \right) + \beta \cdot E_t \left[\hat{\pi}_{t+1} - \frac{(1-n)}{n} \left(\hat{q}_{t+1} - \hat{q}_t \right) \right].$$

$$(11.10)$$

Hence, $\hat{\pi}_t$ is the deviation of Consumer Price Index (CPI) inflation from its target; $x_t \equiv \left(\hat{Y}_t^H - \hat{Y}_t^N \right)$ is the domestic output gap; $\left(\hat{Y}_t^F - \hat{Y}_t^N \right)$ is the difference between foreign output and domestic natural output; and the parameter ω_p, defined in the next section, is the elasticity of the marginal cost with respect to the producer's output.

As is familiar to the reader, in the Calvo-type price-updating model, the term κ captures the degree of price flexibility:

$$\kappa = \frac{(1-\alpha)(1-\alpha\beta)}{\alpha}.$$

The term $(1 - \alpha)$ in this equation stands for the probability of receiving a price-updating signal.

The variable $\hat{q}_t$ denotes the proportional deviation of the real exchange rate from its steady-state level, as defined by

$$\hat{q}_t = \hat{\varepsilon}_t + \hat{P}_{F,t} - \hat{P}_t,$$

where $\hat{P}_{F,t}$ is the proportional deviation of the foreign-price index from its steady-state level.

Recall that the focus of attention of this chapter is the inflation-output trade-off as captured by the slope of the aggregate supply curve:

$$\psi_1 \equiv \frac{\kappa n \omega_p}{1 + \omega_p \theta}.$$

Thus, the slope of the aggregate supply curve decreases with $1 - n$, the degree of good-trade openness; the slope increases with the degree of price flexibility κ.

Other terms in the aggregate supply curve formulation capture the effects on the domestic inflation of foreign output shocks, foreign wage shocks, and past, present, and future real exchange rate shocks.

11.2.2 Perfect Mobility of Goods and Capital but Not of Labor
In the case of perfect international mobility of goods and capital, but with no labor mobility, the aggregate supply curve is given by[7]

$$\widehat{\pi}_t = \kappa \cdot \left[\frac{\omega \cdot n}{1 + \omega \theta} \cdot x_t + \frac{\omega \cdot (1-n)}{1 + \omega \theta} \cdot \left(\widehat{Y}_t^F - \widehat{Y}_t^N \right) + \frac{(1-n)}{n} \cdot \widehat{q}_t \right]$$

$$+ \frac{(1-n)}{n} \cdot \left(\widehat{q}_t - \widehat{q}_{t-1} \right) + \beta \cdot E_t \left[\widehat{\pi}_{t+1} - \frac{(1-n)}{n} \left(\widehat{q}_{t+1} - \widehat{q}_t \right) \right], \tag{11.11}$$

where $\omega = \omega_p + \omega_w$ is the elasticity of marginal cost with respect to domestic output; it includes the expression

$$\omega_p = \frac{1 - \chi}{\chi},$$

the elasticity of the desired price with respect to output (for given wages). It is inversely related to the degree of returns to scale. It also includes the expression

$$\omega_w \equiv \frac{\phi}{\chi}.$$

This is the elasticity of demanded wage with respect to output (consisting of the labor-disutility elasticity and the labor-output elasticity). Because $\omega_w > 0$, we have $\omega > \omega_p$. Therefore, shutting off the migration channel (particularly outward migration) raises the slope of the aggregate supply curve.[8] In this case, the slope of the Phillips curve is

$$\psi_2 \equiv \frac{\kappa n \omega}{1 + \omega \theta}.$$

11.2.3 International Mobility of Goods without Capital Mobility and Labor Mobility
If the domestic economy is not integrated to the international financial market, then there is no possibility of consumption smoothing, and we have that the value of aggregate current spending equals the value of aggregate domestic output:

$$\widehat{P}_{C,t} \widehat{C}_t = \widehat{P}_{Y,t} \widehat{Y}_t \quad ; \quad \widehat{P}_{C,t} \widehat{C}_t^N = \widehat{P}_{Y,t} \widehat{Y}_t^N,$$

where $\widehat{P}_{C,t}$ is the CPI-based price level, and $\widehat{P}_{Y,t}$ is the GDP deflator.

In this case, the aggregate supply curve is

$$
\hat{\pi}_t = \kappa \cdot \left[\frac{(\omega \cdot n + \sigma)}{1 + \omega \theta} \cdot x_t + \frac{\omega \cdot (1-n)}{1 + \omega \theta} \cdot \left(\hat{Y}_t^F - \hat{Y}_t^N \right) + \frac{(1-n)}{n} \cdot \hat{q}_t \right]
$$

$$
+ \frac{(1-n)}{n} \cdot \left(\hat{q}_t - \hat{q}_{t-1} \right) + \beta \cdot E_t \left[\hat{\pi}_{t+1} - \frac{(1-n)}{n} \left(\hat{q}_{t+1} - \hat{q}_t \right) \right].
$$

(11.12)

For the case of perfect mobility of goods with no mobility of capital and labor, the slope of the Phillips curve is equal to

$$
\psi_3 \equiv \frac{\kappa (n\omega + \sigma)}{1 + \omega \theta}.
$$

The slope of the aggregate supply curve is *steeper* than in the previous case.

11.2.4 The Fully Closed Economy

Because with the trade account closed, the consumption of each good equals domestic production of the good, production is fully diversified; namely, $n = 1$. If, in addition, the capital account is closed and in-migration and out-migration are not possible, the aggregate supply curve becomes

$$
\hat{\pi}_t = \frac{\kappa}{1 + \omega \theta} \cdot (\omega + \sigma) \cdot x_t + \beta E_t \hat{\pi}_{t+1}.
$$

(11.13)

In this case, the slope of the Phillips curve is

$$
\psi_4 \equiv \frac{\kappa (\omega + \sigma)}{1 + \omega \theta},
$$

where σ is the intertemporal consumption elasticity of substitution. The slope of the Phillips curve is steeper than in the previous case.

11.2.5 Comparison Across International-Mobility Regimes

We can now offer a systematic ranking of the slope of the aggregate supply curve across various openness regimes. One can verify that $\Psi_1 < \Psi_2 < \Psi_3 < \Psi_4$.

This means that in every successive round of the opening up of the economy, globalization contributes to flatten the aggregate supply curve. The intuition is that when an economy opens up to trade in goods, it tends to specialize in production but to diversify in consumption. This means the number of domestically produced goods ($= n$) is less than the number of domestically consumed goods ($= 1$). Consequently, the commodity composition of the consumption and output baskets, which are identical if the trade account is closed, are different when trade in goods is possible. As a result, the correlation between fluctuations in output and in consumption (which is equal to unity in the case of a closed trade account) is less than unity if the economy is opened to international trade in goods.

When the capital account is open, then the correlation between fluctuations in consumption and domestic output is further weakened: this is because with open capital accounts, the representative household can smooth consumption through international borrowing and lending and thereby separate current consumption from current output. The inflation effects of shocks to the marginal cost are therefore reduced because the fluctuations in labor supply are also smoothed as a consequence of the consumption smoothing.

Out-migration reduces the output elasticity of the marginal cost [compare equation (11.8) and equation (11.9)]. This implies that in the presence of out-migration, shocks to domestic output will have smaller effects on inflation compared to those in a closed economy.[9]

When the economy opens up to in-migration, the proportional factor, z_t, of the marginal cost curve is lowered. Therefore, the effect of demand shocks on inflation is weakened.

11.3   Utility-Based Loss Function

Distortions in the New Keynesian equilibrium can be grouped into two types:

1. Consumption smoothing in the presence of fluctuating output. (Fluctuations of the output gap, which are correlated with consumption, are welfare reducing.)
2. Labor allocation in the presence of price rigidity.

Because an efficient allocation of the labor supply requires an equal division of labor across differentiated goods (recall that the disutility of labor is a convex function), any cross-good dispersion in output (the level of output for goods whose prices have been updated is different than the level of output of goods whose prices were not updated) is distortionary. *Recall*: Given that not all the prices are updated simultaneously, inflation generates a distortion.

These two distortion types are to be minimized in the loss function.

The utility-based loss function, which captures distortions 1 and 2, is[10]

$$L = E_0 \sum_{t=0}^{\infty} \beta^t \left[\hat{\pi}_t^2 + \lambda (x_t - x^*)^2 \right],$$ (11.14)

where x^* is the (log) ratio of the nondistorted aggregate output and the monopolistic-competitive distorted output, under perfect price flexibility; and the parameter λ is the weight of the output-gap term relative to the inflation term. We can show that

$$\lambda = \frac{\psi_i}{\theta} \; ; i = 1, 2, 3, 4,$$

where ψ_i is the slope of the aggregate supply curve (the inverse of the sacrifice ratio), and θ is the elasticity of substitution across differentiated goods. Recall that in the previous subsection, we demonstrated that

$$\psi_1 < \psi_2 < \psi_3 < \psi_4.$$

Thus, the ranking of the relative weight of the output-gap term in the loss function is

$$\lambda_1 < \lambda_2 < \lambda_3 < \lambda_4.$$

Opening up an economy to trade in goods and capital flows weakens the correlation between the fluctuations in the output gap and the fluctuations in consumption. Recall that the representative household welfare depends on consumption, not on domestic output. Therefore, the output-gap weight in the loss function falls as an economy opens up to trade and capital assets.

With migration, the representative household's income and output are separated one from the other. Because consumption levels are associated with the income levels (not GDP levels), fluctuations of domestic output become less important to the representative household compared to the case of no migration. Thus, the output-gap weight in the loss function declines when migration is allowed.

We thus establish that the output-gap weight in the utility-based loss function decreases with the opening up of the economy in every successive round of opening up.

11.3.1 Optimal Monetary Policy

In this subsection, we use the utility-based loss function, along with the aggregate supply and aggregate demand relationships, to formulate an optimal monetary policy rule under discretion.

The approximated aggregate demand equation is

$$x_t = E_t x_{t+1} - \sigma^{-1}\left(\hat{i}_{H,t} - E_t \hat{\pi}_{t+1} - \hat{r}_t^n\right), \tag{11.15}$$

where $\hat{r}_t^n$ is the deviation of the natural rate of real interest from steady state.

The approximated (real) interest-parity equation is

$$\hat{q}_t = E_t \hat{q}_{t+1} + \left(\hat{i}_{F,t} - E_t \hat{\pi}_{F,t+1}\right) - \left(\hat{i}_{H,t} - E_t \hat{\pi}_{t+1}\right). \tag{11.16}$$

The optimal monetary policy rule is obtained by choosing the path of $\hat{\pi}_t$, x_t, and $\hat{q}_t$ so as to minimize the loss function subject to the aggregate supply equation, aggregate demand equation, and the (real) interest parity rule, in every period $t = 1,2, \dots ,\infty$.

The optimal policy rule (under discretion) depends on the degree of openness:[11]

$$\hat{i}_{H,t} = \hat{r}_t^n + \gamma_\pi \cdot E_t \hat{\pi}_{t+1} + \gamma_x \cdot x_t + \gamma_u \cdot \hat{u}_t, \tag{11.17}$$

where $\hat{u}_t$ collects terms from the right-hand side of the aggregate supply curve (apart from the inflation expectations and the output gap) and where the elasticity of the policy-determined interest rate, with respect to the inflation expectations, depends on the degree of openness, as follows:

I. Perfect mobility of labor, capital, and goods:

$$\gamma_\pi = 1 + \frac{\left(1 + \dfrac{\Pi_q}{\psi_1}\sigma\right)}{1 + \theta(\psi_1 + \Pi_q \sigma)}\sigma\theta\beta \quad ; \quad \gamma_x = \frac{\sigma\left[1 + \theta(\psi_1 + \Pi_q \sigma)\psi_1\right]}{\beta}. \tag{11.18}$$

II. No labor mobility; perfect mobility of capital and goods:

$$\gamma_\pi = 1 + \frac{\left(1 + \dfrac{\Pi_q}{\psi_2}\sigma\right)}{1 + \theta(\psi_2 + \Pi_q \sigma)}\sigma\theta\beta \quad ; \quad \gamma_x = \frac{\sigma\left[1 + \theta(\psi_2 + \Pi_q \sigma)\psi_2\right]}{\beta}. \tag{11.19}$$

III. No labor mobility; no capital mobility; perfect goods mobility:

$$\gamma_\pi = 1 + \frac{\left(1 + \dfrac{\Pi_q}{\psi_3}\sigma\right)}{1 + \theta(\psi_3 + \Pi_q \sigma)}\sigma\theta\beta \quad ; \quad \gamma_x = \frac{\sigma\left[1 + \theta(\psi_3 + \Pi_q \sigma)\psi_3\right]}{\beta}. \tag{11.20}$$

IV. Closed economy:

$$\gamma_\pi = 1 + \frac{1}{1+\theta\psi_4}\sigma\theta\beta \quad ; \quad \gamma_x = \frac{\sigma\left[1+\theta\psi_4^2\right]}{\beta}. \tag{11.21}$$

Here,

$$\Pi_q \equiv \frac{(1-n)}{n}(1+\kappa-\beta)$$

is the aggregate supply elasticity of inflation with respect to the real exchange rate. Note that in the closed economy case, $\Pi_q = 0$.

The expression for γ_π demonstrates that the optimal monetary policy under discretion becomes more aggressive with respect to inflation when the economy opens up to migration, trade in goods, and capital flow. In contrast, the expression for γ_x demonstrates that the monetary policy becomes more benign toward fluctuations in the output gap in every globalization round when the economy opens up.[12]

11.4 Solving for the Dynamic Equilibrium

In this section, we derive the closed-form solution to the equilibrium levels of inflation and output gap. We use the following procedure in the derivation of the closed-form solution. First, we write the system in a matrix notation. Second, we use the method of undetermined coefficients to solve for the state-space equilibrium form.

11.4.1 Equilibrium Equations in Matrix Notation
Substituting the optimal policy rule (11.17) into the aggregate demand (11.15), and then substituting the result in a generic aggregate supply curve, we can rearrange the system using the following matrix notation:

$$\begin{bmatrix} x_t \\ \hat{\pi}_t \end{bmatrix} = Q \cdot E_t \begin{bmatrix} x_{t+1} \\ \hat{\pi}_{t+1} \end{bmatrix} + R \cdot \hat{u}_t, \tag{11.22}$$

where the matrices of parameters are defined as follows:

$$Q \equiv \begin{bmatrix} \dfrac{1}{1+\gamma_x/\sigma} & \dfrac{1-\gamma_\pi}{\sigma+\gamma_x} \\[4ex] \dfrac{\psi}{1+\gamma_x/\sigma} & \beta - \dfrac{\psi(\gamma_\pi-1)}{(\sigma+\gamma_x)} \end{bmatrix} \quad ; \quad R \equiv \begin{bmatrix} -\dfrac{\gamma_u}{\sigma+\gamma_x} \\[4ex] 1 + \dfrac{\psi\cdot\gamma_u}{(\sigma+\gamma_x)} \end{bmatrix}.$$

Note that in the writing of the equilibrium system, we make a simplification. Although the real exchange rate, $\hat{q}_t$, is an endogenous variable in our model, we simplify by assuming that it has an AR(1) representation.

We assume that the generic term that collects variables from the right-hand side of the aggregated supply curve, $\hat{u}_t$, satisfies the following exogenous AR(1) process:

$$\hat{u}_t = \rho \cdot \hat{u}_{t-1} + \tilde{u}_t , \tag{11.23}$$

where the parameter ρ is smaller than 1 in absolute value, and the disturbance term, $\tilde{u}_t$, follows a white-noise process.

11.4.2   The Solution

We guess that equation (11.22) has the following state-space representation:

$$\begin{bmatrix} x_t \\ \hat{\pi}_t \end{bmatrix} = F \cdot \hat{u}_t , \tag{11.24}$$

where the parameter matrix, F, is a matrix of order 2×2. Substituting the guessed solution from equation (11.24) into equation (11.22), and using the exogenous process from equation (11.23), we get:

$$F \cdot \hat{u}_t = [Q \cdot F \cdot \rho + R] \cdot \hat{u}_t . \tag{11.25}$$

Because the parameter ρ is a scalar, we are allowed to rewrite equation (11.25) with ρ pre-multiplying the matrix F. Thus, we can use the method of undetermined coefficients to solve for the matrix F:

$$F = (I_{2\times2} - Q \cdot \rho)^{-1} \cdot R. \tag{11.26}$$

Substituting for the matrices Q and R, we get that

$$F = \frac{1}{G} \begin{bmatrix} -\gamma_u[\sigma + \gamma_x - \rho\beta + \rho\psi(\gamma_\pi - 1)] + \rho(1-\gamma_\pi)(\sigma + \gamma_x + \psi\gamma_u) \\ \\ \dfrac{-\gamma_u\rho\psi + \left(1 + \dfrac{\gamma_x}{\sigma} - \rho\right)(\sigma + \gamma_x + \psi\gamma_u)}{\sigma} \end{bmatrix} ;$$

$$G \equiv (\sigma + \gamma_x - \sigma\rho)\{\sigma + \gamma_x - \rho[\beta + \psi(1-\gamma_\pi)]\} + \rho^2\psi(\gamma_\pi - 1)\sigma.$$

Table 11.1
Impulse-Response Parameter Values

Parameter	Symbol	Value
The Calvo parameter	α	0.35
Time discount factor	β	0.99
CRRA[1]	σ	1.00
CES[2]	θ	5.00
MC[3] elasticity with respect to own output	ω_p	0.25
Wage demand elasticity with respect to domestic output	ω_w	5.00
Domestically produced goods	n	0.75
Persistence of the cost-push shock	ρ	0.80

1. Constant relative risk aversion
2. Constant elasticity of substitution
3. Marginal cost

11.5 Impulse Responses to Shocks

At this stage, we can compute the impulse response of the equilibrium inflation and the equilibrium output gap to shocks. We illustrate by computing impulse responses to a cost-push shock. The impulse-response parameter values are presented in table 11.1.

Figure 11.1 depicts the impulse response—of the equilibrium inflation and output gap—to a serially correlated cost-push shock under different regimes of openness.

Figure 11.1 demonstrates that as the economy opens up, the equilibrium inflation response to a cost-push shock would be more moderate, while at the same time, the equilibrium output-gap response to the same shock is more erratic.

11.6 Effects of Changes in Parameters

Figure 11.2 illustrates the solution sensitivity to the share of domestically produced goods, n, and to the substitution elasticity across goods, θ, which is inversely related to the producer market power; both structural parameters are related to the degree of openness. Figure 11.2 shows that as the import share grows (i.e., as n falls), equilibrium-output elasticity, with respect to a cost-push shock, becomes more negative. At the same time, equilibrium-inflation elasticity, with respect to the same shock, is not monotonic: it falls as long as the import share

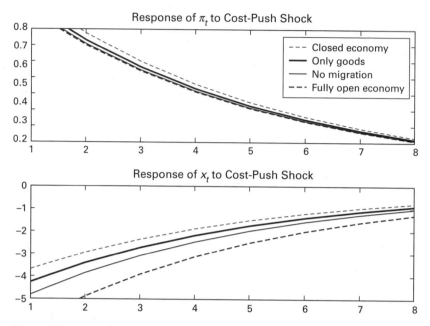

Figure 11.1
Impulse Response of Inflation and Output Gap to a Serially Correlated Cost-Push Shock

grows from 0 to 25 percent, but it increases if import share grows further. If we assume that monopolistic power falls with openness, we have another channel through which globalization influences equilibrium inflation and output. As monopolistic power falls (i.e., as θ grows), equilibrium-output elasticity, with respect to a cost-push shock, becomes more negative. However, equilibrium-inflation elasticity again responds ambiguously: if import share is smaller than 25 percent, this elasticity falls together with the monopolistic power, but it grows otherwise. Altogether, it implies that our analytical conclusion is limited to the case where economies are open, but only up to a certain degree. However, this does not necessarily weaken our argument, as the degree of openness is restricted anyway; for instance, by the no-Ponzi-game assumption, the import share must be below 50 percent.

11.7 Concluding Remarks

In this chapter, we analyzed the effects of international mobility of goods, labor, and finance, within a New Keynesian global economy with a representative household and fully arbitraged economic

Equilibrium-Inflation Elasticity with Respect to a Cost-Push Shock

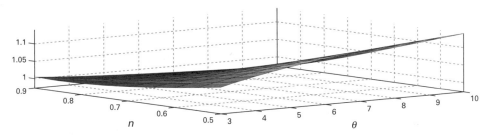

Equilibrium-Output Elasticity with Respect to a Cost-Push Shock

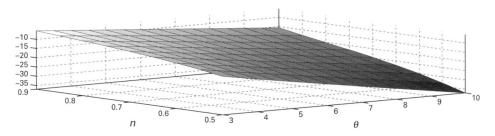

Figure 11.2
Solution Sensitivity to Structural Parameters Under the Open-Economy Case

framework, on (1) the Phillips curve; (2) the weights of inflation and output gap in the approximated, utility-based loss function; (3) the utility-based interest rate rule under discretion; and (4) the equilibrium inflation and output gap. We demonstrate how an endogenously determined monetary policy, which is guided by the welfare criterion of the representative household, becomes more aggressive with regard to inflation fluctuations but more benign with respect to output-gap fluctuations when the economy opens up to in-migration and out-migration, trade in goods, and capital flows. To concentrate on the inflation-output trade-off, we treat the real exchange rate as an exogenous variable unaffected by the globalization regimes. Exploration of the effects of globalization on the real exchange rate in our framework is left for future research.

The chapter assumes that the flex-price markup is constant, unaffected by globalization forces. But there has been some evidence of greater restraints on domestic prices and wage growth in sectors more exposed to international competition, such as textiles and electronics.

Chen, Imbs, and Scott (2004) analyzed disaggregated data for EU man-
ufacturing over the period 1988–2000. They find that increased openness lowers prices by reducing markups and by raising productivity.
In response to an increase in openness, markups show a steep short-run
decline, which partly reverses later, while productivity rises in a manner
that increases over time. If globalization reduces the markup, our
model predicts that this effect, by itself, leads to a more forceful anti-
inflation policy and lessens the attention given by the policy maker to
the fluctuations in economic activity. One can conjecture that more
frequent price updating steepens the trade-off between inflation and
activity; however, to our knowledge, neither theory nor empirical evidence exists in support of any systematic relationship between globalization and frequency of price updating. Notably, Gopinath and
Rigobon (2007) report that the time frequency of price adjustment of
U.S. imported goods trended downward, on average, during the Great
Moderation.

The New Keynesian model, presented in this chapter, was used to
provide the theoretical underpinning for monetary and fiscal policy
during the Great Moderation. However, after the ensuing crisis, a surge
of remodeling efforts has taken place. The ongoing research effort aims
at developing an analytical framework that integrates credit frictions
and asset price bubbles, as presented in chapters 5–8, into the macroeconomic analytical framework. The inclusion of such elements in the
macroeconomic model will help explain the reasons for a switch from
the macroeconomic tranquility of the Great Moderation to a global
financial crisis and also underpins the monetary and fiscal policy in the
era of the Great Recession.

12 Leveraging, De-leveraging, and the Liquidity Trap

As discussed in chapter 3, Japanese growth has been impeded by "zombie banks," deflation, the liquidity trap conjectured by Paul Krugman early in the 1990s, faulty banking policy, and the aftermath of stock and real estate market speculation. The Bank of Japan has tenaciously pursued a zero-interest, expansionary money policy, in tandem with high deficit spending that has raised the national debt to 150 percent of GDP. Japan's bubble-burst savings rose (consumption collapsed), the natural interest rate (needed for full-employment general equilibrium) turned negative, and the money interest rate reached the lower bound of zero, rendering monetary policy impotent. The actual real interest rate immediately after the crash and for decades to come often was slightly positive, the combined effect of modestly falling prices (due partly to collapsed demand and retail liberalization in an otherwise *keiretsu* price-fixed environment) and a zero money interest rate. This created a small Keynesian output gap (albeit with negligible unemployment) that was addressed with fiscal deficit spending, but it is still possible to argue that deflation and a liquidity trap kept and still keeps Japan's GDP and employment below its full competitive potential. Krugman (2010a, 2010b) contends that Japan's liquidity trap was the first manifested since the Great Depression. The second episode of liquidity traps across many of the OECD (Organisation for Economic Co-operation and Development) countries came in 2008. The global financial crisis, featuring the collapse of global equity, bond, and housing markets, unleashed a frenzy of advice and emergency policy intervention aimed at stemming the hemorrhaging, bolstering aggregate effective demand, and repairing regulatory lapses to restore business confidence (see chapter 3).

The full-arbitrage, representative agent, New Keynesian model that is described in chapter 11, which assumes that credit flows freely (i.e., the absence of any borrowing limits), is incapable of capturing key features of these awesome events.

Because of full arbitrage, interest parities prevail across all assets and all maturities. This modeling approach seems a reasonable approximation in a period such as the Great Moderation.[1] The failure prior to the 2008 crisis to predict the crash in asset prices opened the door wide for an effort to bring in contractual and financial frictions into the macroeconomic analytical framework.

As we emphasize in chapter 6, a central problem in the credit market is that lenders are reluctant to make loans because they cannot easily determine whether a prospective borrower has resources to repay the loan. If the loan is made, the lender is concerned whether the borrower will engage in risky behavior that could lower the probability that the loan will be repaid. Collateral reduces this information asymmetry problem because high-quality collateral (i.e., assets that are easily valued and easy to take control of) significantly decreases the losses to the lender if the borrower defaults on the loan. High-quality collateral also reduces the moral hazard problem because the borrower is reluctant to engage in excessively risky behavior because now he or she has something to lose.

The key feature missing from the traditional macroeconomic model described above is the role of financial intermediaries. Clearly, the 2008 crisis has shown that financial intermediary capital has a crucial role in the economy, and losses incurred by financial intermediaries can have strong spillover effects to the rest of the economy. Recently, Gertler and Kiyotaki (2011) and Rampini and Viswanathan (2011) added a financial intermediary sector (albeit the crisis is driven by panic; unlike Holmstrom and Tirole [1997]) and analyzed the dynamic interactions between this sector and the rest of the economy. Introducing this sector into macroeconomic models enables elaborate discussions on various policies conducted by governments during the recent crisis in the attempt to stimulate the economy via the financial intermediation sector. Such policies are discussed by Gertler and Kiyotaki (2011).

A different angle on the role of credit frictions in the macroeconomy is provided by Eggertsson and Krugman (2012). They study a model with heterogeneous agents, where patient agents lend and impatient agents borrow subject to a collateral constraint. If, for some reason, the collateral requirement becomes tighter, impatient agents will have to go into a process of de-leveraging, reducing the aggregate demand. This excess saving leads to a reduction in the natural interest rate that might become negative, and the nominal (policy) interest rate hits the zero bound, putting the economy into a liquidity trap. Then, traditional monetary policy becomes impossible, but fiscal policy regains some potency. Their model is presented in this chapter.

Eggertsson and Krugman (2012) develop a stylized New Keynesian model where consumers are constrained by borrowing limits because of some contractual frictions, as discussed in previous chapters.[2] In their model, unanticipated tightening in the credit market, manifested as a fall in borrowing limits, forces consumers to cut spending. The borrowing-limit shock triggers a vicious circle, whereby spending cuts lead to falling prices, which raise the real value of the consumer nominal debt. The ensuing debt overhang depresses consumption spending further, which leads to an additional fall in the price level and consumer spending, and so on.[3] The Eggertsson-Krugman model therefore captures a key feature of the Great Recession: a credit market shock led to a transitional de-leveraging period with depressed demand and a liquidity trap. All these effects are present in a small-scale, stylized, New Keynesian model.

12.1 The Natural Rate of Interest, the Lower Bound, and the Output Gap

To understand monetary policy under economic depression, we begin the analysis with a technical issue: how the natural interest rate is affected by a decrease in borrowing limits. In a flexible-price endowments model, impatient agents borrow from patient agents, whereas the former are subject to a borrowing limit. When the debt limit unexpectedly falls, impatient consumers are forced to cut spending, which through a standard general equilibrium mechanism lowers the natural interest rate all the way to become negative. The next step in developing the model allows the consumer debt to take the form of nominal obligations. In this case, the shock to the borrowing limit has a magnified effect on the natural interest rate, because the depressed demand that follows the shock lowers the price level, thereby raising the real value of debt overhang and lowering further consumer spending. Consequently, the nominal interest rate is pushed toward the zero lower bound. At this stage of developing the analytical framework into a full-fledged New Keynesian model, Eggertsson and Krugman (2012) introduce nominal price rigidity; consequently, output becomes variable.

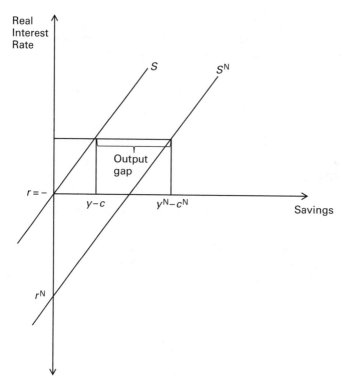

Figure 12.1
Liquidity Trap

We begin with a description of the connection between the natural rate of interest, the lower bound, and the output gap. Figure 12.1 helps us to understand the general equilibrium liquidity trap situation. It summarizes a story line told in this chapter: a shock that tightens credit flows from savers to borrowers; consumption decisions burdened by a debt overhang, de-leveraging phase, where the natural rate of interest falls; the nominal rate of interest reaches its lower bound and price deflation emerges; and output falls because of weakened aggregate demand.

The natural rate of interest, r^N, which clears the goods market under flexible prices, where the saving schedule is S^N, is negative. In the next section, we will see how a discrete fall in borrowing limits (which may happen under meltdown of market values of collateral assets) could push the S^N schedule to the right during the period of de-leveraging, a process in which debtors are forced to pay down their debt at the same time, leading to a negative natural rate of interest. The de-leveraging is the other side of depressed consumption, which pushes the real interest rate down. If the lower bound for the nominal interest rate is reached, then with the aid of the Fisher equation,

$$i = 0 = r + \pi,$$

the liquidity-trapped real interest rate is equal to the negative inflation rate. That is, the *actual real* interest rate, r, is equal to the rate of *deflation*, $-\pi$.

Consequently, a gap is formed between the actual real interest rate and the natural rate of interest. Conjointly, there is another gap between the level of *actual* output, Y, which anchors the S schedule, and the *natural* (flexible-price) *output*, Y^N, which anchors the S^N schedule. Accordingly, in figure 12.1, the output gap is measured by the horizontal difference between the *actual*-saving schedule, S, and the *flexible-price* saving schedule, S^N. The widened output slackness is a direct consequence of the financial meltdown, which triggered the de-leveraging process.

12.2 The Natural Rate of Interest

To understand how severe tightening in the credit market causes a fall in the natural rate of interest, we start with a pure-endowment economy, a special case of the perfect price flexibility model.

Consider a continuum of households (with a mass equaling 1). Households are of two types: *patient*, with a low discount rate, denoted by s, and *impatient*, with high discount rate, denoted by b. Each one of these two representative households gets a constant endowment $(1/2)Y$ each period. Borrowing and lending take the form of risk-free bonds denominated in the consumption good, as in an indexed bond case.

They utility function is

$$\sum_{t=0}^{\infty} \beta(i)^t \log c_t(i), \tag{12.1}$$

where $i = $ s or b, and $\beta(s) = \beta > \beta(b)$.

The budget constraint of each individual household is

$$D_t(i) = (1 + r_{t-1})D_{t-1}(i) - \frac{1}{2}y + C_t(i), \tag{12.2}$$

where D denotes debt, and $i = $ s or b.

A borrowing limit exists (inclusive of next-period interest rate payments), D^{high}, so that at any period-t debt,

$$(1+r_t)D_t(i) \le D^{high} > 0. \tag{12.3}$$

We assume that this bound is at least strictly lower than the maximum repayment capacity, the present discounted value of output of each agent; that is, $D_{high} < (1/2) [\beta/(1 - \beta)]Y$. [Later, we will see that the equilibrium interest rate is equal to $(1-\beta)/\beta$, which is used for the discounting operation.)

Consumption of the saver satisfies a consumption Euler equation in each period (C denotes consumption):

$$\frac{1}{C_t^s} = (1+r_t)\beta \frac{1}{C_{t+1}^s}. \tag{12.4}$$

The impatient household borrows up to the borrowing limit:

$$C^b = \frac{1}{2}Y - \frac{r}{1+r}D^{high}. \tag{12.5}$$

The goods-market clearing condition is

$$Y = C^s + C^b, \tag{12.6}$$

implying

$$C^a = \frac{1}{2}Y + \frac{r}{1+r}D^{high}. \tag{12.7}$$

Equations (12.4), (12.5), and (12.6) imply that the nonstochastic, steady-state, real interest rate is determined by the discount factor of the *patient* consumer. That is, the equilibrium value of the natural interest rate is

$$r^N = (1-\beta)/\beta.$$

Suppose that the debt limit falls *unexpectedly and discretely* from D^{high} to D^{low}.[4] How does the shock affect the natural real interest? This is what we explore next.

12.3 Borrowing Limit and the Natural Interest Rate

We assume that the transition to the new steady state, where borrowers already fully adjusted their consumption decisions after the shock, takes only one period. Denote short-run variables with S and long-run variables with L. The next-period real interest rate remains

$$r^N = \frac{1-\beta}{\beta}.$$

In the new steady state, the equilibrium rate of interest depends on the saver's discount factor but not on the debt ceiling.

In the short run, as in steady state, we have for the borrower

$$C_L^b = \frac{1}{2}Y - \frac{r}{1+r}D^{low} = \frac{1}{2}Y - (1-\beta)D^{low}, \qquad (12.8)$$

where, in equation (12.8), we substituted for the long-run equilibrium real interest rate. In the short run, however, the borrower needs to de-leverage to satisfy the new borrowing limit. Hence, his budget constraint in the short run is

$$D_S = D^{high} - \frac{1}{2}Y + C_S^b. \qquad (12.9)$$

If before the shock the borrower debt is always rolled over, period by period, now, after the shock, he is more severely constrained because he could borrow up to a lower borrowing limit. Therefore, in order to pay back old debt, the borrower consumption spending must fall during the entire de-leveraging stage of the cycle. Because we made an assumption here that the borrower must de-leverage to the new debt limit within a single period, so that

$$D_S = \frac{D^{low}}{1+r_S},$$

his short-run consumption falls to

$$C_S^b = \frac{1}{2}Y + \frac{D^{low}}{1+r_S} - D^{high}. \qquad (12.10)$$

Short-run goods-market clearing implies

$$C_S^s + C_S^b = Y.$$

The long-run consumption of the saver is

$$C_L^s = \frac{1}{2}Y + \frac{r}{1+r}D^{low} = \frac{1}{2}Y + (1-\beta)D^{low}. \qquad (12.11)$$

Substituting for the consumption of the borrower, we get

$$C_s^s = \frac{1}{2}Y - \frac{D^{low}}{1+r_s} + D^{high}. \tag{12.12}$$

Recall that the consumption decision of the saver satisfies the consumption Euler equation

$$C_L^s = (1+r_s)\beta C_s^s. \tag{12.13}$$

Substitute the short- and long-run consumption of the saver into equation (12.14), and, solving for $1 + r_s$, we get

$$1 + r_s = \frac{\frac{1}{2}Y + D^{low}}{\beta \frac{1}{2}Y + \beta D^{high}}. \tag{12.14}$$

The de-leveraging shock will make the natural rate of interest r_s to become negative if

$$\frac{\frac{1}{2}Y + D^{low}}{\beta \frac{1}{2}Y + \beta D^{high}} < 1. \tag{12.15}$$

Or,

$$\beta D^{high} - D^{low} > \frac{1}{2}\frac{1-\beta}{\beta}Y.$$

Naturally, we can define *debt overhang* by

$$\beta D^{high} - D^{low},$$

and the present value of the representative individual wealth by

$$\frac{1}{2}\frac{1-\beta}{\beta}Y.$$

This condition (12.15) will apply if the debt overhang is larger than wealth.

The interpretation for the negative natural rate of interest is that the saver must be induced to make up for the reduction in consumption by the borrower; thereby raising the level of spending. For this to happen, the natural interest rate must fall, and in the face of a large de-leveraging shock, it must become negative to induce the saver to spend sufficiently more.

12.4   Natural Rate of Interest and Zero-Bound Rate

To make the price level determinate, assume that nominal government debt is traded. This extension enables us to analyze the conditions where a borrowing-limit shock forces the nominal interest rate to attain the zero lower bound. As before, we assume that the long-run equilibrium, with market-clearing stable prices, is restored with a positive (nominal) interest rate after just one transition period.

In the transition period, the Euler equation, which has to be satisfied by the saver, becomes

$$\frac{1}{C_t^s} = (1+i_t)\beta_t \frac{1}{C_{t+1}^s} \frac{P_t}{P_{t+1}}, \qquad (12.16)$$

where P_t is the price level, and i_t is the nominal interest rate. The saver behaves in accordance with the Fisher equation, which must prevail in the short run:

$$1+r_s = (1+i_s)\frac{P_s}{P*}.$$

We impose the zero bound

$$i_t \geq 0.$$

Solving for the price level, we get[5]

$$\frac{P_s}{P*} = \frac{\frac{1}{2}Y + D^{\text{low}}}{\beta\frac{1}{2}Y + \beta D^{\text{high}}} < 1. \qquad (12.17)$$

That is, if a shock pushes the natural (real) rate of interest below zero, the price level must drop now by the amount of $P_s/P*$, so that it can rise into the future long-run equilibrium by the amount of $P*/P_s$, creating the inflation necessary to achieve a negative real interest rate.

This analysis has assumed, however, that the debt behind the de-leveraging shock is indexed (i.e., denominated in terms of the consumption good). But suppose instead that the debt, B_t, is denominated in terms of money. In that case, short-run price-level fall will increase the real value of the preexisting debt. The debt limit is defined, however, in *real* terms, because the ability of the borrower to pay in the future out of his endowment is a real term. Therefore, the fall in the price level after the shock will increase the burden of de-leveraging in real terms. Specifically, let debt be denominated in nominal terms, and the price level is P_S. Then, $D^{\text{high}} = B^{\text{high}}/P_S$.

And, in order to satisfy the debt limit, the indebted agent must make short-run repayments of

$$\frac{B^{\text{high}}}{P_S} - \frac{D^{\text{low}}}{1+r_s}. \tag{12.18}$$

The natural rate of interest becomes

$$1+r_s = \frac{\frac{1}{2}Y + D^{\text{low}}}{\beta\frac{1}{2}Y + \beta\frac{B^{\text{high}}}{P_S}} < 1. \tag{12.19}$$

Hence, as the price level falls, the borrower must pay more, cutting on his consumption spending, and as a consequence the natural rate becomes more negative compared to the index debt case. The natural rate of interest is now endogenous.

12.5   Price Rigidity and the Natural Interest Rate

We now want to move to a fully fledged New Keynesian model with price rigidity and variable output. To do this, we assume that C_t is extended to a Dixit-Stiglitz aggregate of a continuum of goods giving the producer of each good market power with elasticity of demand given by θ. There is also a continuum of firms of measure one, each of which produces one type of the varieties the consumers like.

Type i consumers thus have the following utility function:

$$\sum_{t=0}^{\infty} \beta(i)^t \left\{ u^i[c_t(i)] - v^i[h_t(i)] \right\},$$

where $i = s$ or b,

$$c_t = \left[\int_0^1 c_t(j)^{\frac{\theta-1}{\theta}} \right]^{\frac{\theta}{\theta-1}},$$

and the corresponding price index is

$$p_t = \left[\int_0^1 p_t(j)^{\theta-1} \right]^{\frac{\theta}{\theta-1}}.$$

Of these consumers, a fraction χ_s is savers and a fraction $1-\chi_s$ is borrowers.

Aggregate consumption is thus

$$c_t = \chi_s c_t^s + (1-\chi_s)c_t^b,$$

where c_t is per capita consumption in the economy, c_t^s is per capita saver consumption, and c_t^b is per capita borrower consumption.

The production function is linear in labor. Let a fraction $1-\lambda$ of these monopolistically competitive firms keep their prices fixed for a certain planning period, while the λ fraction of the firms can change their prices all the time.[6]

The log-linearized version of the model generates a linear Phillips curve of the following form:

$$\pi_t = \kappa \hat{Y}_t + E_{t-1}\pi_t,$$

where[7]

$$\kappa \equiv \frac{\lambda}{1-\lambda}\xi, \ \hat{Y}_t \equiv \log\frac{Y_t}{\bar{Y}}, \ \text{and} \ \pi_t \equiv \log\frac{p_t}{p_{t-1}}.$$

The key point is that output is no longer an exogenous endowment as in our last example. Instead, if inflation is different in the short run from what those firms that preset prices expected, then output will be above potential.

Assume that the central bank follows a Taylor rule of the following form:

$$i_t = \max(0, r_t^n + \varphi_\pi \pi_t),$$

where $\phi_\pi > 1$, and r_t^n is the natural rate of interest.[8]

Log-linearizing the consumption Euler equation of savers gives

$$\hat{C}_t^s = E_t \hat{C}_{t+1}^s - \sigma(i_t - E_t\pi_{t+1} - \bar{r}),$$

where

$$\sigma = -\frac{\bar{u}_c^s}{\bar{u}_{cc}^s\bar{Y}}, \ \hat{C}_t^s \equiv \log\left(\frac{c_t^s}{\bar{Y}}\right),$$

and i_t now refers to $\log(1+i_t)$ in terms of our previous notation, and $\bar{r} = \log \beta^{-1}$. Log-linearizing the resource constraint yields

$$\hat{Y}_t = \chi_s \hat{C}_t^s + (1 - \chi_s)\hat{C}_t^b,$$

where

$$\hat{C}_t^b \equiv \log\left(\frac{c_t^b}{\bar{Y}}\right).$$

To close the model, it now remains to determine the consumption behavior of the borrowers, which is again at the heart of the analysis.[9]

We can then see immediately from the Phillips-curve equation

$$\pi_t = \kappa \hat{Y}_t + E_{t-1}\pi_t$$

that $\hat{Y}_L = 0$ so that the economy will revert back to its "flexible-price" equilibrium in the long run as this model has long-run neutrality. The model will then be the flexible-price model we just analyzed.[10]

In the short run, the borrower as in the previous sections needs to de-leverage to meet the borrowing limit. The borrower consumption is thus given by

$$\hat{C}_t^b = \hat{Y}_s - \hat{D} + \gamma_D \pi_s - \gamma_D \beta(i_s - r_L^n - \bar{r}),$$

where

$$\hat{D} \equiv \frac{B^{\text{high}} - \bar{D}}{\bar{Y}}$$

is the debt overhang triggered by the shock; the counterpart of $\beta D^{\text{high}} - D^{\text{low}}$ from section 12.2.

Note that the borrower is liquidity-constrained: his consumption function depends on his current income but not the present value of the sum of present and future income, as is the case of the saver's consumption. The latter is given by

$$\hat{C}_s^s = \hat{C}_L^s - \sigma(i_s - \pi_L - \bar{r}).$$

Substituting the borrower and the saver consumption functions into the overall resource constraint, we obtain

$$\hat{Y}_s = \chi_s\left[\hat{C}_L^s - \sigma(i_s - \pi_L - \bar{r})\right] + (1 - \chi_s)\left[\hat{Y}_s - \hat{D} + \gamma_D \pi_s - \gamma_D \beta(i_s - r_L^n - \bar{r})\right].$$

The short-run real interest rate, when prices were fully flexible, is given by

$$r_s^n \equiv \bar{r} - \frac{1-\chi_s}{\chi_s \sigma + (1-\chi_s)\gamma_D \beta}\hat{D} + \frac{\gamma_D}{\chi_s \sigma + (1-\chi_s)\gamma_D \beta}\pi_s.$$

Substitute the definition of the natural rate of interest and $\hat{C}_L^b \equiv \hat{C}_L^s = \pi_L$. We get

$$\hat{Y}_s = -\frac{\chi_s \sigma + (1-\chi_s)\gamma_D \beta}{\chi_s}(i_s - r_s^n).$$

This equation is the counterpart of the IS schedule in the crude Keynesian model.[11] The de-leveraging shock is assumed to be *unexpected*, so that

$$E_{-1}\pi_s = 0.$$

Then, the aggregate supply equation can be written as

$$\pi_s = \kappa \hat{Y}_s.$$

Substituting the aggregate supply equation into the $\hat{Y}_s$ equation above, and assuming the debt overhang is large enough, so that the zero bound is binding, the effect of the de-leveraging shock on output growth and inflation is given by

$$\hat{Y}_s = \Gamma - \frac{1-\chi_s}{\chi_s - (1-\chi_s)\kappa\gamma_D}\hat{D} < 0$$

$$\pi_s = \kappa\Gamma - \frac{(1-\chi_s)\kappa}{\chi_s - (1-\chi_s)\kappa\gamma_D}\hat{D} < 0,$$

where $\Gamma > 0$.[12]

To sum up, the shock to the borrowing limit that depresses private spending and brings the policy interest rate all the way down to the lower bound leads to deflation and output recession.

12.6 Concluding Remarks

This chapter analyzed the macroeconomic effects of a shock to the borrowing limit that triggers a sudden shift from leveraging to de-leveraging. Such a shock, causing various balance-sheet mismatches, creates major problems of macroeconomic management. On the monetary policy side, it requires adoption of nonconventional monetary policy, with limited effectiveness. Even a zero nominal interest rate may not be low enough to induce the needed private-sector spending. On the fiscal policy side, for a slump to be mitigated, someone (i.e., the government) must spend more to compensate for the fact that private-sector debtors are spending less.

Eggertsson and Krugman (2012) sum up:

The bottom line, then, is that if we view liquidity-trap conditions as being the result of a deleveraging shock, the case for expansionary policies, especially expansionary fiscal policies, is substantially reinforced. In particular, a strong fiscal response not only limits the output loss from a deleveraging shock; it also, by staving off Fisherian debt deflation, limits the size of the shock itself.

The Eggertsson-Krugman model yields important insights for macroeconomic management, in the presence of de-leveraging, and a liquidity-trapped monetary policy; both characterize the Great Recession. But, the development of credit and asset price bubbles that apparently took place, without notice, during the Great Moderation, bursting in 2008 and leading to the Great Recession, is not captured in this framework because the financial sector is not fully incorporated into the New Keynesian framework. Origins of financial crises are analyzed in the next chapter.

Appendix: Multiple (Steady-State) Equilibria Under a Taylor Rule

A continuous Taylor-type interest-rate rule, when combined with the Fisher equation, can generate multiple equilibria in the New Keynesian model. In addition to the intended deterministic steady state at the targeted inflation rate, $\pi = \pi^*$, there is also a low-inflation unintended deterministic steady state, which in fact is likely to be deflationary.

Figure 12.2 plots the Fisher equation, $i = \pi / \beta$, where π is the inflation factor, i is the nominal interest rate factor, and β^{-1} is the real interest-rate factor for discount factor $0 < \beta < 1$. The steady-state Fisher equation arises from the standard household Euler equation for consumption when consumption is at a deterministic steady state. The interest-rate rule $i = 1 + f(\pi)$ is drawn so that it cuts the Fisher inflation from below at the targeted steady state, π^*, in accordance with the Taylor principle. The zero lower bound for the net interest rate $i - 1$ then implies the unintended steady state at π_L, provided that the interest rate rule is *continuous*. In fact, as shown by Benhabib, Schmitt-Grohe, and Uribe (2002), there is a continuum of perfect foresight paths, starting from an initial $\pi = \pi^*$, which converge asymptotically to π_L.[13]

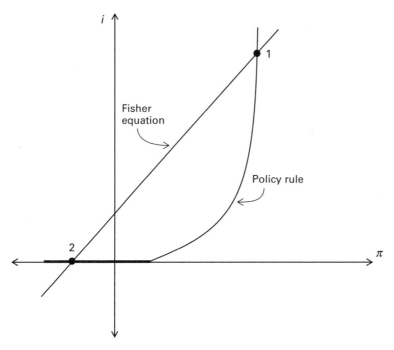

Figure 12.2
Multiple Steady States Under a Continuous Taylor Rule

13   Amplification and Persistency of Shocks in Dynamic Macroeconomic Models

13.1   Introduction

The previous chapter addressed a key development of the New Keynesian macroeconomic paradigm: from an analytical framework that features full capital-market arbitrage, smooth credit, Ricardian-equivalence properties, representative agents, and efficient monetary management, to the framework that incorporates both debt frictions and liquidity-trapped equilibrium. These add-ons to the standard model provide a special role for fiscal policy for aggregate demand management, as private aggregate demand is severely deficient. The analytical framework of the New Keynesian benchmark model is based on the frictionless credit paradigm, capturing to some extent the effects of globalization forces and the worldwide reduction in inflation during the 1990s, which is known as the Great Moderation era. The multiple-agent, credit-friction analytical framework attempts to capture some key features of the period after the 2008 crisis, which is known as the Great Recession era.

13.2   Persistency with Agency Problem

The costly-state-verification framework of Townsend (1979) features an agency problem in which the debtor learns the true payoff of the project, although only ex post, while the lender does not observe it without incurring a cost. The lender will be able to verify the payoff level only if he pays monitoring costs, which depend on the investment size. The monitoring costs that are incurred by the lender are passed on to the borrower through the interest rate charged in the high-payoff states. In the low-payoff states, the borrower surrenders the entire payoff to the lender after state verification by the lender at a cost. Consequently, external financing of an investment project is more costly than internal financing of the same project in this framework. This is, indeed, an optimal debt contract that solves essentially an agency problem, minimizing the socially wasteful costs of monitoring.

Bernanke and Gertler (1989) apply the costly-state-verification framework to a dynamic macroeconomic model. A key implication is that temporary shocks have persistent effects on the real economy through the financial-accelerator channel. A shock to the entrepreneur's net worth that tightens the borrowing limit forces him to downscale his investment. The contracted stock of capital reduces the net worth of new investors, and therefore capital accumulation slows down, and so on. Hence, the shock has persistent effects.

13.2.1   Financial Acceleration

There is a continuum of population of mass 1. A fraction, η, of the population is entrepreneurs, and a fraction $1 - \eta$ is households. Entrepreneurs have exclusive access to an investment technology with which a unit of the consumption good is transformed to ω units of capital goods. Accordingly, each individual entrepreneur's investment yields ωi_t of capital for an input of i_t of consumption goods. The productivity parameter ω is an idiosyncratic, i.i.d., shock, with distribution function G, and $E(\omega) = 1$. That is, while entrepreneurs as a whole safely convert 1 unit of consumption good into 1 unit of capital good, an individual entrepreneur, subject to idiosyncratic shocks, can convert 1 unit of consumption good into ω units of capital goods. The realization of an individual entrepreneur's outcome is only observable to an outsider at a verification cost, μi_t. Thus, the larger is the amount of finance an investment requires from either internal or external sources, the larger would potentially be the monitoring costs.

The optimal debt contract minimizes monitoring costs, which the lender effectively passes on to the borrower through the interest rate, $\bar{\omega}_t$. The latter evidently reflects the lender's monitoring costs. As there is no aggregate uncertainty in the investment process, the household that is the lender (because it has a relatively low discount rate) can fully diversify its debt security purchases across the entire population of the entrepreneurs. Therefore, lending requires no risk premium.

An entrepreneur with net worth n_t who borrows $i_t - n_t$ promises to repay $\bar{\omega}_t i_t$ for all realizations $\omega \geq \bar{\omega}_t$, while for realizations $\omega < \bar{\omega}_t$ he will be audited, and his creditors will receive the investment payoff ωi_t net of auditing costs, μi_t. For a given investment size i_t, the auditing thresh-old $\bar{\omega}_t$ is set so that the lenders break even,

$$\left\{ \int_0^{\bar{\omega}_t} (\omega - \mu) dG(\omega) + [1 - G(\bar{\omega}_t)] \bar{\omega}_t \right\} i_t q_t = i_t - n_t,$$

where q_t is the price of capital in terms of the consumption good.

An entrepreneur with net worth n_t then chooses i_t to maximize his expected payoff:

$$\max_{i_t} \int_{\bar{\omega}_t}^{\infty} (\omega - \mu) dG(\omega) i_t q_t,$$

subject to the above break-even condition.

The solution of this optimization problem is a linear optimiza-tion rule,

$$i_t = \psi(q_t) n_t,$$

where q_t is the period t price of capital, and $\psi'(q_t)$ is positive.

Aggregate investment is given by

$$I_t = \psi(q_t) N_t,$$

where N_t denotes the aggregate net worth of entrepreneurs.

Therefore, aggregate investment is increasing in both the price of capital and the net worth. The reason is that both higher capital price and higher net worth require a lower auditing threshold. Lower monitoring costs reduce the borrowing costs and lead to higher investment.

The aggregate production function, $Y_t = f(K_t, L_t)$, exhibits constant returns to scale.

13.2.2 Equilibrium Dynamics

Dividing the entrepreneur's payoff by net worth yields the entrepre-neur's rate of return on its *internal* funds:

$$\rho(q_t) = \int_{\bar{\omega}_t}^{\infty} (\omega - \mu) dG(\omega) \psi(q_t) q_t > 1.$$

The rate of return on internal funds, the marginal efficiency of invest-ment, is larger than 1 because of the agency costs associated with the financing of the investment. Entrepreneurs are risk neutral, while households are risk averse.

As is standard, the return to holding 1 unit of capital from period t to period $t + 1$ is given by

$$R_{t+1}^k = \frac{A_{t+1}f'(K_{t+1}) + q_{t+1}(1-\delta)}{q_t},$$

where $A_{t+1}f'(K_{t+1})$ is equal to the period $t + 1$ capital rental rate, and δ is the capital depreciation rate.

As is standard, a consumption-saving decision by the risk-averse household is derived from the Euler condition

$$u'(c_t) = \bar{\beta}E_t\left[R_{t+1}^k u'(c_{t+1})\right],$$

where $u'(c)$ denotes the marginal utility of consumption of the (risk-averse) household.

The risk-neutral entrepreneur's Euler condition is

$$1 = \beta E_t\left[R_{t+1}^k \rho(q_{t+1})\right],$$

where the factor $\rho(q_{t+1}) > 1$ is the return on the entrepreneur's internal funds; the entrepreneur discount factor is denoted by β (which is smaller than the household discount factor, $\bar{\beta}$); and $\rho(q_{t+1})(>1)$ stands for the period $t + 1$ return on the entrepreneur's internal funds that are financing the investment.

The dynamics of this model work as follows. Period $t - 1$ investment adds the period t capital stock to the depreciated value of the period $t - 1$ capital yield (as is standard). Therefore, period $t - 1$ investment and period t productivity level, A_t, determine wage and rental rates in period t, and therefore the period t net worth of the entrepreneurs. Period t net worth, N_t, in turn determines the supply curve of capital for period $t + 1$:

$$K_{t+1}^s = S\left[E(R_{t+1}^k), N_t\right].$$

Period t expected demand for capital stock, based on expected period $t + 1$ returns, is then given by

$$E(A_{t+1})f'(K_{t+1}^d) = E(R_{t+1}^k).$$

In equilibrium,

$$K_{t+1}^s = K_{t+1}^d.$$

Consider now a negative temporary productivity shock in period t. It lowers the period t wage rate and period t aggregate net worth. The increase in period t borrowing frictions causes period $t + 1$ capital stock to decline, triggering a fall in the period $t + 1$ wage rate. The fall in the wage rate implies lower period $t + 1$ net worth for the next-generation entrepreneurs. Thus, the period t shock generates a *persistent* effect through a financial accelerator into the following future periods.

13.3   Amplification and Persistency with Incomplete Contracts

Kiyotaki and Moore (1997) focus on the dynamic implications of capital market illiquidity in the presence of endogenously determined collateral constraints on borrowing. They apply the incomplete contract theory to formulate a dynamic general equilibrium model that features fire-sale stock market phenomena and persistent upturns and downturns of economic activity. Amplifications of shocks occur when capital that is used in the productive sector has to be sold at fire-sale prices to the investors to be used in the nonproductive sector.

13.3.1   Fire-Sale Pricing and Amplification Effects
Assume the existence of a continuum of risk-neutral investors of two types: productive and unproductive. They operate in two sectors: productive and unproductive. The fraction in the population of productive agents is η, and the fraction in the population of unproductive agents is $1 - \eta$. Productive-investor investment technology is linear, using k_t units of capital input in period t to yield $(\alpha)k_t$ in period $t + 1$. Unproductive-investment technology exhibits diminishing returns. Investing k_t units of capital input in period t yields output $F(k_t)$ in period $t + 1$ ($F' > 0$, $F'' < 0$).

Investment is irreversible, and aggregate capital stock is fixed, $\bar{K}$.

Unproductive investors have also a relatively low discount rate. In equilibrium, they end up lending to the more productive investors whose discount rate is relatively high.

The borrowing constraint is given by

$$Rb_t \leq q_{t+1}k_t,$$

where b denotes the amount of debt, q denotes the price of capital, and R denotes the risk-free rate of interest. The more productive investor borrows to the limit and does not consume any of the products that he produces. The interest rate is therefore determined by the subjective discount rate of the unproductive investor, the lender,

$$R = \frac{1}{\bar{\beta}},$$

where $1/\bar{\beta}$ is the reciprocal of the unproductive investor's discount factor.

Let $[(\alpha + q_t)k_{t-1} - Rb_{t-1}]$ denote the productive investor's net worth in period $t - 1$; αk_{t-1} is his tradable output, $q_t k_{t-1}$ is his asset holdings from the previous period, and Rb_{t-1} is the market value of maturing debt. Thus, period t demand for productive assets, k_t, is given by

$$k_t = \frac{1}{q_t - \frac{1}{R} q_{t+1}} [(\alpha + q_t)k_{t-1} - Rb_{t-1}].$$

The unproductive investor chooses to hold the stock of capital $\bar{k}_t$, which yields the same return as the risk-free rate:

$$R = \frac{\bar{F}'(\bar{K}_t) + q_{t+1}}{q_t}.$$

As is standard, the productive-capital price evolves according to the difference equation:

$$q_t - \frac{1}{R} q_{t+1} = \frac{1}{R} \bar{F}'\left(\frac{\bar{K} - \eta K_t}{1 - \eta}\right).$$

The capital-market clearing condition is

$$\eta k_t + (1 - \eta)\bar{k}_t = \bar{K}.$$

To simplify notation, we denote by $M(k_t)$ the (discounted) marginal product:

$$\frac{1}{R} \bar{F}'\left(\frac{\bar{K} - \eta K_t}{1 - \eta}\right) = M(k_t).$$

As in the standard asset price equation, the asset price is the discount sum of present and future returns to capital:

$$q_t = \sum_{s=0}^{\infty} \frac{1}{R^s} M(k_{t+s}).$$

13.3.2 Dynamics

The steady-state productive asset price and the steady-state marginal productivity of capital must jointly satisfy the conditions

$$q^* - \frac{1}{R} q^* = a,$$

$$\frac{1}{R}\overline{F}'\left(\frac{\overline{K}-\eta K^*}{1-\eta}\right) = a.$$

Suppose now the economy is in the steady state in period $t-1$, but in period t there is an unexpected one-time shock that reduces production of all investors by the factor $1-\Delta$. The percentage change in the productive agents' asset holdings $\widehat{K}_t$ for a given percentage change in asset price $\widehat{q}_t$ is given by

$$\widehat{k}_t = -\frac{\xi}{1+\xi}\left(\Delta - \frac{R}{R-1}\widehat{q}_t\right),$$

where ξ denotes the elasticity asset supply with respect to the interest rate at the steady state. In the following periods, the percentage change in the productive agents' asset holdings, $\widehat{K}_{t+s}$, is

$$\widehat{k}_{t+s} = \frac{\xi}{1+\xi}\widehat{k}_{t+s-1}.$$

Thus, the shock in period t, which reduces the capital holdings of a productive investor, persists into the indefinite future.

The percentage change in asset price, $\widehat{q}_t$, is

$$\widehat{q}_t = \frac{\frac{1}{\xi}(R-1)}{R}\sum_{s=0}^{\infty}\frac{1}{R^s}\widehat{k}_{t+s}.$$

Similarly, the fall in the asset price continues many periods after the realization of the shock in period t.

The percentage changes as a function of the shock size:

$$\widehat{k}_t = -\left(1+\frac{1}{(1+\xi)(R-1)}\right)\Delta$$

$$\widehat{q}_t = -\frac{1}{\xi}\Delta.$$

Now, decompose the equilibrium changes in period t into a *static* part and a *dynamic* part. One can get

$$\widehat{K}_t = -\Delta - \frac{1}{(1+\xi)(R-1)}\Delta$$

$$\widehat{q}_t = -\frac{R-1}{R}\frac{1}{\xi}\Delta - \frac{1}{R}\frac{1}{\xi}\Delta.$$

The *static* part is the first term on the right-hand side of these expressions, and the *dynamic* part is the second term on the right-hand side of these expressions.

In sum, Kiyotaki and Moore (1997) were able to derive the entire time path (impulse responses). The short-run amplification effect of the shock is triggered by a reallocation of capital from the productive sector to the less productive sector. Capital holdings have to be sold at fire-sale prices to the investors in the less productive sector, which causes the price of capital to drop. The shock also causes future declines in asset prices and output.

13.4 Financial Intermediary and Panic-Based Equilibrium

This section addresses how financial intermediaries work to amplify real economy shocks in a dynamic-stochastic setup. There are two complementary approaches to incorporation of financial intermediaries: these concern the interactions between banking distress and the real economy. First, the moral hazard built into the incentive structure faced by a financial intermediary as a borrower needs to be explicitly recognized (Gertler and Kiyotaki 2011). Second, the balance-sheet problem associated with maturity mismatch of the financial intermediary, which triggers bank runs, needs to be addressed. Gertler and Kiyotaki (2013) introduce such a mechanism, which can trigger bank runs, to a dynamic general equilibrium macroeconomic framework. Their goal is to develop a simple macroeconomic model of banking instability that features both a financial accelerator and bank runs. The balance-sheet problem that underpins the effect known as *financial accelerator* is due to an agency problem. A bank's ability to attract funds depends on its own capital, as in Holmstrom and Tirole (1993). Contraction of bank capital raises the cost of bank credit, slows the economy, and depresses asset prices further. Maturity mismatch triggers bank runs because banks, as in Diamond and Dybvig (1983), hold imperfectly liquid assets but issue short-term debt, and there exists a bank run equilibrium.

13.4.1 Bank Runs
In Gertler and Kiyotaki (2013), there are two agents: households and a banker-entrepreneur. Each type is a continuum of measure unity. Bankers intermediate funds between households and productive assets.

There are two goods: capital, K, and consumption good, C. Capital can be held and managed by households, K^h, or by bankers, K^b:

$$K_t^b + K_t^h = \bar{K} = 1,$$

where $\bar{K}$ is total holding of capital (with a zero depreciation rate).

Capital held and managed by bankers in period t, K_t^b, yields $K_t^b Z_{t+1}$ units of output in terms of consumption goods in period $t + 1$, a linear production function with a stochastic productivity coefficient. Similarly, the capital managed by households serves as an input in a linear production function with stochastic productivity coefficient, Z_{t+1}. But, in the case of the household, there is an additional management cost, $f(K_t^h)$, in terms of the consumption good. The management cost function is strictly convex for low-intensity utilization of capital and is a linear segment for high utilization of capital, as follows:

$$f(K_t^h) = \begin{cases} \dfrac{\alpha}{2}(K_t^h)^2, & \text{for } K_t^h \leq \bar{K}^h \\[2mm] \alpha\bar{K}^h\left(K_t^h - \dfrac{\bar{K}^h}{2}\right), & \text{for } K_t^h > \bar{K}^h. \end{cases}$$

This formulation captures the role of financial intermediaries. They are key to management of the economy capital stock. When they fail, management of capital becomes inefficient.

13.4.2 The Household
Households choose whether to invest directly by managing capital or to save and deposit their savings in the banks. They maximize expected utility

$$U_t = E_t\left(\sum_{i=0}^{\infty} \beta^i \ln C_{t+i}^h\right)$$

subject to a sequential budget constraint

$$C_t^h + D_t + Q_t K_t^h + f(K_t^h) = Z_t W^h + R_t D_{t-1} + (Z_t + Q_t)K_{t-1}^h,$$

where β denotes the subjective discount factor, Q_t denotes the market price of capital, and D_t denotes the household bank deposits. Each household also receives an endowment of nondurable goods, Z_t, yielding income $Z_t W^h$ in period t.

Households' first-order maximization conditions are

$$E_t(\Lambda_{t,t+1}R_{t+1}) = 1$$

$$E_t(\Lambda_{t,t+1}R_{t+1}^h) = 1$$

$$\Lambda_{t,t+i} = \beta^i \frac{C_t^h}{C_{t+i}^h}$$

$$R_{t+1}^h = \frac{Z_{t+1} + Q_{t+1}}{Q_t + f'(K_t^h)},$$

where $\Lambda_{t,t+s}$ denotes the household's marginal rate of substitution between consumption in period $t + 1$ and t, and R_{t+1}^h denotes the household's return from direct capital holdings. Observe that as long as they hold at least some capital directly, households, along with banks, help determine the market price of capital; otherwise, only banks determine the market price. It turns out that if households hold capital directly in the range in which the management cost is quadratic, the market price of capital tends to be decreasing in the share of capital held by households. This feature of the model becomes important during a banking crisis where households withdraw their deposits from the banks and shift their savings to direct holding of capital. The severity of the drop in asset prices depends, then, on the convex segment of the management cost function.

13.4.3 The Banker-Entrepreneur

Banks finance their holding of capital by issuing deposits to households and by drawing on their own equity, n_t. Because of moral hazard, banks are constrained in their ability to attract deposits from the household. We assume that the bank utility function is linear. Their subjective discount factor is identical to that of households. Because of the differences between households and banks in marginal utility, the former will be creditors and the latter will be borrowers. To ease the burden of the financial-friction constraint, banks will have incentive to save by accumulating their earnings. Banks also have a finite expected lifetime. Each banker has survival probability σ each period. Banker-entrepreneurs consume only at the end of their lifetimes. Every period, a new banker enters, and the number of banks that enter is equal to the number of exiting banks, so that the total number of banks is constant over time. Exiting banks remove their equity in the bank, n_t, and spend it on consumption in the last minute of life. They are replaced by new bankers with an initial equity stake in the bank, w^b. That is, bankers who are risk neutral enjoy utility from consumption in the period they exit.

The bank value function, in a recursive representation, is $V_t = E_t[\beta(1 - \sigma)n_{t+1} + \beta\sigma V_{t+1}]$.

The banker's expected utility at the end of period t is

$$V_t = E_t\left[\sum_{i=1}^{\infty}\beta^i(1-\sigma)\sigma^{i-1}c_{t+i}^b\right].$$

During each period, banks finance their asset holdings with deposits and equity. Thus, the existing bank balance sheet in period t is $Q_t k_t^b = d_t + n_t$, and bank equity evolves as follows:

$$n_t = (Z_t + Q_t)k_{t-1}^b - R_t d_{t-1}.$$

The new banker in period t has a net worth, n_t, which is equal to the initial endowment, w^b. For new bankers in period t, we have

$$n_t = w^b.$$

Exiting banks use their bank equity to consume:

$$c_t^b = n_t.$$

There is a moral hazard problem for banks because at the end of the period, a banker can divert a fraction θ of assets for personal use, at the cost of bankruptcy in the beginning of the next period (as in Holmstrom and Tirole [1998]; see chapter 6). For households to be willing to finance bank operations by their deposits, it must be the case that the market value of the bank exceeds the gains to the bank from asset diversions:

$$\theta Q_t k_{t-1}^b \leq V_t.$$

Bank value, V_t, is maximized by choosing the banker capital holdings, k_t^b, and the deposit finance, d_t. The maximization is subject to the incentive compatibility constraint, $\theta Q_t k_{t-1}^b \leq V_t$, and the bank equity accumulation rule, $n_t = (Z_t + Q_t)k_{t-1}^b - R_t d_{t-1}$. The market-determined values Q_t and R_t are beyond the control of a banker and taken as given in the maximization.

The first-order conditions are typically forward looking. One can use the guess-and-verify method to solve for the recursive expression for the bank value function, which is

$$V_t = \mu_t Q_t k_t^b + v_t n_t,$$

where $\mu_t = (v_{kt}/Q_t) - v_t$ is interpreted as the marginal excess value of assets over deposits for an additional unit of k_t^b. Rewriting the incentive constraint as $\theta Q_t k_t^b \leq \mu_t Q_t k_t^b + v_t n_t$, it can be verified that the constraint is binding if and only if the marginal value from an additional unit of k_t^b, μ_t, if the bank does not divert assets, is positive, but smaller than the marginal gain from diverting assets, θ. Therefore, the incentive constraint leads to a limit of the leverage ratio,

$$\frac{Q_t k_t^b}{n_t} = \frac{v_t}{\theta - \mu_t}.$$

We denote by $\phi_t = Q_t k_t^b / n_t$ the maximum leverage ratio, which satisfies with strict equality the incentive constraint. As the bank issues more deposits, its incentive to divert funds increases. The maximum leverage ratio limits the portfolio size to the point where the incentive to divert the debt to private uses is balanced by the cost of losing the holdings of the bank.

Solving the recursive expression of holdings value, the marginal gain from asset management without diversion, μ_t, is the discounted excess return per unit of assets,

$$\mu_t = \beta E_t [(R_{t+1}^b - R_{t+1}) \Omega_{t+1}], \quad R_{t+1}^b = \frac{Z_{t+1} + Q_{t+1}}{Q_t}.$$

v_t is the discounted cost per unit of deposits,

$$v_t = \beta R_{t+1} E_t (\Omega_{t+1}),$$

where Ω_{t+1} is a (probability) weighted average of the future marginal value of the net worth of a bank:

$$\Omega_{t+1} \equiv 1 - \sigma + \sigma (v_{t+1} + \phi_{t+1} \mu_{t+1}).$$

When the incentive constraint is not binding, unlimited arbitrage by banks will make excess returns equal to zero, implying $\mu_t = 0$.

A financial crisis involves a sharp increase in excess returns on assets and a drop in asset prices. Note that in the above recursive relationship, excess return (endogenously determined), μ_t, depends on future excess return (endogenously determined), μ_{t+1}.

13.4.4 Market-Clearing Conditions
The total net worth of bankers is

$$N_t = \sigma[(Z_t + Q_t)K_{t-1}^h - R_t D_{t-1}] + (1 - \sigma)w^b,$$

where $(1 - \sigma)w^b$ is the total endowment of the entering banks.

Total assets held by the banking system are equal to holdings by the surviving and entering bankers. Total assets are also equal to total net worth times the leverage ratio in the banking system:

$$Q_t K_t^b = \phi_t N_t.$$

The total consumption of exiting bankers is

$$C_t^b = (1 - \sigma)[(Z_t + Q_t)K_{t-1}^h - R_t D_{t-1}].$$

The total output is the sum of output from capital, household endowments, and bank endowments.

The resource constraint is

$$Y_t = Z_t + Z_t W^h + W^b = f(K_t^h) + C_t^h + C_t^b.$$

Note that even though fluctuations in gross output, Y, are driven by productivity shocks only, fluctuations in net output, $Y - f(K^h)$, are driven by endogenous shifts in the stock of capital managed by households. During bank runs, households switch from depositing their saving in banks to holding and managing capital directly. Consequently, net output falls sharply.

13.4.5 Ex Post Bank Runs
As in Diamond and Dybvig (1983) (see chapter 5), an ex post bank run is possible if individual depositors believe that the other households will not roll over their deposits with the bank. The excess withdrawals of deposits cause the bank to fail. At each period before the realization of returns, households can decide to withdraw all their deposits, and banks have to liquidate capital. Households then acquire capital directly. To understand the mechanics of bank runs, consider a benchmark simple case in which bank runs are not expected when bank deposits are made in period $t - 1$; that is, households attach zero probability to the possibility of a run in period t.

A bank run occurs if the liquidation value of bank assets, $(Z_t + Q_t^*)K_{t-1}^b$, falls short of the bank's liabilities to the depositors, $R_t D_{t-1}$; that is,

$$(Z_t + Q_t^*)K_{t-1}^b < R_t D_{t-1}.$$

Bank runs depend, among other things, on the *liquidation* price of capital, Q_t^*. The liquidation price is determined as follows. Assume that once liquidated, the whole banking system collapses. The liquidation price is determined by an equilibrium where no bank exists, and thus households manage all capital. For simplicity, the no-bank equilibrium will exist indefinitely after the crisis; that is, $1 = K_{t+i}^h$ for all $i \geq 0$.

The liquidation price is

$$Q_t^* = E_t \left[\sum_{i=1}^{\infty} \Lambda_{t,t+i} (Z_{t+i} - \alpha \bar{K}^h) \right] - \alpha \bar{K}^h.$$

The condition that bank asset value, $(Z_t + Q_t^*)K_{t-1}^b$, falls short of the bank's liabilities to depositors, $R_t D_{t-1}$, is

$$R_t^{b*} \equiv \frac{Z_t + Q_t^*}{Q_{t-1}} < R_t \left(1 - \frac{1}{\phi_{t-1}} \right).$$

Namely, the rate of return on bank investment falls short of the rate the bank has to pay its depositors, adjusting for the bank leverage.

13.4.6   Probability of Bank Runs

To restore rational expectation in the model, assume that bank runs are anticipated when bank deposits are made.

In the event of a bank run, some but not all depositors will recover the principal and the interest. We attach a recovery probability based on the ratio between post-crisis bank assets and their liabilities. Accordingly, the probability is

$$x_{t+1} = \frac{(Q_{t+1}^* + Z_{t+1})k_t^b}{\bar{R}_{t+1} d_t}.$$

Denote by ι the fraction of the depositors who will be paid (the share). The deposit rate promised in period t for those who will be fully paid is derived as follows.

Assume that households in period t attach a probability x_{t+1} under the assumption that only a fraction of the depositors will be paid back, and all the rest will lose their entire deposits. In the case of no bank runs, the depositor gets what was promised to him or her in period t, $\bar{R}_{t+1}$,

$$\bar{R}_{t+1} = \frac{1 - E_t(\iota_{t+1}\Lambda^*_{t,t+1}R^{b*}_{t+1})^{\frac{\phi_t}{\phi_t-1}}}{E_t[(1-\iota_{t+1})\Lambda_{t,t+1}]}.$$

That is, the realized return to depositors depends on whether a run occurs, as well as on whether in the event of a run a depositor is paid back or not:

$$R_{t+1} = \begin{cases} \bar{R}_{t+1}, \text{No bank run} \\[2ex] \bar{R}_{t+1}, \text{prob} = x_{t+1} \\[2ex] 0, \text{ prob} = 1 - x_{t+1}. \end{cases}$$

The equilibrium risk-adjusted deposit rate can be solved from the depositor (intertemporal) condition

$$1 = \bar{R}_{t+1}E_t[(1-\iota_{t+1})\Lambda_{t,t+1} + \iota_{t+1}x_{t+1}\Lambda^*_{t,t+1}].$$

The return to holdings of capital by banks,

$$R^{b*}_t \equiv \frac{Z_t + Q^*_t}{Q_{t-1}} < R_t\left(1 - \frac{1}{\phi_{t-1}}\right),$$

is equal to the ratio of the dividends plus the crisis value to the no-crisis value of capital. We can define the leverage ratio as $\phi_t = v_t/\theta - \mu_t$.

An increase in the perceived probability of a bank run has harmful effects on the economy even if a bank run does not materialize. Because the deposit rate increases, bank net worth shrinks, contracting bank credit flows. In addition, an increase in the probability reduces the excess value of bank assets and pushes down the leverage ratio.

The spread between the deposit rate and the risk-free rate is soaring, but because the risk-free rate is driven down by the increasing managerial cost, the deposit rate actually goes down. The anticipation is still exogenous at the moment.

13.5 Concluding Remarks

Gertler and Kiyotaki (2013) develop a dynamic, stochastic, general equilibrium macroeconomic model that features both financial-accelerator effects and bank runs. Diamond and Dybvig (1983) previously showed that a bank run is possible if individual depositors believe that other households will not roll over their deposits with the bank, causing the bank to fail. Bank balance-sheet conditions affect not only the cost of bank credit but also whether runs are possible. Triggered by aggregate shocks in the real economy, causing severe deteriorations of macroeconomic conditions due to amplification effects through financial accelerators, bank asset value falls short of liabilities. The ensuing runs on banks feed back into the macroeconomy, causing a sharp decline in output.

Epilogue

Historical patterns of booms and busts typically exhibit frequent small recessions interrupted by rare but deep and long recessions. These patterns, however, have not been adequately captured by the traditional macroeconomic models. Traditional macroeconomic models, used often by central banks and many other policy-making institutions, are not capable of delivering crisis features in history: frequent small recessions punctuated by rare depressions. A major challenge to the macroeconomic research effort is to come to grips with the modeling failure and to offer empirically testable dynamic macromodels, which can combine interactions among the monetary, financial, and real sectors, consistent with the empirical regularities of business cycles.

Financial intermediaries, which have largely been omitted from the traditional macroeconomic framework, were treated simply like a "veil" that exists between savers and investors; not as a source of crisis by themselves. Financial frictions, however, have first-order effects on economic activity, both in the short and the long runs.

The major financial frictions that I highlight in this book, and for which I provide the analytical mechanisms that trigger crises or make their aftermath much worse, are coordination failures, incentive problems under asymmetric information, credit frictions, and contractual frictions. I have also highlighted the possible fragility of some caged-like monetary-fiscal arrangements, such as the single-currency area, fixed exchange rates, or an international gold standard.

Recent Crisis Literature

Several papers have identified important externalities that are associated with financial frictions. Stiglitz (1982) and Geanakoplos and Polemarchakis (1986) pointed to inefficiencies that are associated with incomplete markets in general equilibrium settings. In Lorenzoni (2008) and Jeanne and Korinek (2013), funding constraints depend on endogenously determined market prices. Although each individual takes market prices as given, they are endogenously determined by the collective actions of market participants. Hart and Zingales (2013) develop a general equilibrium framework for the study of the efficiency aspects of government intervention during the business cycle, when human capital is not pledgeable and cannot serve as collateral. They identify a fundamental economic inefficiency that justifies intervention (from an ex ante perspective).

A massive amount of intellectual effort has been invested recently in trying to integrate the literature on credit frictions into macroeconomic models in order to understand the effect that credit frictions have on macroeconomic fluctuations. Going back to Bernanke and Gertler (1989) and Kiyotaki and Moore (1997), economic theory has shown that credit frictions cause amplification and persistence of small economic shocks. Bernanke and Gertler (1989), Kiyotaki and Moore (1997), and Bernanke, Gertler, and Gilchrist (1999) analyze how financial frictions and temporary shocks have persistent effects on economic activity. Because temporary shocks affect the current net worth of borrowers, which determines their borrowing limit, and because net worth takes time to rebuild, these effects are persistent beyond the current period. Financial frictions can also lead to amplification because they trigger reallocation of capital from highly productive sectors, whose stock prices decline, into low-productivity sectors. Brunnermeier and Sannikov (2010) developed a continuous time model where they can pin down the location of the steady state endogenously. In previous literature (with log linear approximations around a deterministic steady state), the long-run equilibrium is exogenously determined, and shocks do not have permanent effects. Recently, Gertler and Kiyotaki (2011, 2013) and Rampini and Viswanathan (2011) add a financial-intermediary sector to macroeconomics modeling in order to analyze the dynamic interactions between this sector and the rest of the economy. Financial frictions with endogenously determined steady state imply that sizeable shocks can push the system away from the steady state into a crisis regime. The effects of post-crisis de-leveraging on output and their policy implications, in the presence of a liquidity-trapped interest rate, are analyzed by Eggertsson and Krugman (2012). Financial intermediation institutions, such as banks, with their exposure to risk and leverage cycles, are features that were also recently embedded into dynamic, stochastic, general-equilibrium analytical frameworks (e.g., Gertler and Kiyotaki 2013).

The role played by a central bank's inflation credibility in self-fulfilling debt crises has been studied by Calvo (1998) and Aguiar, Farhi, and Gopinath (2013). Extreme commitment to low inflation eliminates the option to inflate away the debt in a crisis. Such a strong commitment is equivalent to issuing foreign currency debt or joining a single-currency area, making the economy vulnerable to country-specific rollover risk because it has to default explicitly on its debt during a crisis. In contrast, a weak commitment to inflation renders the economy vulnerable to rollover risks if the government issues only domestic currency bonds. This flexibility to inflate away the debt, rather than to default explicitly on its debt, potentially reduces the country's exposure to self-fulfilling crises. But in tranquil times, inflation is relatively high. Therefore, an intermediate inflation credibility can achieve the proper balance between the country's exposure to rollover risk and costly inflation during tranquil times.

Expanding the Tool Kit of the Central Bank

Changing the composition of central bank assets between foreign and domestic assets (as in the case of sterilized foreign exchange rate market interventions) can have real economic effects in the presence of liquidity shortages.

It is well known that if there is perfect asset substitutability between foreign and domestic assets, the money supply can fully adjust to bring expected rates of return on domestic and foreign currency bonds into equilibrium, as in the standard interest parity. Sterilized foreign-exchange-market intervention by the monetary authorities, where the domestic money supply is unchanged, is incapable of pushing the exchange rate up or down. However, the proposition may change in the presence of imperfect asset substitutability, where domestic and foreign bonds command a different liquidity premium. In this case, sterilized foreign-exchange-market intervention could effectively change the value of the foreign currency in terms of domestic currency. A sterilized purchase of foreign assets may change the liquidity premium that domestic bonds command, relative to foreign bonds, even though the money supply is left unchanged. A similar outcome may result when foreign exchange intervention changes market views of future foreign-exchange-market interventions.[1]

Similarly, liquidity-based imperfect asset substitution between domestic government and domestic private-sector bonds during liquidity crises can be exploited by the central bank.[2]

Recently, Mian and Sufi (2014) argued that the policy response to the 2008 financial crisis focused too much on banks while neglecting over-indebted homeowners. The deterioration of the household balance sheet was the proximate dominant cause in the fall of consumption, the main component of aggregate demand, thus prolonging the Great Recession that followed the financial crisis. Mian and Sufi suggest that the policy package needs to focus on mortgage relief.

Dynamic Policy Issues

Currently, dynamic general equilibrium models are still unable to address some key policy questions:

1. How should monetary authorities guarantee financial stability? One means is assuming the lender-of-last-resort function, as advocated by Bagehot in the nineteenth century.[3] That is, during periods of financial panic, the central bank can provide liquidity to ease the panic.[4]
2. If inflation expectations are low, aggregate-demand cum aggregate-supply management points to low interest rates. But low rates may reinforce the asset-price bubble. How should monetary policies address warning signals from the rising asset prices, especially housing prices, in the presence of low economic activity?
3. When the risk of contagion in the markets is large, in the immediate aftermath of the collapse of too-big-to-fail banks, how should policy makers extend assistance to the rest of the financial system so as not to exacerbate moral hazard behavior by the financial system because it expects to be bailed out in major downturns?
4. In a depressed economy, when should the fiscal authority begin a process of reduction of debt that was inflated during the period of low economic activity? Furthermore, how soon to begin fiscal austerity to tackle demographically based unfunded liabilities of the government?
5. When should the monetary authority begin a monetary policy of substantial tightening for an economy that is recovering from a financial crisis?

During monetary conditions where short-run interest rates approach zero, the monetary transmission mechanism is broken, prices are stable, and the labor market is weak, the central bank typically uses nonconventional monetary measures, such as buying long-term government bonds and corporate bonds. The consequences of premature tightening are a rise in the yield of the bonds of highly rated governments. A rise in yields on long-term bonds may lead to rising long-term borrowing costs for the private sector.[5]

Significant progress has been made by recent research on the transmission of money to the real economy, through the friction-prone financial intermediary sector, and also by research on the effects of fiscal policy in the presence of financial frictions. Yet, a dynamic general equilibrium theory of crises that would be useful for policy guidance remains in a developmental stage.

The book surveys the development of the late twentieth- and early twenty-first-century macroeconomic analytical framework from the pre-2008 paradigm of modern macroeconomic thinking, which served as the workhorse of policy making. The pre-2008 crisis paradigm provided the theoretical backbone for the conduct of monetary policy during the Great Moderation period. The financial crisis triggered new thinking, especially in the area of macroeconomics. A new paradigm is emerging.

Notes

Preface

1. David Romer (2013) counts six episodes in the United States during the past 30 years where serious financial turmoil posed grave macroeconomic risks: some of the adverse consequences were avoided and others not. (1) Paul Volcker disinflation in combination with severe recession and bank exposure to Latin American debt caused many major banks to be in serious trouble. (2) The 1987 stock market crash was a significant financial shock. (3) The savings and loan crisis of the late 1980s and early 1990s did some damage to the economy through misallocation of investment and impaired lending and somewhat more damage to the government budget through the direct costs of the bailout. (4) The Russian debt crisis and the collapse of Long-Term Capital Management in 1998 created the instability of the world financial system. (5) The dot-com bubble and bust of the late 1990s and early 2000s caused a considerable misallocation of investment and a short-term recession. (6) The housing-price collapse and financial meltdown in 2007–2008, which led to the Great Recession.

Chapter 1

1. Bernanke conjectured that China and other Asian nations amassed huge foreign currency reserves after 1998 to protect themselves against capital flight, causing them to become lenders to the rest of the world.

2. Figure 1.1 tracks world industrial production from June 1929, the start of the Great Depression, and compares it to a corresponding track starting from April 2008, the beginning of the Great Recession. It appears that the tracks of the Great Depression and the Great Recession follow similar patterns in the first 12 months after the initial shock, indicating roughly similar initial financial shock in both cases in terms of intensity and global effects.

3. The term *divine coincidence* refers to a situation where stabilizing inflation is the same as stabilizing output in the medium and long runs. In the theoretical New Keynesian Dynamic Stochastic General Equilibrium (DSGE) models with representative agents, there is no difference in the real side of the macroeconomic equilibrium, and its representative household welfare, between a single mandate (i.e., managing inflation) and a dual mandate (i.e., jointly managing inflation and employment) of the central bank.

Chapter 2

1. This chapter is based on Razin and Rosefielde (2011).

2. *Derivative* is a generic term for swaps, futures, options, and composites that do not have any intrinsic value (proprietary claims to interest, dividends, or asset appreciation), their worth depending derivatively on promises to acquire, sell, swap, and insure securities not yet owned. They take many forms including equity, foreign exchange, interest, commodity, credit (credit default swaps [CDSs]), mortgage-backed, and packaged derivatives. Simple, or common, derivatives are called "vanilla"; more complex instruments are dubbed "exotic." Their primary purposes are leveraging and hedging risk (e.g., traditional short sales) for personal portfolio management or speculation, but this has broadened into "shadow banking," where large institutions use derivative instruments to manage their financial operations. They serve legitimate business purposes, but also facilitate arbitrage as a business in itself (hedging business) and leveraged speculation (including gambling with other people's money; e.g., Nick Leeson and the Barings Bank fiasco). All are traded either on exchanges or over-the-counter and bear "counterparty" risk as well as security risk because "promises" can be broken. "Performance" risk is another seldom considered problem, because even if promises are kept, ownership rights to the assets underlying derivatives like mortgage-backed securities are often obscure and unenforceable. According to the Bank for International Settlements, the total notional worth of derivatives worldwide was $684 trillion in June 2008.

3. Dooley, Folkerts-Landau, and Garber (2003) contend that the periphery undervalues its currency to foster export-led growth in order to facilitate the rural to urban employment process and to enable technology transfer from the center, causing embedded trade and financial flow imbalances (cf. Eichengreen 2004).

4. Bloomberg, Real Estate Economic Institute, Japan, Home Price Indices, as of March 18, 2009.

5. Westerners once knew this but have forgotten; see Benedict (1946).

6. A hyperdepression is any depression greater than the great American depression of 1929; see Maddison (2003b, 298).

7. Caballero, Hoshi, and Kashyap (2006) contend the zombie banks crowd the market and the resulting congestion has real effects on the healthy firms in the country. They find the cumulative distortionary impact of investment and employment to be substantial (cf. Akiyoshi and Kobayashi 2008). For a detailed historical review of the Japanese banking crisis, see Kanaya and Woo (2000).

8. The authors find that small, undercapitalized firms were the primary victims of the credit crunch. These firms contribute little to Japanese productivity growth, undercutting the claim that the financial crisis caused Japan's two lost decades.

9. Paul Krugman contends that after Japan's bubble burst, savings rose (consumption collapsed), the natural interest rate (needed for full employment general equilibrium) turned negative, and the money interest rate reached the lower bound of zero, rendering monetary policy impotent. The actual real interest rate immediately after the crash and for decades to come often was slightly positive, the combined effect of modestly falling prices (due partly to collapsed demand and retail liberalization in an otherwise *keiretsu* [financial conglomerate] price-fixed environment) and a zero money interest rate. This created a small Keynesian output gap (albeit with negligible unemployment) that was addressed with fiscal deficit spending, but it is still possible to argue that deflation and

a liquidity trap kept, and still keeps, Japan's GDP and employment below its full competitive potential. Krugman (2010a, 2010b) contends that Japan's liquidity trap was the first manifested since the Great Depression and sends a signal to monetary authorities like Ben Bernanke to be alert to the danger. He recommends that Japan's and America's output gaps should be closed with quantitative easing (central bank purchase of medium- and long-term government securities) and inflationary expectations nurtured through a Phillip's mechanism. The suggestion is sound in principle (albeit controversial) for contemporary America. Japan's institutions prevent its economy from attaining natural output levels. There may be a gap between Japan's achieved and potential institutionally constrained GDP, but it is impossible to measure these gaps reliably (see Krugman 1998a, 2010a, 2010b; cf. Aoki and Saxonhouse 2000; Stiglitz 2010).

10. It is unclear whether Krugman (2010) ascribes Japan's second lost decade, 2000–2010, to a liquidity trap.

11. The graying of the population means that with low fertility rates and high longevity rates, the ratio of retired people to working-age people is increasing. Japan's population growth had slowed noticeably by 1990 and was still positive when its financial crisis hit. Deaths first began exceeding births in 2007, and the trend will not be swiftly reversed. Demographers are currently forecasting that more than one in three Japanese will be over age 65 in 2055, with the working-age cohort falling by more than a third, to 52 million. Immigration could alleviate the pressure, but the Japanese are resolutely opposed to it because of unvoiced fears of being inundated by the Chinese. The long-term demographic prospect for China, including the possibility for expanded immigration, mimics the Japanese pattern because of Deng Xiaoping's one child per family policy and xenophobia (see Eberstadt 2007, 2010).

12. Rajan and Zingales (1998b) contend that "hot" money in Asia is white hot, because in the absence of the rule of contract law, in a relationship-based culture, short-term foreign investors are especially wary.

13. Argentina's money supply contracted sharply because constitutionally its money base was tied peso for peso to its foreign reserves, which wreaked havoc on business activity when hot money fled the country under its fixed foreign exchange regime.

14. Hong Kong's currency board, however, was successfully defended by massive foreign reserve sales and purchases of private equities.

15. *Crony capitalism* is a vague term often used to describe market economies, especially in the Third World, where business depends heavily on patronage in closed, privileged networks of officials, relatives, and friends that thrive even though under other circumstances their companies would fail the competitive test. These systems are considered morally hazardous, corrupt, inefficient, and ripe for disaster (see Pempel 1999).

16. The term *Washington Consensus* was coined by John Williamson in 1989 to describe 10 standard reforms advocated in Washington, D.C., for ameliorating crises and promoting sustainable growth in developing countries. These reforms include fiscal discipline, structural investments (in education, etc.), tax rationalization, market-determined interest rates, competitive exchange rates, trade liberalization, privatization, deregulation, and rule of law (see Blustein 2001; Williamson 2002).

17. Stiglitz (2011) argues that controls can dampen the destabilizing effects of productive and financial regional and global integration; see also Lee and Jang (2010).

18. The only thing that really links Russia's 1998 financial crisis to Asia's is the demonstration effect. When the Asian bubble burst in July 1997, Europeans started to reassess

Russia's creditworthiness, after being assured by Anders Aslund, the IMF, World Bank, and the G-7 that Russia had become a "capitalist market economy" on the road to recovery. The real story is that Yeltsin officials, after scamming their own people innumerable times including the infamous 1996 "Loan for Shares" swindle of the millennium, began a massive issue of GKOs (*Gosudarstvennoye Kratsrochoye Obyazatel'stvo* ["government short-term obligations"]) designed to entice foreign hot money by paying 150 percent interest, at a time when Russia could not cover its budgetary expenses with tax revenues hopelessly in arrears. Yeltsin insiders knew that the obligations could not be met, but also saw opportunities for self-enrichment and played the situation that way. They secured a $22.6 billion IMF rescue package on July 13, 1998, swapping GKOs for long-term Eurobonds to string the process out, before finally repudiating their GKO and euro-denominated obligations, and abruptly devaluing on August 17, 1998. In the Asian case, foreign capital fled because private sector risks had increased. By contrast in the Russian case, foreign capital fled because carry traders realized that the Russian government was intent on ripping them off. The only question was when, not if, the Kremlin would strike (see Aslund 1995; Goldman 2003; Rosefielde and Hedlund 2009).

Chapter 3

1. This chapter is based on Razin and Rosefielde (2012).

2. The term refers to situations where stabilizing inflation is the same as stabilizing output.

3. Bernanke, Bertaut, DeMarco, and Kamin (2011) have provided convincing evidence that foreign investors during the 2000s preferred what they perceived to be safe American financial assets, particularly U.S. treasuries and agency-sponsored collateralized debt obligations. Although European foreign trade surpluses were smaller than China's, they leveraged their balance sheets, issuing large volumes of external dollar liabilities to finance purchases of U.S. mortgage-based securities, stoking the American housing bubble (see Bernanke et al. 2011).

4. Subprime mortgages involved loans to people likely to encounter difficulty maintaining their repayment schedules. ARMs allowed homeowners to borrow inexpensively, but obligated them to pay more if interest rates rose. Additionally, during the new millennium it was common for banks to waive down payments, enabling "owners" to walk away from their properties when housing prices (and values) fell, leaving banks with a huge inventory of bankruptcy repossessions and distressed sales. The Clinton administration pushed subprime lending. The value of U.S. subprime mortgages in 2007 was $1.3 trillion. In an inflationary environment, driven in part by people borrowing from their home's inflationary premium, home buying was transformed into a speculative game. The ratio of global liquidity to global GDP quadrupled in the period 1980–2007; doubling in the period 2000–2007. Cross-border capital flows increased by a factor of 10 in the period 1990–2007 from $1.1 trillion to $11.2 trillion. Derivatives rose from virtually zero in 1990 to $684 trillion in 2007. American nonfinancial debt outpaced GDP growth since 2007 by $8 trillion (see Mills 2009, 51). There is controversy about whether it is credit supply versus credit demand that posed the binding constraint in various crises. While in theory, regulations (such as on-capital requirements) would cause credit supply to fall after a shock to capital, there is also regulatory forbearance that attenuates this factor. In the global financial crisis, and in particular in Europe, this regulatory forbearance played an important role. As a consequence of the shift out of money markets investing in asset-backed commercial paper, the market for asset-backed commercial

paper and hence financing of those relying on commercial paper dried up. Corporates then turned to bank lines, perversely causing bank credit to increase in the initial stages of the global financial crisis, which banks then sought to wind down.

5. The dot-com bubble began shortly after Federal Reserve chairman Alan Greenspan's "irrational exuberance" speech on December 5, 1996. For proof that dot-com stocks were grossly overvalued, see Delong and Magin (2006). The NASDAQ composite index peaked at 5,132.52 on March 10, 2000, and bottomed at 1,108.49 on October 10, 2002. The Enron accounting scam, tied to energy deregulation and lax accounting by Arthur Anderson, also contributed to the slaughter.

6. Nobel Prize laureates Myron Scholes and Robert Merton, famous for devising a new method for valuing derivatives, were members of Long-Term Capital Management's board of directors.

7. Richard Bowen III testified to the Financial Crisis Inquiry Commission that mortgage underwriting standards collapsed in the final years of the U.S. housing bubble (2006–2007). Sixty percent of mortgages purchased by Citicorp from some 1,600 mortgage companies were defective. Clayton Holdings reported in parallel testimony that only 54 percent of mortgage loans met their originators' underwriting standards.

8. Jack Boogle, founder of Vanguard Group, privately estimated that $40 trillion of the $41 trillion traded on world stock exchanges in year 2009 was speculative. The institutional share of American stock market investment has risen in the past two decades from 8 percent to 70 percent.

9. American housing prices peaked in early 2005, and the Case-Shiller home price index began falling in 2006. Prices plunged 34 percent thereafter, bottoming in 2009, and are expected to continue declining in 2011 despite more than a trillion dollars of government support. On December 24, 2009, the Treasury Department pledged unlimited support for the next 3 years to Fannie Mae and Freddie Mac, despite $400 billion in losses. The bubble was predicted by Robert Shiller in 2000; see Shiller (2000), *Irrational Exuberance*, and Shiller (2008), *The Subprime Solution: How Today's Global Financial Crisis Happened, and What to Do About It*. As early as 1997, Federal Reserve chairman Alan Greenspan fought to keep derivatives unregulated, a goal codified in the Commodity Futures Modernization Act of 2000. Derivatives such as credit default swaps (CDSs) were used to hedge or speculate against particular credit risks. Their volume increased 100-fold in the period 1998–2008, with estimates of the debt ranging as high as $47 trillion. Total over-the-counter derivative notional value rose to $683 trillion by June 2008. Warren Buffet described the phenomenon as "financial weapons of mass destruction" (*The Economist*, September 18, 2008).

10. Debt obligations issued by nation-states are called *sovereign debt*. Superficially, it might be supposed that sovereign bonds are more secure than their corporate equivalents, but the reverse often is the case because under the doctrine of sovereign immunity, countries cannot be forced to honor their obligations. Creditors' only recourse is passively to accept rescheduling, interest reductions, or even repudiation (see Eaton and Fernandez 1995). Sovereign debt initially played a subsidiary role in the 2008 financial crisis. The collapse of Iceland's main banks and 77 percent stock market plunge in September 2008 prompted ratings agencies to cut Iceland's sovereign debt rating drastically from AAA to BBB. The IMF arranged a rescue package on November 19, 2008, but the cat was out of the bag. Suddenly, investors became aware that the scope of the global financial crisis might be much wider than earlier supposed, raising the specter of a worldwide financial collapse that did not disappear until March 2009. Nonetheless,

sovereign debt fears reemerged in 2010 due to credit rating reductions for Greek, Irish, Portuguese, and Spanish sovereign debt that forced the European Union to intervene in defense of these members. The rescue involved loans for conditionality, where credit-impaired sovereigns were compelled to pledge the adoption of austerity measures reducing their structural deficits. The problem expanded later to include Ireland, Spain, Italy, and others. Additionally, many worry that if rating cuts contingent on budgetary debt reductions do not cease, it could force the European Union to abandon the euro as a common currency, and even result in the EU's dissolution.

11. Morici contends that Congress and the White House made no compromise whatsoever in extending and expanding the Bush tax cuts, including a temporary 33 percent cut in poor and middle-class social security taxes, ballooning the federal deficit to $1.5 trillion in 2011; to say nothing of off-budget deficits 10 times as large.

12. Bear Stearns, founded in 1923, had survived the 1929 Wall Street crash and achieved celebrity status in the new millennium because of Lewis Ranieri's pioneering innovation of the mortgage-backed securitization business. Its problems became public in June 2007 when the company pledged a $3.2 billion collateralized loan (collateralized debt obligation; CDO) to rescue one of its hedge funds. CDOs were thinly traded, and when Bear Stearns encountered liquidity problems, Merrill Lynch seized $850 million worth, but only realized $100 million in forced liquidation. During the week of July 16, 2007, Bear Stearns acknowledged that its two CDO-supported hedge funds had lost nearly all their value amid a rapid decline in the subprime mortgages market. On March 14, 2008, the Federal Reserve Bank of New York agreed to grant Bear Stearns a $25 billion loan collateralized by free and clear assets from Bear Stearns in order to provide liquidity for 28 days. The deal, however, was changed two days later into a forced bailout when the Federal Reserve decided that the loan would be given to Bear Stearns's shotgun bride, J.P. Morgan, enticed into the marriage by a $35 billion nonrecourse Federal Reserve loan. The action approved by Ben Bernanke, putting public money at risk, was justified by the necessity of preventing systemic failure and forestalling the need for further intervention.

13. The Dow Jones Industrial Average peaked October 9, 2007, at 14,164 and bottomed March 9, 2008, at 6,470. In early September 2008, it traded around 11,500, just where it stood at the end of 2010.

14. Lending institutions were abruptly required to write their illiquid mortgage assets down to rapidly falling current values, forcing them to sell securities to raise capital and generating a vicious downward credit spiral.

15. Both firms were subsequently delisted from the New York Stock Exchange in June 2010 because their share prices fell below $1.

16. According to Alan Blinder and Mark Zandi (2010), the breakdown of the American $1 trillion countercrisis fiscal stimulus package is divisible into two baskets: spending increases ($682 billion) and tax cuts ($383 billion). The Economic Stimulus Act of 2008 spent $170 billion. The American Recovery and Reinvestment Act of 2009 disbursed another $582 billion on infrastructure ($147 billion; including $109 billion for "nontraditional" infrastructure); transfers to state and local governments ($174 billion: Medicaid $87 billion, education $87 billion), transfers to persons ($271 billion: social security $13 billion, unemployment assistance $224 billion, food stamps $10 billion, and COBRA payments $24 billion). Tax cuts under the 2009 act totaled $190 billion, allocated to businesses ($40 billion), making work pay ($64 billion), first-time home buyer tax credit ($14 billion), and individuals ($72 billion). Subsequently, the government also provided $55 billion of

extended unemployment insurance benefits. More than 90 percent of the stimulus was targeted at bolstering aggregate effective demand through transfers and tax rebates in the post-1960s Heller fashion, rather than in direct investment assistance (traditional infrastructure, business tax credits, and first-time home buyer credits) as Keynes himself recommended.

17. Bernard Madoff, non-executive chairman of NASDAQ and founder of Bernard L. Madoff Investment Securities, LLC, was sentenced to 150 years' imprisonment and forfeiture of $17 billion for a Ponzi scheme fraud costing investors $10 billion to $20 billion, which was exposed by the 2008 financial crisis. Robert Stanford, chairman of the Stanford Financial Group, was charged with a similar fraud. His trial took place in 2012.

18. The Dodd-Frank Act contains 16 titles, strewn with prohibitions, rules, and rate fixing. It is difficult to render a summary judgment, but it has been criticized for not addressing the too-big-to-fail issue and indulging political goals at the expense of regulatory goals.

19. A study by the Federal Reserve Bank of St. Louis comes to the conclusion that affordable housing requirements played a negligible role. Available at http://research .stlouisfed.org/conferences/gse/Van_Order.pdf. This study also shows how private label securitization gained market share at the expense of the agencies. Competition from private labels did cause the agencies to take more risk, which resulted in the large losses and conservatorship, but at a late stage of the game (2005–2006), hence the conclusion that government mandates on the agencies were not the cause of the expansion of subprime lending.

20. The figure includes unfunded social security obligations.

21. "The Perfect Bailout: Fannie and Freddie Now Directly to Wall Street," Yahoo! Finance, February 2, 2011. U.S. Treasury secretary Tim Geithner provided Fannie Mae and Freddie Mac with as much credit as they needed to purchase toxic mortgages held by banks at prices that will not produce book losses. This amounts to a stealthy taxpayer-funded bailout, giving a green light to all parties to repeat the reckless lending that caused the 2008 financial crisis, confident that they will reap the gains and taxpayer will eat the losses.

22. Wallison and Pinto (2012) contend that the Dodd-Frank Act allows the administration to substitute the Federal Housing Administration (FHA) for Fannie Mae and Freddie Mac as the principal and essentially unlimited provider of subprime mortgages at taxpayers' expense. Since the 2008 government takeover of Fannie Mae and Freddie Mac, the regulator of these government-sponsored enterprises has restricted them to purchase of high-quality mortgages, with affordable housing requirements mandated in 1992 relaxed. This reduces the future risk, but the good is entirely negated by shunting the old destructive practices to the FHA on the pretext of supporting the soundness of the entire mortgage industry. The gambit, in the usual way, allows the administration to present a prudent face with regard to Fannie Mae and Freddie Mac, while diverting attention from the $400 billion loss previously racked up by Fannie Mae and Freddie Mac, and recklessly reprising the Housing and Urban Development Administration's (HUD) prior destructive policies. Wallison, Pollock, and Pinto (2011) report that the U.S. government sponsored 27 million subprime policies. To correct the situation, they recommend that the government get out of the housing finance business. Government regulation should be restricted to ensuring mortgage credit quality. Assistance to low-income families should be on-budget. Fannie Mae and Freddie Mac should be privatized.

Chapter 4

1. This chapter is based on Razin and Rosefielde (2012).

2. European Financial Stability and Integration Report 2010, European Commission, Economic Staff Working Paper, Brussels, April 11, 2011.

3. The GIIPS group should also include Cyprus, whose GDP is a mere 0.2 percent of the euro zone economy, but it had an oversized banking sector due to its tax havens. Cyprus banks were teetering and the sovereign debt bank failure loop accelerating as a result of contagion from Greece.

4. Kaiser and Starie (2009).

5. The term *supranational community* was coined by Jean Monnett, head of France's General Planning Commission.

6. The members of CMEA were the Soviet Union, Poland, East Germany, Hungary, Czechoslovakia, Romania, Bulgaria, Cuba, Vietnam, and Mongolia.

7. The supranational entitlement and moral hazard problem mirrors domestic disorders often said to cause euro-sclerosis, but is potentially more pernicious because governments can borrow more than individuals.

8. See Daniel Gros and Niels Thygesen (1999), *European Monetary Integration*: After the demise of the Bretton Woods system in 1971, most European Economic Community (EEC) members agreed to maintain stable foreign exchange rate parities. Fluctuations were restricted to no more than 2.25 percent (the European "currency snake"). The system was replaced by the European Monetary System (EMS), and the European Currency Unit (ECU) was defined. It fixed parities, set an exchange rate mechanism (ERM), extended European credit facilities, and created a European Monetary Cooperation Fund that allocated the ECU to member central banks in exchange for gold and U.S. dollar deposits. The German deutschemark was the de facto anchor because of its relative strength and the country's low-inflation policies. In the early 1990s, the EMS was strained by conflicting macroeconomic policies in Germany and England. England and Italy withdrew in 1992. Speculative attacks on the French franc led to widening the band to 15 percent in August 1993.

9. See Mundell (1961), McKinnon (1963), Kenen (1967), and De Grauwe (2000, 2010).

10. The same argument holds for North America. Canada's economy has performed well without forging a monetary union with the United States.

11. Mundell (1963).

12. A *tri-lemma* is a situation in which someone faces a choice among three options, each of which comes with some inevitable problems, so that not all the three underlying policy objectives can be simultaneously accomplished. In international finance, the tri-lemma stems from the fact that, in most nations, economic policy makers would like to achieve the following goals.

First, make the country's economy open to international capital flows, because by doing so, policy makers of a country enable foreign investors to diversify their portfolios overseas and achieve risk sharing. The country also benefits from the expertise brought to the country by foreign investors. Second, use monetary policy as a tool to help stabilize inflation, output, and the financial sector in the economy. This is achieved as the central bank can increase the money supply and reduce interest rates when the economy is depressed and reduce money growth and raise interest rates when it is overheated. Moreover, the central bank can serve as a lender of last resort in case of financial panic. Third, maintain stability in the exchange rate. This is because a volatile exchange rate, at times driven by speculation, can be a source of broader financial volatility and makes it harder for households and businesses to trade in the world economy and for investors to plan for the future. The problem, however, is that a country can only achieve adequately two of these three goals. By attempting to maintain a fixed exchange rate and capital mobility, the central bank loses its ability to control the interest rate or equivalently the monetary base—its policy instruments—as the interest rate becomes anchored to the world interest rate by the interest rate parity, and the monetary base is automatically adjusted. This is the case of individual members of the EMU. In order to keep control over the interest rate or equivalently the money supply, the central bank has to let the exchange rate float freely, as in the case of the United States. The tri-lemma here involves favorable options, but picking any two precludes acquiring the third. There is an important distinction between a problem and a tri-lemma. A problem has a solution, while a tri-lemma is a constraint that must be continually managed.

13. The ECB sets euro-zone-wide interest rates, but if these rates are inappropriate for distressed economies like Greece, Athens lacks an independent currency to remedy the problem. Likewise it has no national central bank to act as "lender of last resort." The ECB cannot act as a lender of last resort for Greek banks because it does not easily get a mandate from its board to do so for political reasons and because regulation of banks and deposit insurance is mostly in the hands of national authorities.

14. Not all "internal depreciations" are intolerable. The reunification of East and West Germany provides a relatively painless example. Germany held wages down and increased productivity to alleviate unemployment and cope with income transfers flowing to the former Communist East.

15. Greece paid Goldman $300 million to help it hide its ballooning debts, according to http://www.businessinsider.com/henry-blodget (February 2010).

16. The Cyprus financial crisis is a case in point. In March 2013, Cyprus was forced to temporarily keep its banks shut as it tried to find a way out of the banking crisis. If it failed to convince the euro zone that it had a viable alternative to bailing-in depositors (making depositors share in the losses), then the ECB could have decided that Cypriot banks were no longer eligible for the euro system's emergency loans, known as Emergency Liquidity Assistance (ELA), which is now the only thing keeping the island's banks afloat. Without the euro-zone bailout provision of liquidity, Cyprus had no central bank to prop up its banks like a non-euro-zone country does. So, Cyprus could have become an economy with no money or it would have had to exit the EMU and start printing its own currency to keep its banking system running. After the bailout, Cyprus is on the verge of an unprecedented financial experiment: imposing controls on money transfers in an economy that doesn't have its own currency. This is consistent with the international finance tri-lemma: Pre-crisis Cyprus chose a fixed exchange rate, free capital mobility, and no monetary independence; afterward, Cyprus was forced to have capital controls and a fixed exchange rate potentially to stabilize the economy through the provision of a liquidity channel.

17. De Grauwe (2011).

18. The new Greek bonds issued to the banks would have long maturities of up to 30 years and low interest rates according to the Institute of International Finance, the group

representing private sector creditors. French president Nicolas Sarkozy estimated that the rates would average 4.5 percent.

19. Miguel Kiguel (2011), "Argentina and Greece: More Similarities than Differences in the Initial Conditions." Argentina, like Greece, was confronted with a conundrum. It sought to restore access to the international capital market (sovereign debt problem) by raising taxes and cutting public expenditures to pay down its indebtedness . But, in doing so it risked making repayment more difficult by plunging the economy into a deep depression. Kiguel argues that Argentina's budget cutting had precisely this adverse effect and cautions the EU accordingly. His preferred solution is to hold the line on deficit spending insofar as possible and promote productivity and competition with nondeflationary tactics. Another complementary approach that he fails to consider is steamrolling vested political interests, streamlining government services, and earmarking savings for debt repayment. The structural similarities between Argentina and Greece that guide Kiguel's recommendation are (1) loss of devaluation option (currency board and dollarization in the Argentinian case; replacement of the drachma with the euro in the Greek case), (2) loss of access to the international capital market (excess sovereign debt), and (3) loss of monetary options due to dollar/euro-ization. On the policy front, both Argentina and Greece tried to acquire external assistance and ultimately failed to obtain enough. They also resorted to deflation to spur competitiveness but here too were unsuccessful.

20. Obstfeld (2013) claims that "Consideration of financial stability needs does, however, add a powerful extra argument (mentioned earlier) for constraining governments to avoid large debts. In a banking union, the credibility of the communal fiscal backstop depends on all members maintaining sufficient fiscal space. Absent strong fiscal norms, there would be a tendency for each individual country to free ride on the fiscal strength of its partners."

21. Unlike the EMU, the U.S. single-currency area came after the establishment of a political and fiscal union. Alexander Hamilton (1757–1804), who served in President George Washington's cabinet as secretary of the Treasury from 1789 to 1795, executed a program of fiscal integration among the states of the newly independent United States. The new Congress under the Constitution, granting taxing powers to pass on the federal level, enabled Hamilton to formulate and execute a plan for establishing federal-level public credit to service the national debt. The assumption of state debts, and the ability to service foreign debts, enabled the United States to take out new loans in the foreign capital markets. Together with the debt restructuring program, Congress chartered a national bank, issuing the dollar currency as the legal tender in all states.

22. Kantor (2012). Spanish and Irish banks won't receive direct aid from the new European bailout fund.

23. Sargent (2012).

24. The EU sovereign debt crisis is emblematic, not unique. The union's energy policy, which requires the unanimous agreement of 27 members, is similarly in disarray. The consensus strategy is window dressing and a reference point for devising schemes to beat the program. The rhetoric is a united vision; the reality is 27 independent strategies to exploit the vision. See Scott (2012).

25. The GIIPS countries have been forced to introduce severe austerity programs since 2011. In an interesting study, De Grauwe and Ji (2012) ask the question: Where did the forces that led these countries into austerity come from? Are these forces the result of deteriorating economic fundamentals (e.g., the increase in the debt to output ratio) or

were the austerity dynamics forced by fear and panic that erupted in the financial markets and then gripped policy makers. They claim that the evidence supports the second hypothesis.

26. The euro zone is currently on a path converging toward banking union: a union that covers all major banks and which includes resolution powers in case of bankruptcy, deposit insurance, and regulation of financial services. The ECB, through the 2012 Outright Monetary Transactions policy, an unlimited government bond-buying scheme subject to EU oversight of the borrower budget, supported the progress made by governments in agreeing to reinforce monetary union with greater fiscal union and banking union.

27. Bordo and James (2013) argue that there is also an incompatibility of fixed exchange rates and capital mobility with financial stability. When countries joined the gold standard, it bestowed a seal of approval that prompted a big influx of foreign money. That pumped up credit, driving an expansion of domestic banks that often ended in grief. Under the gold standard, a strong state could support wobbly banks and investors; in pre-war Russia, for example, the central bank was called the "Red Cross of the bourse." But a weak state could easily forfeit investors' confidence, as happened to Argentina in its 1980 debt-and-banking crisis. That same story has been repeated in the brief history of the euro. Money cascaded into peripheral Europe, causing banking booms and housing bubbles. In the bust that followed, the task of recapitalizing banks has caused both the Irish and Spanish states to buckle.

Part II

1. Chapter 8 reviews the analytics of currency crises, and chapter 11 reviews the analytics of the liquidity trap—the macroeconomic phenomenon that may follow a severe financial crisis.

Chapter 5

1. Sections 5.1–5.5 are Based on Goldstein and Razin (2013a, 2013b).

2. See also Bryant (1980).

3. This reasoning explains why bank runs happen in equilibrium given a fixed demand-deposit contract. A key question in the literature that followed Diamond and Dybvig (1983) is whether bank runs will still happen when contracts are set endogenously. The general answer is that bank runs are indeed part of equilibrium in this broader sense. Papers addressing this issue include Postlewaite and Vives (1987), Calomiris and Kahn (1991), Allen and Gale (1998), Cooper and Ross (1998), Diamond and Rajan (2001a), Peck and Shell (2003), and Goldstein and Pauzner (2005). This section is based on Goldstein and Pauzner (2005).

4. Throughout this chapter, we make the common assumption that with a continuum of i.i.d. random variables, the empirical mean equals the expectations with probability 1 (see Judd 1985). We assume no aggregate uncertainty.

5. Note that any von Neumann–Morgenstern utility function, which is well defined at 0, can be transformed into an equivalent utility function that satisfies $u(0) = 0$.

6. This sharp outcome is obtained when the noise in the signal approaches zero. For larger noise, the transition from attack to no-attack will not be so abrupt, but rather there

will be a range of partial attack. This does not matter for the qualitative message of the theory.

7. Early work in this direction is in Zhang (2011).

8. If $\mu = 1$, the entrepreneur has enough income in period 1 to pay back consumers (investors) and still leave some surplus [$t(x) > 0$ for some x values]. In this case, the first-best level of reinvestment, $y^{FB} = b - 1 > 0$, will be chosen whenever x is large enough.

9. The intertemporal consumption-based asset-pricing model predicts that an asset's current price is equal to the expectation, conditioned on current information, of the product of the asset's payoff and a representative consumer's intertemporal marginal rate of substitution (IMRS). Compare it to the standard full-contingent-markets pricing formula for a safe asset, $q = E_0[(IMRS) \cdot 1] = 1$, and to the liquidity-based formula, $q = 1 + E_0[m(x)] > 1$.

Chapter 6

1. This chapter is based on Goldstein and Razin (2013a, 2013b).

2. Strictly speaking, the financial intermediaries here are not intermediating between the outside investors and the entrepreneurs, but rather providing a different type of financing that can relax financial constraints via monitoring.

Chapter 7

1. See also Shiller (1981).

2. There is also a macroliterature analyzing bubbles in models with symmetric information. For example, Tirole (1985) demonstrates the possibility of a bubble in an overlapping-generations model.

3. Allen and Gorton (1993) explicitly model an agency problem leading to bubbles in the financial market.

4. The price of the risky asset Y, which delivers 1 unit of the good in state U and R units of the good in state D, in terms of units of Arrow-D security, is given by

$$\frac{1 - q_U^{h_1}}{q_U^{h_1}} R + 1 = \frac{q_U^{h_1} + (1 - q_U^{h_1})R}{q_U^{h_1}}.$$

The price of the safe asset X in terms of the Arrow-D security is

$$\frac{1 - q_U^{h_1}}{q_U^{h_1}} + 1 = \frac{1}{q_U^{h_1}}.$$

Therefore the relative price of the risky asset in terms of the safe asset is

$$q_U^{h_1} + (1 - q_U^{h_1})R.$$

Chapter 8

1. This chapter is based on Goldstein and Razin (2013a, 2013b).

2. See a formal exposition in Piersanti (2012).

3. The model by Krugman (1979) builds on an earlier paper by Salant and Henderson (1978) about a speculative attack on gold reserves.

4. Note that self-fulfilling speculative attacks can also result from a first-generation model, as demonstrated by Obstfeld (1986).

5. For a broad review of the global-game methodology and its various applications, see Morris and Shin (2003). There is also a large literature that followed the original developments, analyzing conditions under which the unique-equilibrium result fails to hold (see, e.g., Angeletos and Werning 2006; Hellwig, Mukherji, and Tsyvinski 2006).

6. For empirical evidence on the twin crises, see Kaminsky and Reinhart (1999).

7. For a broad description of the events around the crisis, see Radelet and Sachs (1998). The importance of capital flows was anticipated by Calvo (1998).

8. For a broader review, see the collection of articles in Claessens and Forbes (2001).

Chapter 9

1. Helpman and Razin (1978, chap. 13) also extend the two-period open economy framework to an infinite-horizon, general equilibrium, dynamic model of trade in assets and goods. The infinite-horizon framework allows trade-offs between consumption and portfolio investment, interactions between trade in goods and factor allocations, as well as interactions between trade in goods and trade in assets.

2 See Gourinchas and Rey (2013). They emphasize the unique "exorbitant privilege" of the United States, which provides the world with reserve currency. U.S. Treasury bills are "safe haven" assets as a result. The United States borrows at the world's safe interest rate on its securities and invests abroad in high-return, and more risky, securities.

3. Prasad (2011) documents that, in fact, FDI now constitutes the major share of external liabilities of emerging markets. These shifts in stocks imply equally (or more) sharp shifts in underlying flows.

4. See Kose, Prasad, Rogoff, and Wei (2006) for a survey of the literature on the volatility and risk of debt flows.

5. See the appendix to this chapter for an asymmetry of information between domestic and foreign investors.

6. See chapter 6.

7. Only good projects are viable: $p^H R(1 + \varepsilon) - (1 + R)I > 0 > p^L R(1 + \varepsilon) - (1 + R)I + B$.

8. See Razin, Sadka, and Yuen (1998).

Chapter 10

1. For a survey of theories of capital flows in the presence of frictions, see Kirabaeva and Razin (2013).

Chapter 11

1. This chapter is based on Binyamini and Razin (2008). See also Gali (2008) for a comprehensive treatise of the open-economy New Keynesian model.

2. Similarly, Mishkin (2007) writes about the U.S. inflation-output trade-off: "The finding that inflation is less responsive to the unemployment gap, suggests that fluctuations in resource utilization will have smaller implications for inflation than used to be the case.

From the point of view of policy makers, this development is a two-edged sword: On the plus side, it implies that an overheating economy will tend to generate a smaller increase in inflation. On the negative side, however, a flatter Phillips curve also implies that a given increase in inflation will be more costly to wring out of the system."

3. For some related literature, see Artstein (2002) and Friedman and Suchoy (2004).

4. Borio and Filardo (2007) present cross-country evidence in support of their contention that global factors have recently become empirically more relevant for domestic inflation determination. But Ihrig et al. (2007) have shown that their result is very specific to the econometric method used. Based on cross-country analysis, Badinger (2007) finds that globalization is also correlated with more aggressive policy toward inflation. Tetlow and Ironside (2007), although not dealing with globalization, find that for the United States, the slope of the Phillips curve has—largely and continuously—lessened during recent years.

5. Following Razin and Yuen (2002), Razin and Loungani (2007) demonstrate that globalization flattens the Phillips curve and changes the inflation-output weights in the reduced-form welfare-based loss function of the central bank in favor of inflation control. These aspects of globalization are also addressed by Clarida (2008) in a model with imported raw materials in addition to imported finished goods.

6. This approach to migration was originally suggested by Engler (2007).

7. Razin and Yuen (2002) were among the first to extend the closed-economy New Keynesian framework to an open economy with trade in goods and in capital assets. Gali and Monacelli (2005) analyze the effect of exchange rate movements on inflation.

8. See also Engler (2007).

9. If the economy imports intermediate goods, there is also a real exchange rate effect. The real exchange rate affects the inflation-output trade-off, even in the absence of other cost-push shocks. Clarida, Gali, and Gertler (1999) discuss this effect.

10. We derive the utility-based loss function along the lines of Woodford (2003). We assume that foreign producers use a local currency pricing strategy and they update prices at the same frequency as that of domestic producers. Note also that we abstract from the money term in the utility function.

11. Cecchetti et al. (2007) suggest that aggressive monetary policy is the key explanation for the flattening of the trade-off. They argue that the disinflationary impact of globalization is limited and partly attributable to the fixed exchange rate regime in some of the East Asian countries. They analyze empirically the change in the ex post Taylor rule from the high-inflation era to the low-inflation era. Our theory can provide an explanation for this change in the Taylor rule.

12. Note, however, that in the closed economy, the real-exchange-rate channel shuts off, decreasing the degree of optimal response to output gap. This point is illustrated by comparing the parameter for the closed economy, equation (11.21), with those for open economies, equations (11.18)–(11.20).

Chapter 12

1. However, the development of credit and asset price bubbles that apparently took place without notice during the Great Moderation, bursting in 2008 and leading to the Great Recession, is not captured in this framework.

2. Earlier, in the Keynesian literature the discount factor shock as the cause of a liquidity trap was explored in Eggertsson and Woodford (2003), Christiano (2004), Eggertsson (2006), and Christiano, Eichenbaum, and Rebelo (2011).

3. Recall that Irving Fisher (1933) famously argued that the Great Depression was caused by a vicious circle of this kind.

4. The shock captures the phenomenon of a sudden realization that assets were overvalued and that peoples' collateral constraints were too lax.

5. If $P_S = P^*$, we get

$$1 + i_s = (1 + r_s)\frac{P^*}{P_s} = \frac{\frac{1}{2}Y + D^{low}}{\beta\frac{1}{2}Y + \beta D^{high}} < 1.$$

That is, maintaining a constant price level would require a negative nominal interest rate if condition (12.9) is satisfied. Obviously, negative nominal interest rate cannot happen. We must substitute $i_s = 0$ into the expression above.

6. As is standard in the monopolistic competition model with preset pricing. We assume that the firms are committed to sell whatever is demanded at the price.

7. The parameter ξ is defined by Eggertsson and Krugman (2012).

8. A caveat here is that a continuous Taylor-type interest-rate rule, when combined with the Fisher equation, necessarily leads to multiple equilibria in the New Keynesian model. However, the multiple equilibrium analysis ignores the possibility that even at the zero lower bound, central banks have used quantitative and qualitative easing measures, which can lower interest rates at longer maturities. In addition to the intended deterministic steady state at the targeted inflation rate $\pi = \pi^*$, there is a low-inflation deterministic steady state, which in fact is likely to be deflationary.

9. As before, in order to simplify exposition, we split the model into "short run" and "long run" with an unexpected shock occurring in the short run.

10. We have already seen that in the long run, $\hat{C}_L^b \equiv \hat{C}_L^s = 0$. Also note that the policy rule implies a unique bounded solution for the long run in which $i_L = r_L^n = \bar{r}$ and $\pi_L = 0$. Another caveat here involves the determination of the long-run price level. Given the Taylor rule we have just specified, prices will not revert to some exogenously given P^*. Instead, they will be stabilized after the initial shock, so that prices will remain permanently at the short-run equilibrium level P_S.

11. Eggertsson and Krugman interpret the schedule in this way: "Consider what happens if i_s falls, other things equal. First, savers are induced to consume more than they otherwise would. Second, this higher consumption leads to higher income for both borrowers and savers. And because borrowers are liquidity-constrained, they spend their additional income, which leads to a second round of income expansion, and so on. Once we combine this derived IS curve with the assumed Taylor rule, it's immediately clear that there are two possible regimes following a deleveraging shock. If the shock is relatively small, so that the natural rate of interest remains positive, the actual interest rate will fall to offset any impact on output. If the shock is sufficiently large, however, the zero lower bound will be binding, and output will fall below potential."

12. $\Gamma = \dfrac{\chi_s\sigma + (1 - \chi_s)\gamma_D\beta}{\chi_s - (1 - \chi_s)\kappa\gamma_D}\bar{r} < 0.$

See the appendix in Eggertsson and Krugman (2012) for further derivations.

13. We do not have here, however, a fully specified, microfounded model of the dynamics about how one gets to those long-term equilibria. The low inflation equilibrium in figure 12.2 appears to be unstable according to a dynamic mechanism whereby an interest rate below the natural rate will drive up the inflation rate. The multiple-equilibria issue, observed by Benhabib, Schmitt-Grohe, and Uribe (2001, 2002), in the context of perfect foresight self-fulfilling expectations, is also studied under adaptive learning in Evans and Honkapohja (2009), Evans, Guse, and Honkapohja (2008), and Evans and Honkapohja (2010). Mertens and Ravn (2010) offer an interesting empirical application.

Epilogue

1. Indeed, during the recent liquidity crisis, the Israeli government accumulated foreign exchange reserves through sterilized interventions in the foreign exchange market in order to boost the domestic aggregate demand without triggering a housing bubble by excessive monetary expansion and low interest rates. Specifically, as is known, countries that have no external capital controls, such as Israel, cannot usually have both monetary independence *and* successful management of the exchange rate through sterilized interventions unless there are exceptional situations of liquidity trap, or imperfect credit flows, internal and external, due to liquidity and credit risks. Without such exceptional risks, Israel cannot have a successful sterilized intervention, so that the currency depreciates while maintaining a relatively high interest rate to avoid a real estate bubble, unless prudential macroeconomic policies introduce credit flow barriers.

2. An asset swap by the central bank can change market supply of liquidity and produce real effects. The liquidity shortage after the 2008 crises gave a unique opportunity for the Federal Reserve to experiment in such unconventional monetary policy.

3. Walter Bagehot, *Lombard Street: A Description of the Money Market* (1873).

4. The Federal Reserve failed to meet its original 1913 mandate to maintain financial stability during the widespread bank failures and the collapse of money and credit that followed the 1929 stock market crash. It "rediscovered" the lending-of-last-resort function during the 2008 crisis.

5. International capital flows can abruptly change direction after monetary tightening in the United States. Such capital-flow shifts can initiate major readjustments of currency values across the world once the imminent monetary tightening in the United States is anticipated.

References

Abreu, Dilip, and Markus Brunnermeier. 2003. Bubbles and crashes. *Econometrica* 71:173–204.

Acharya, Viral, Hyun Song Shin, and Tanju Yorulmazer. 2011. Fire sale FDI. *Korean Economic Review* 27 (2):163–202.

Aghion, Philippe, Philippe Bacchetta, and Abhijit Banerjee. 2001. Currency crises and monetary policy in an economy with credit constraints. *European Economic Review* 45: 1121–1150.

Aguiar, Mark, Emmanuel Farhi, and Gita Gopinath. 2013. Crisis and commitment: Inflation, credibility, and the vulnerability to sovereign debt crises. NBER Working Paper 19516, National Bureau of Economic Research, Inc., Cambridge, MA.

Aguiar, Mark, and Gita Gopinath. 2005. Fire-sale foreign direct investment and liquidity crises. *Review of Economics and Statistics* 87:439–452.

Aguiar, Mark, and Gita Gopinath. 2006. Defaultable debt, interest rates and the current account. *Journal of International Economics* 69:64–83.

Akerlof, George A. 1970. The market for lemons: Quality uncertainty and the market mechanism. *Quarterly Journal of Economics* 84:488–500.

Akiyoshi, Fumio, and Keiichi Kobayashi 2008. Banking crisis and productivity of borrowing firms: Evidence from Japan. RIETI discussion paper, Tokyo.

Allen, Franklin, and Douglas Gale. 1994. Limited market participation and volatility of asset prices. *American Economic Review* 84:933–955.

Allen, Franklin, and Douglas Gale. 1998. Optimal financial crises. *Journal of Finance* 53:1245–1284.

Allen, Franklin, and Douglas Gale. 2000a. Bubbles and crises. *Economic Journal* 110:236–255.

Allen, Franklin, and Douglas Gale. 2000b. Financial contagion. *Journal of Political Economy* 108:1–33.

Allen, Franklin, and Gary Gorton. 1993. Churning bubbles. *Review of Economic Studies* 60 (4):813–836.

Allen, Franklin, Stephen Morris, and Hyun S. Shin. 2006. Beauty contests and iterated expectations. *Review of Financial Studies* 19:719–752.

Angeletos, George-Marios, and Ivan Werning. 2006. Crises and prices: Information aggregation, multiplicity, and volatility. *American Economic Review* 96:1720–1736.

Angeletos, George-Marios, Christian Hellwig, and Alessandro Pavan. 2006. Signaling in a global game: Coordination and policy traps. *Journal of Political Economy* 114:452–484.

Aoki, Masahiko, and Gary Saxonhouse. 2000. *Finance, Governance, and Competitiveness in Japan*. London: Oxford University Press.

Artstein, Yael. 2002. The flexibility of the Israeli labor market. In *The Israeli Economy, 1985–1998*, ed. A. Ben-Bassat. Cambridge, MA: MIT Press.

Aslund, Anders. 1995. *How Russia Became a Market Economy*. Washington, DC: Brookings Institution.

Atkeson, Andrew. 1991. International lending with moral hazard and risk of repudiation. *Econometrica* 59:1069–1089.

Bacchetta, Philippe, and Eric van Wincoop. 2006. Can information heterogeneity explain the exchange rate determination puzzle? *American Economic Review* 96:552–576.

Badinger, H. 2007. *Globalization, Taylor Rules, and Inflation*. mimeo. Vienna, Austria: Wirtschaftsuniversität Wien.

Baker, Malcolm, C. Fritz Foley, and Jeffrey Wurgler. 2004. Stock market valuations and foreign direct investment. New York University Working Paper no. SC-AM-04-05, New York.

Barlevy, Gadi. 2008. Economic theory and asset bubbles. *Economic Perspectives* 31 (3):44–59.

Barro, Robert, and David B. Gordon. 1983. Rules, discretion and reputation in a model of monetary policy. *Journal of Monetary Economics* 12:101–121.

Bean, Charles. 2006. Globalization and inflation. *Bank of England Quarterly Bulletin* Q4:468–475.

Benedict, Ruth. 1946. *The Chrysanthemum and the Sword: Patterns of Japanese Culture*. Boston: Houghton Mifflin.

Benhabib, Jess, Stephanie Schmitt-Grohe, and Martin Uribe. 2001. Avoiding liquidity traps. Center for Economic Policy Research, discussion paper 2948, London.

Benhabib, Jess, Stephanie Schmitt-Grohe, and Martin Uribe. 2002. Avoiding liquidity traps. *Journal of Political Economy* 110 (3) 535–563.

Bentolila, S., J. J. Dolaldo, and J. F. Jimeno. 2007. Does immigration affect the Phillips curve? Some evidence for Spain. mimeo. Madrid: CEMFI.

Berle, Adolph Augustus, and Gardiner C. Means. 1932. *The Modern Corporation and Private Property*. Piscataway, NJ: Transaction Books.

Bernanke, Ben S. 1983. Nonmonetary effects of the financial crisis in the propagation of the Great Depression. *American Economic Review* 73:257–276.

Bernanke, Ben S. 2005. The global saving glut and the US current account deficit. Speech to the Board of Governors of the Federal Reserve System (USA), March 10. Available at http://www.federalreserve.gov/boarddocs/speeches/2005/20050414/default.htm.

Bernanke, Ben S. 2012. Monetary Policy since the Onset of the Crisis. Board of Governors of the Federal Reserve System. Available at http://www.federalreserve.gov/newsevents/speech/bernanke20120831a.htm?et_cid=21721275&et_rid=yosafat.inkai.juara@gmail.com.

Bernanke, B., C. Bertaut, L. P. DeMarco, and S. Kamin. 2011. International capital flows and returns to safe assets in the United States, 2003–2007. Federal Reserve System, International Financial Discussion Paper No. 1014.

Bernanke, Ben S., and Mark Gertler. 1989. Agency costs, net worth, and business fluctuations. *American Economic Review* 79:14–31.

Bernanke, Ben S., Marc Gertler, and Simon Gilchrist. 1999. The financial accelerator in quantitative business cycle framework. In *Handbook of Macroeconomics*, vol. 1, ed. John Taylor and Michael Woodford, 1341–1393. New York: Elsevier.

Bernardo, Antonio, and Ivo Welch. 2004. Liquidity and financial market runs. *Quarterly Journal of Economics* 119:135–158.

Binyamini, Alon, and Assaf Razin. 2008. Inflation-output tradeoff as equilibrium outcome of globalization. *Israel Economic Review* 6 (1):109–134.

Blustein, Paul. 2001. *The Chastening: Inside the Crisis That Rocked the Global Financial System and Humbled the IMF.* New York: Public Affairs.

Bordo, Michael, and Harold James. 2013. The European crisis in the context of the history of previous financial crises. NBER Working Paper 19112, National Bureau of Economic Research, Inc., Cambridge, MA.

Borio, C., and A. Filardo. 2007. Globalisation and inflation: New cross-country evidence on the global determinants of domestic inflation. Unpublished paper. Bank for International Settlements, Basel, Switzerland.

Blinder, A., and M. Zandi. 2010. How the Great Recession was brought to an end. Accessed June 27, 2011. Available at www.economy.com/mark-zandi/documents/End-of-Great-Recession.pdf.

Brunnermeier, Markus, and Lasse Pedersen. 2009. Market liquidity and funding liquidity. *Review of Financial Studies* 22:2201–2238.

Brunnermeier, Markus, and Yuliy Sannikov. 2010. A macroeconomic model with a financial sector. National Bank of Belgium Working Paper 236, Brussels, Belgium.

Bryant, John. 1980. A model of reserves, bank runs, and deposit insurance. *Journal of Banking & Finance* 4:335–344.

Bulow, Jeremy I., and Kenneth S. Rogoff. 1989. Sovereign debt: Is to forgive or forget? *American Economic Review* 79:43–50.

Caballero, Ricardo J., Takeo Hoshi, and Anil K. Kashyap. 2006. Zombie lending and depressed restructuring in Japan. NBER Working Paper 12129, National Bureau of Economic Research, Inc., Cambridge, MA.

Caballero, Ricardo, and Arvind Krishnamurthy. 2001. International and domestic collateral constraints in a model of emerging market crises. *Journal of Monetary Economics* 48:513–548.

Calomiris, Charles. 1990. Is deposit insurance necessary? A historical perspective. *Journal of Economic History* 50:283–295.

Calomiris, Charles, and Gary Gorton. 1991. The origins of banking panics: models, facts, and bank regulation. In *Financial Markets and Financial Crises*, ed. Glen Hubbard, 109–174. Chicago: University of Chicago Press.

Calomiris, Charles, and Charles Kahn. 1991. The role of demandable debt in structuring optimal banking arrangements. *American Economic Review* 81:497–513.

Calvo, Guillermo. 1983. Staggered prices in a utility-maximizing framework. *Journal of Monetary Economics* 12:383–398.

Calvo, Guillermo. 1998. Capital flows and capital-market crises: The simple economics of sudden stops. *Journal of Applied Econometrics* 1:35–54.

Calvo, Guillermo, and Enrique Mendoza. 2000. Rational contagion and the globalization of securities markets. *Journal of International Economics* 51:79–113.

Caramazza, Francesco, Luca Ricci, and Ranil Salgado. 2004. International financial contagion in currency crises. *Journal of International Money and Finance* 23:51–70.

Carlsson, Hans, and Eric van Damme. 1993. Global games and equilibrium selection. *Econometrica* 61:989–1018.

Cecchetti, Stephen G., Peter Hooper, Bruce C. Kasman, Kermit L. Schoenholtz, and Mark W. Watson. 2007. Understanding the evolving inflation process. Paper presented at the U.S Monetary Policy Forum, Washington, D.C., March 9.

Chancellor, Edward. 2000. *Devil Take the Hindmost: A History of Financial Speculation*. New York: Plume.

Chang, Roberto, and Andres Velasco. 2001. A model of financial crises in emerging markets. *Quarterly Journal of Economics* 116:489–517.

Chen, N., J. Imbs, and A. Scott. 2004. Competition, globalization and the decline of inflation. *Journal of International Economics* 63 (1):93–118, 312.

Christiano, Lawrence J. 2004. Why do firms hold inventories? 2004 Meeting Papers 814, Society for Economic Dynamics.

Christiano, Lawrence, Martin Eichenbaum, and Sergio Rebelo. 2011. When is the government spending multiplier large? *Journal of Political Economy* 119 (1):119–133.

Claessens, Stijn, Michael P. Dooley, and Andrew Warner. 1995. Portfolio capital flows: Hot or cold? *World Bank Economic Review* 9:153–170.

Claessens, Stijn, and Kristin Forbes, eds. 2001. *International Financial Contagion*. Boston: Kluwer Academic.

Clarida, Richard. J. 2008. Reflections on monetary policy in the open economy. In *NBER International seminar on Macroeconomics 2008*, ed. Jeffrey Frankel and Christopher Pissarides. Chicago: University of Chicago Press.

Clarida, Richard, Jordi Gali, and Mark Gertler. 1999. The science of monetary policy: A New Keynesian perspective. *Journal of Economic Literature* 37 (4):1661–1707.

Cooper, Russell, and Thomas W. Ross. 1998. Bank runs: Liquidity costs and investment distortions. *Journal of Monetary Economics* 41:27–38.

Cruces, Juan J., and Christoph Trebesch. 2013. Sovereign defaults: The price of haircuts. *American Economic Journal: Macroeconomics* 5:190–228.

Dallago, Bruno, and Chiara Guglielmetti. 2011. The Eurozone Crisis: Institutional Setting, Structural Vulnerability, and Policies. Working Paper, Autonomous Province of Trento, OPENLOC.

Dasgupta, Amil. 2004. Financial contagion through capital connections: A model of the origin and spread of bank panics. *Journal of the European Economic Association* 2:1049–1084.

De Grauwe, Paul. 2000. *Economics of Monetary Union*. New York: Oxford University Press.

De Grauwe, Paul. 2010. The Greek crisis and the future of the Eurozone. *Inter Economics* 45:89–93.

De Grauwe, Paul. 2011. The European Central Bank as a lender of last resort. VoxEU.org, August 18.

De Grauwe, Paul, and Yuemei Ji. 2012. Self fulfilling crises in the Eurozone: An empirical test. *Journal of International Money and Finance* 34:15–36.

Delong, J. B., and K. Magin. 2006. A short note on the size of the dot-com bubble. NBER Working Paper 12011, National Bureau of Economic Research, Inc., Cambridge, MA.

De Long, J. Bradford, Andrei Shleifer, Lawrence Summers, and Robert Waldman. 1990. Noise trader risk in financial markets. *Journal of Political Economy* 98:703–738.

Diamond, Douglas W., and Philip H. Dybvig. 1983. Bank runs, deposit insurance, and liquidity. *Journal of Political Economy* 91:401–419.

Diamond, Douglas W., and Raghuram Rajan. 2001. Banks, short term debt, and financial crises: Theory, policy implications, and applications. *Carnegie-Rochester Center Series on Public Policy* 54:37–71.

Dooley, Michael P., David Folkerts-Landau, and Peter Garber. 2003. The revived Bretton Woods system. NBER Working Paper 10332, National Bureau of Economic Research, Inc., Cambridge, MA.

Dooley, Michael P., and Inseok Shin. 2000. Private inflows when crises are anticipated: a case study of Korea. NBER Working Paper 7992, National Bureau of Economic Research, Inc., Cambridge, MA.

Dow, James. 2004. Is liquidity self-fulfilling? *Journal of Business* 77:895–908.

Eaton, Jonathan, and Raquel Fernandez. 1995. Sovereign debt. In *Handbook of International Economics*, volume 3, ed. Gene M. Grossman and Kenneth Rogoff, 2031–2077. Amsterdam: Elsevier North-Holland.

Eaton, Jonathan, and Mark Gersovitz. 1981. Debt with potential repudiation: Theoretical and empirical analysis. *Review of Economic Studies* 48:289–309.

Eberstadt, Nicholas. 2007. China's one-child mistake. *Wall Street Journal*, September 17.

Eberstadt, Nicholas. 2010. What population growth—and decline—means for the global economy. *Foreign Affairs* 89 (6):54–64.

Eggertsson, Gauti. 2006. The deflation bias and committing to being irresponsible. *Journal of Money, Credit and Banking* 36:283–321.

Eggertsson, Gauti B., and Paul Krugman. 2012. Debt, deleveraging, and the liquidity trap: A Fisher-Minsky-Koo approach. *Quarterly Journal of Economics* 127 (3):1469–1513.

Eggertsson, Gauti, and Michael Woodford. 2003. The zero bound on interest rates and optimal monetary policy. *Brookings Papers on Economic Activity* 1:212–219.

Eichengreen, Barry. 2004. Global imbalances and the lessons of Bretton Woods. NBER Working Paper 10497, National Bureau of Economic Research, Inc., Cambridge, MA.

Eichengreen, Barry. 2012. When currencies collapse: Will we replay the 1930s or the 1970s. *Foreign Affairs* 91:117–134.

Eichengreen, Barry, and Kevin H. O'Rourke. 2009. A tale of two depressions. VoxEU.org.

Eichengreen, Barry, Andrew Rose, and Charles Wyplosz. 1996. Contagious speculative attacks: First tests. *Scandinavian Journal of Economics* 98:463–484.

Eisfeldt, Andrea L., and Adriano A. Rampini. 2006. Capital reallocation and liquidity. *Journal of Monetary Economics* 53:369–399.

Evans, George W., Eran Guse, and Seppo Honkapohja. 2008. Liquidity traps, learning and stagnation. *European Economic Review* 52:1438–1463.

Evans, George W., and Seppo Honkapohja. 2009. Expectations, deflation traps and macroeconomic policy. CEPR Discussion Paper No. 7397.

Evans, George W., and Seppo Honkapohja. 2010. Does Ricardian equivalence hold when expectations are not rational? University of Oregon Economics Department, Working Paper 2010-13, Eugene, OR.

Farhi, Emmanuel, and Jean Tirole. 2012. Collective moral hazard, maturity mismatch and systemic bailouts. *American Economic Review* 102:60–93.

Ferguson, Niall. 2008. *The Ascent of Money: A Financial History of the World*. New York: Penguin.

Ferguson, Niall. 2010. Complexity and collapse. *Foreign Affairs* 89 (2): 18–32.

Fisher, Irving. 1933. The debt-deflation theory of great depressions. *Econometrica* 1:337–357.

Flood, Robert, and Peter Garber. 1984. Collapsing exchange-rate regimes, some linear examples. *Journal of International Economics* 17:1–13.

Fostel, Ana, and John Geanakoplos. 2012. Tranching, CDS, and asset prices: How financial innovation can cause bubbles and crashes. *American Economic Journal: Macroeconomics* 4 (1):190–225.

Fratzscher, Marcel. 1998. Why are currency crises contagious? *Weltwirtschaftliches Archiv* 134 (4):664–691.

Friedman, Amit, and Tanya Suchoy. 2004. The NAIRU in Israel: An unobserved components approach. *Israel Economic Review* 2 (2):125–154.

Friedman, Milton. 1968. The role of monetary policy. *American Economic Review* 58:1–17.

Gali, Jordi. 2008. *Monetary Policy, Inflation, and the Business Cycle: An Introduction to the New Keynesian Framework*. Princeton, NJ: Princeton University Press.

Gali, Jordi. 2013. Monetary policy and rational asset price bubbles. NBER Working Paper 18806, National Bureau of Economic Research, Inc., Cambridge, MA.

Gali, Jordi, and Tomasso Monacelli. 2005 Monetary policy and exchange rate volatility in a small open economy. *Review of Economic Studies* 72: 707–734.

Geanakoplos, John. 1997. Promises, promises. In *The Economy of Evolving Complex Systems, II,* ed. W. B. Arthur, S. Durlauf, and D. Lane, 285–320. Reading, MA: Addison-Wesley.

Geanakoplos, John. 2003. Liquidity, default, and crashes: Endogenous contracts in general equilibrium. In *Advances in Economics and Econometrics: Theory and Applications (Eighth World Congress) Volume II,* ed. M. Dewatripont, L. P. Hansen, and S. J. Turnovsky, 170–205. Cambridge, UK: Cambridge University Press.

Geanakoplos, John. 2010. Solving the present crisis and managing the leverage cycle. *Federal Reserve Bank of New York Economic Policy Review* (August):101–131.

Geanakoplos, John D., and Herakles M. Polemarchakis. 1986. Existence, regularity and constrained suboptimality of competitive allocations when the asset structure is incomplete. In *Uncertainty, Information and Communication: Essays in Honor of K.J. Arrow,* vol. 3, ed. W. P. Hell, R. M. Starr, and D. A. Starrett, 65–95. New York: Cambridge University Press.

Geanakoplos, John, and William R. Zame. 1997. Collateralized asset markets. Unpublished. Yale University.

Gennotte, Gerard, and Hayne Leland. 1990. Market liquidity, hedging, and crashes. *American Economic Review* 80:999–1021.

Gerlach, Stefan, and Frank Smets. 1995. Contagious speculative attacks. *European Journal of Political Economy* 11:45–63.

Gertler, Mark, and Nobuhiro Kiyotaki. 2011. Financial intermediation of credit policy in business cycle analysis. In *Handbook of Monetary Economics,* volume 3B, ed. Benjamin M. Friedman and Michael Woodford, 45–90. Amsterdam: Elsevier.

Gertler, Mark, and Nobuhiro Kiyotaki. 2013. Banking, liquidity and bank runs in an infinite-horizon economy. NBER Working Paper 19129, National Bureau of Economic Research, Inc., Cambridge, MA.

Glick, Reuven, and Andrew Rose. 1999. Contagion and trade: Why are currency crises regional? *Journal of International Money and Finance* 18:603–617.

Goldman, Marshall. 2003. *The Privatization of Russia: Russian Reform Goes Awry.* London: Routledge.

Goldstein, Itay. 2005. Strategic complementarities and the twin crises. *Economic Journal* 115:368–390.

Goldstein, Itay, and Alexander Guembel. 2008. Manipulation and the allocational role of prices. *Review of Economic Studies* 75:133–164.

Goldstein, Itay, and Ady Pauzner. 2004. Contagion of self-fulfilling financial crises due to diversification of investment portfolios. *Journal of Economic Theory* 119:151–183.

Goldstein, Itay, and Ady Pauzner. 2005. Demand deposit contracts and the probability of bank runs. *Journal of Finance* 60:1293–1328.

Goldstein, Itay, and Assaf Razin. 2006. An information-based trade off between foreign direct investment and foreign portfolio investment. *Journal of International Economics* 70:271–295.

Goldstein, Itay, and Assaf Razin. 2013a. Review of theories of financial crises. NBER Working Paper 18670, National Bureau of Economic Research, Inc., Cambridge, MA.

Goldstein, Itay, and Assaf Razin. 2013b. Three branches of theories of financial crises. NBER Working Paper No. 18670.

Goodfriend, Marvin. 2011. Central banking in the credit turmoil: An assessment of Federal Reserve practice. *Journal of Monetary Economics* 58 (1):1–12.

Gopinath, Gitta, and Roberto Rigobon. 2007. Sticky borders. *Quarterly Journal of Economics* 123 (2):531–575.

Gourinchas, Pierre-Olivier, and Hélène Rey. 2013. External adjustment, global imbalances and valuation effects. NBER Working Paper 19240, National Bureau of Economic Research, Inc., Cambridge, MA.

Gros, Daniel, and Niels Thygesen. 1999. *European Monetary Integration*. London: Longman.

Hart, Oliver D., and Luigi Zingales. 2013. Liquidity and inefficient investment. NBER Working Paper 19184, National Bureau of Economic Research, Inc., Cambridge, MA.

Hayek, F. A. 1945. The use of knowledge in society. *American Economic Review*, 35, (4):519–530.

Hellwig, Christian, Arijit Mukherji, and Aleh Tsyvinski. 2006. Self-fulfilling currency crises: The role of interest rates. *American Economic Review* 96:1769–1787.

Helpman, Elhanan, and Assaf Razin. 1978. *A Theory of Trade under Uncertainty*. New York and London: Academic Press.

Holmstrom, Bengt, and Jean Tirole. 1993. Market liquidity and performance monitoring. *Journal of Political Economy* 101 (4):678–699.

Holmstrom, Bengt, and Jean Tirole. 1997. Financial intermediation, loanable funds, and the real sector. *Quarterly Journal of Economics* 112:663–691.

Holmstrom, Bengt, and Jean Tirole. 1998. Private and public supply of liquidity. *Journal of Political Economy* 106:1–40.

Holmström, Bengt, and Jean Tirole. 2001. LAPM: A liquidity-based asset pricing model. *Journal of Finance* 56 (5):1837–1867.

Iacoviello, Matteo. 2005. House price, borrowing constraints, and monetary policy in the business cycle. *American Economic Review* 95:739–764.

Ihrig, J., S. Kamin, D. Lindner, and J. Marquez. 2007. Some simple tests of the globalization and inflation hypothesis. International Finance Discussion Papers 891. Washington: Board of Governors of the Federal Reserve System.

Jeanne, Olivier, and Anton Korinek. 2013. Macroprudential regulation versus mopping up after the crash. NBER Working Paper 18675, National Bureau of Economic Research, Inc., Cambridge, MA.

Judd, Kenn L. 1985. The law of large numbers with a continuum of IID random variables. *Journal of Economic Theory* 58 (2):19–25.

Kaiser, Wolfram, and Peter Starie eds. 2009. *Transnational European Union: Towards a Common Political Space.* London: Routledge.

Kaminsky, Graciela L., Richard Lyons, and Sergio L. Schmukler. 2004. Managers, investors, and crises: Mutual fund strategies in emerging markets. *Journal of International Economics* 64:113–134.

Kaminsky, Graciela, and Carmen Reinhart. 1999. The twin crises: The causes of banking and balance-of-payments problems. *American Economic Review* 89:473–500.

Kaminsky, Graciela, and Carmen Reinhart. 2000. On crises, contagion, and confusion. *Journal of International Economics* 51:145–168.

Kaminsky, Graciela L., Carmen M. Reinhart, and Carlos A. Vegh. 2003. The unholy trinity of financial contagion. *Journal of Economic Perspectives* 17:51–74.

Kanaya, Akihiro, and David Woo. 2000. The Japanese banking crisis of the 1990s: Sources and lessons. International Monetary Fund Working Paper 00/7, Washington DC.

Kantor, James. 2012. Germany spoils party with refusal on bank aid. *International Herald Tribune*, October 20–21, p. 9.

Keister, Todd. 2012. Bailouts and financial fragility. No. 473. Staff Report. Federal Reserve Bank of New York.

Kenen, Peter B. 1967. Toward a supranational monetary system. In *Issues in Banking and Monetary Analysis*, ed. Giulio Pontecorvo, Robert P. Shay, and Albert G. Hart, 59–77. New York: Holt, Reinhart and Winston.

Keynes, J. M. 1936. *The General Theory of Employment, Interest and Money.* London: Macmillan.

Kiguel, Miguel. 2011. Argentina and Greece: More similarities than differences in the initial conditions. CEPR VOX, August 16.

Kirabaeva, Koralai, and Assaf Razin. 2013. Composition of capital flows. In *Handbook of Financial Globalization (GLFI)—The Evidence and Impact of Financial Globalization, GLFI3,* ed. Gerard Caprio, 103–120. Amersterdam: Elsevier Science and Technology.

Kiyotaki, Nobuhiro, and John Moore. 1997. Credit cycles. *Journal of Political Economy* 105:211–248.

Kocherlakota, Narayana R. 2000. Creating business cycles through credit constraints. *Federal Reserve Bank of Minneapolis Quarterly Review* 24:2–10.

Kodres, Laura, and Matthew Pritsker. 2002. A rational expectations model of financial contagion. *Journal of Finance* 57:769–799.

Kose, M. Ayhan, Eswar Prasad, Kenneth S. Rogoff, and Shang-Jin Wei. 2009. Financial globalization and economic policies. Center for Economic Policy Research, Discussion Paper 7117, London.

Krugman, Paul. 1979. A model of balance-of-payments crises. *Journal of Money, Credit and Banking* 11:311–325.

Krugman, Paul. 1998a. *Bubble, Boom, Crash: Theoretical Notes on Asia's Crisis.* Cambridge, MA: MIT Mimeo.

Krugman, Paul. 1998b. *What Happened to Asia*. Cambridge, MA: MIT Mimeo.

Krugman, Paul. 1999. Balance sheets, the transfer problem, and financial crises. *International Tax and Public Finance* 6:459–472.

Krugman, Paul. 2000. Fire sale FDI. Available at http://web.mit.edu/krugman/www/FIRESALE.htm.

Krugman, Paul. 2010a. How much of the world is in a liquidity trap? *New York Times* blog, March 17.

Krugman, Paul. 2010b. The Third Depression. *New York Times*, June 27.

Krugman, Paul. 2014 (forthcoming). Currency regimes, capital flows, and crises. *IMF Economic Review*.

Kydland, Finn E., and Edward C. Prescott. 1982. Time to build and aggregate fluctuations. *Econometrica* 50:1345–1371.

Lane, Philip. 1997. Inflation in open economies. *Journal of International Economics* 42:327–347.

Lee, Sook-Jong, and Hoon Jang. 2010. *Toward Managed Globalization: The Korean Experience*. Seoul: East Asia Institute.

Levinson, Marc. 2010. Faulty Basel: Why more diplomacy won't keep the financial system safe. *Foreign Affairs* 89 (3): 76–89.

Lorenzoni, Guido. 2008. Inefficient credit booms. *Review of Economic Studies* 75:809–833.

Loungani, P., A. Razin, and C. Yuen. 2001. Capital mobility and the output-inflation tradeoff. *Journal of Development Economics* 64:255–274.

Lucas, Robert E., Jr. 1975. An equilibrium model of the business cycle. *Journal of Political Economy* 83 (6):1113–1144.

Lucas, Robert E., Jr. 2000. Some macroeconomics for the 21st century. *Journal of Economic Perspectives* 14:159–168.

Lucas, Robert E., Jr. 2003. Macroeconomic priorities. *American Economic Review* 93:1–14.

Maddison, Angus. 2003a. *Development Center Studies The World Economy: Historical Statistics*. Geneva: OECD Publishing.

Maddison, Angus. 2003b. *The World Economy: Historical Statistics*. Paris: OECD Publishing.

Mankiw, N. Gregory. 2010. The trilemma of international finance. Available at: http://www.nytimes.com/2010/07/11/business/economy/11view.html.

Martin, Alberto, and Jaume Ventura. 2012. Economic growth with bubbles. *American Economic Review* 102:3033–3058.

McKinnon, Ronald I. 1963. Optimum currency areas. *American Economic Review* 53: 717–725.

McKinnon, R., and H. Pill. 1996. Credible liberalizations and international capital flows: The overborrowing syndrome. In *Financial Deregulation and Integration in East Asia*, ed. T. Ito and A. Krueger. Chicago: University of Chicago Press.

Mendoza, Enrique. 2010. Sudden stops, financial crises and leverage. *American Economic Review* 100:1941–1966.

Mertens, Karel, and Morten O. Ravn. 2010. Fiscal policy in an expectations driven liquidity trap. CEPR Discussion Paper 7931.

Mian, Atif, and Amir Sufi. 2014. *House of Debt: How They (and You) Caused the Great Recession, and How We Can Prevent It from Happening Again*. Chicago: University of Chicago Press.

Milesi-Ferretti, Gian Maria, and Assaf Razin. 1997. Current account sustainability: Selected East Asian and Latin American experiences. NBER Working Paper No. 5791, National Bureau of Economic Research, Inc., Cambridge, MA.

Milesi-Ferretti, Gian Maria, and Assaf Razin. 2000. Current account reversals and currency crises, empirical regularities. In *Currency Crises*, ed. Paul Krugman, 285–326. Chicago: University of Chicago Press.

Mills, Q. 2009. *World Financial Crisis 2008–2010: What Happened, Who Is to Blame and How to Protect Your Money*. Amazon, NY: Create Space.

Minsky, Hyman. 1982. *Can It Happen Again?: Essays on Instability and Finance*. New York: M. E. Sharpe.

Mishkin, Frederic S. 1999. Central banking after the crisis. *Journal of International Money and Finance* 18 (4):709–723.

Mishkin, Fredric S. 2007. Remarks given at the Annual Macro Conference, Federal Reserve Bank of San Francisco, San Francisco, California, March 23.

Miyajima, Hideaki, and Yishay Yafeh. 2007. Japan's banking crisis: An event-study perspective. *Journal of Banking & Finance* 31 (9):2866–2885.

Morris, Stephen, and Hyun S. Shin. 1998. Unique equilibrium in a model of self-fulfilling currency attacks. *American Economic Review* 88:587–597.

Morris, Stephen, and Hyun S. Shin. 2003. Global games: Theory and applications. In *Advances in Economics and Econometrics*, ed. Mathias Dewatripont, Lars P. Hansen, and Stephen Turnovsky, 56–114. Cambridge, UK: Cambridge University Press.

Morris, Stephen, and Hyun S. Shin. 2004. Liquidity black holes. *Review of Finance* 8:1–18.

Morris, Stephen, and Hyun S. Shin. 2012. Contagious adverse selection. *American Economic Journal: Macroeconomics* 4:1–21.

Mundell, Robert A. 1961. A theory of optimum currency areas. *American Economic Review* 51:657–664.

Mundell, Robert A. 1963. Capital mobility and stabilization policy under fixed and flexible exchange rates. *Canadian Journal of Economics and Political Science* 29:475–485.

Obstfeld, Maurice. 1986. Rational and self-fulfilling balance of payments crises. *American Economic Review* 76:72–81.

Obstfeld, Maurice. 1994. The logic of currency crises. NBER Working Paper 4640, National Bureau of Economic Research, Inc., Cambridge, MA.

Obstfeld, Maurice. 1996. Models of currency crises with self-fulfilling features. *European Economic Review* 40:1037–1047.

Obstfeld, Maurice. 2013. Finance at center stage: Some lessons of the Euro crisis. CEPR Discussion Paper 9415, London.

Ozdenoren, Emre, and Kathy Yuan. 2008. Feedback effects and asset prices. *Journal of Finance* 63:1939–1975.

Pagano, Marco. 1989. Trading volume and asset liquidity. *Quarterly Journal of Economics* 104:255–274.

Peck, James, and Karl Shell. 2003. Equilibrium bank runs. *Journal of Political Economy* 111:103–123.

Pempel, T. J., ed. 2009. *The Politics of the Asian Crisis*. Ithaca, NY: Cornell University Press.

Phelps, Edmund S. 1967. Phillips curves, expectations of inflation and optimal unemployment over time. *Economica* 34 (135):254–281.

Phillips, Alban W. 1958. The relation between unemployment and the rate of change of money wage rates in the United Kingdom, 1861–1957. *Economica* 25:283–299.

Piersanti, Giovanni. 2012. *The Macroeconomic Theory of Exchange Rate Crises*. Oxford: Oxford University Press.

Postlewaite, Andy, and Xavier Vives. 1987. Bank runs as an equilibrium phenomenon. *Journal of Political Economy* 95 (3):485–491.

Prasad, Eswar. 2011. Role reversal in global finance. Proceedings of the 2011 Jackson Hole Symposium, Federal Reserve Bank of Kansas City. Available at http://www .kansascityfed.org/.

Radelet, Steven, and Jeffrey Sachs. 1998. The East Asian financial crisis: Diagnosis, remedies, prospects. *Brookings Papers on Economic Activity* 1:1–74.

Rajan, Raghuram, and Luigi Zingales. 1998a. Financial dependence and growth. *American Economic Review* 88:559–586.

Rajan, Raghuram, and Liugi Zingales. 1998b. Which capitalism: Lessons from the Asian crisis. *Journal of Applied Corporate Finance* 11:40–48.

Rampini, Adriano, and S. Viswanathan. 2011. Financial intermediary capital. AFA 2013 San Diego Meetings Paper.

Razin, A., and P. Loungani. 2007. Globalization and equilibrium inflation-output tradeoffs. In *NBER International Seminar on Macroeconomics 2005*, ed. Jeffrey A. Frankel and Christopher Pissarides. Cambridge, MA: MIT Press.

Razin, Assaf, and Steven Rosefielde. 2011. Currency and financial crises of the 1990s and 2000s. NBER Working Paper 16754, National Bureau of Economic Research, Inc., Cambridge, MA.

Razin, Assaf, and Steven Rosefielde. 2012. A tale of politically-failing single-currency area. NBER Working Paper 18352, National Bureau of Economic Research, Inc., Cambridge, MA.

Razin, Assaf, Efraim Sadka, and Chi-Wa Yuen. 1998. A pecking order theory of capital flows and international tax principles. *Journal of International Economics* 44:45–68.

Razin, Assaf, and Chi-Wa Yuen. 2002. The New Keynesian Phillips curve: Closed economy vs. open economy. *Economic Letters* 75 (1):1–9.

Reinhart, Carmen, and Daniel Rogoff. 2009. *This Time Is Different: Eight Centuries of Financial Folly*. Princeton, NJ: Princeton University Press.

Rey, Hélène. 2013. *Dilemma not Trilemma: The Global Financial Cycle and Monetary Policy Independence*. Federal Reserve Bank of Kansas City, Jackson Hole. Available at http://www.kansascityfed.org.

Rodrik, Dani, and Andres Velasco. 1999. Short term capital flows. NBER Working Paper 7364, National Bureau of Economic Research, Inc., Cambridge, MA.

Romer, D. 1993. Openness and inflation: Theory and evidence. *Quarterly Journal of Economics* CVII (4):869–904.

Romer, David. 1998. A new assessment of openness and inflation: Reply. *Quarterly Journal of Economics* CXII (2):649–652.

Romer, David. 2013. Preventing the next catastrophe: Where do we stand? Available at: http://blog-imfdirect.imf.org/2013/05/03/preventing-the-next-catastrophe-where-do-we-stand/.

Rogoff, K. 2003. Disinflation: An unsung benefit of globalization? *Finance & Development* 40 (4):55–56.

Rogoff, K. 2004. Globalization and global disinflation. In *Monetary Policy and Uncertainty: Adapting to a Changing Economy*, proceedings of the 2003 Jackson Hole symposium sponsored by the Federal Reserve Bank of Kansas City.

Rosefielde, Steven. 2005. Russia: An abnormal country. *European Journal of Comparative Economics* 2 (1):3–16.

Rosefielde, Steven, and Stefan Hedlund. 2009. *Russia Since 1980: Wrestling with Westernization*. Cambridge, UK: Cambridge University Press.

Salant, Stephen, and Dale Henderson. 1978. Market anticipation of government policies and the price of gold. *Journal of Political Economy* 86:627–648.

Samuelson, Paul. 1958. An exact consumption-loan model of interest with or without the social contrivance of money. *Journal of Political Economy* 66:467–482.

Sargent, Thomas J. 2012. Nobel lecture: United States then, Europe now. *Journal of Political Economy* 120:1–40.

Schneider, Martin, and Aaron Tornell. 2004. Balance sheet effects, bailout guarantees and financial crises. *Review of Economic Studies* 71:883–913.

Scott, Jesse. 2012. *New Challenges for Energy Security: Growing Energy Demand Versus Environmental Constraints, "Energetika XXI: Economy, Policy."* St. Petersburg, Russia: Ecology.

Shiller, Robert J. 1981. Do stock prices move too much to be justified by subsequent changes in dividends? *American Economic Review* 71 (3):421–436.

Shiller, R. 2000. *Irrational Exuberance*. Princeton, NJ: Princeton University Press.

Shiller, R. 2008. *The Subprime Solution: How Today's Global Financial Crisis Happened, and What to Do About It*. Princeton, NJ: Princeton University Press.

Shleifer, Andrei, and Daniel Treisman. 2005. A normal country: Russia after communism. *Journal of Economic Perspectives* 19 (1):151–174.

Shleifer, Andrei, and Robert Vishny. 1997. The limits to arbitrage. *Journal of Finance* 52:35–55.

Sims, Christopher A. 2012. Gaps in the institutional structure of the euro area. *Financial Stability Review* 16:217–223.

Stiglitz, Joseph E. 1982. Information and capital markets. In *Financial Economics: Essays in Honor of Paul Cootner*, ed. William F. Sharpe and Cathryn Cootner, 118–158. Engelwood Cliffs, NJ: Prentice Hall.

Stiglitz, Joseph E. 1996. Some lessons from the East Asian miracles. *World Bank Research Observer* 11 (2):151–177.

Stiglitz, Joseph E. 2010 New $600 billion stimulus fuels fears of currency wars. *Democracy Now*, November 5, 11–24.

Stiglitz, Joseph E. 2011. Watchdog: Government pay rules and few lasting effects. *Associated Press Online*, February 10.

Stiglitz, Joseph E., and Andrew Weiss. 1981. Credit rationing in markets with imperfect information. *American Economic Review* 71:393–410.

Sturzenegger, Federico, and Jeronim Zettelmeyer. 2006. *Debt Defaults and Lessons from a Decade of Crises*. Cambridge, MA: MIT Press.

Taleb, Nassim. 2010. *Black Swan: The Impact of the Highly Improbable*. New York: Random House.

Tetlow, R., and B. Ironside. 2007. Real-time model uncertainty in the United States: The Fed, 1996–2003. *Journal of Money, Credit and Banking* 39 (7):1533–1561.

Tirole, Jean. 1985. Asset bubbles and overlapping generations. *Econometrica* 53:1499–1528.

Tobin, James, and Stephen Golub. 1998. *Money Credit and Capital*. New York: Irwin/McGraw-Hill.

Tong, Hui, and Shang-Jin Wei. 2011. The composition matters: Capital inflows and liquidity crunch during a global economic crisis. *Review of Financial Studies, Society for Financial Studies* 24 (6):2023–2052.

Townsend, Robert M. 1979. Optimal contracts and competitive markets with costly state verification. *Journal of Economic Theory* 21:265–293.

Tsyrenikov, Viktor. 2007. Capital inflows and moral hazard. Working Paper, Cornell University, Ithaca, NY.

Van Rijckeghem, Caroline, and Beatrice Weder. 2001. Sources of contagion: Is it finance or trade. *Journal of International Economics* 54:293–308.

Vavilov, Andrey. 2010. *The Russian Public Debt and Financial Meltdowns*. Basingstoke, UK: Palgrave Macmillan.

Wallison, P. J., and E. Pinto. 2010. How the government is creating another bubble. AEI Articles and Commentary, December 27.

Wallison, Peter J., and Edward J. Pinto. 2012. Free fall: How government policies brought down the housing market. American Enterprise Institute, Washington DC, April 26.

Wallison, Peter, Alex Pollock, and Edward Pinto. 2011. Taking the government out of housing finance: Principles for reforming the housing finance market. AEI Online. Available at www.aei.org/module/1/the-government-mortgage-complex.

Wedel, J. 2009. *Shadow Elites: How the World's New Power Brokers Undermine Democracy, Government and the Free Market*. New York: Basic Books.

White, W. 2010. Some Alternative Perspectives on Macroeconomic Theory and Some Policy Implications. Federal Reserve Bank of Dallas Globalization and Monetary Policy Institute, Working Paper No. 54.

Williamson, John. 2002. What Washington means by policy reform. In *Latin American Adjustment: How Much Has Happened?*, ed. John Williamson. Washington, DC: Institute for International Economics.

Woodford, Michael. 2003. *Interest and Prices: Foundations of a Theory of Monetary Policy*. Princeton, NJ: Princeton University Press.

Wynne, M. A., and E. K. Kersting 2007. Openness and inflation. Federal Reserve Bank of Dallas, Staff Paper No. 2.

Zhang, Yu. 2011. Essays on banking. Ph.D. dissertation, Department of Economics, Cornell University, unpublished.

Index